D0965665

The Inviting Life

AN INSPIRATIONAL GUIDE
TO HOMEMAKING,
HOSTING, AND OPENING THE
DOOR TO HAPPINESS

Laura Calder

appetite

Appetite by Random House® and colophon are registered trademarks of Penguin Random House LLC.

Library and Archives Canada Cataloguing in Publication is available upon request.
ISBN: 9780147530523
eBook ISBN: 9780147530530

Book and cover design by Jennifer Griffiths

Cover art and drawings throughout by and © Laura Calder

Printed and bound in China

Published in Canada by Appetite by Random House®,
a division of Penguin Random House Canada Limited.

www.penguinrandomhouse.ca

10 9 8 7 6 5 4 3 2 1

appetite
by RANDOM HOUSE

Penguin
Random
House

This book is dedicated to

PETER

my beloved co-host in life.

Do remember to forget
Anger, worry and regret
Love while you've got love to give
Live while you've got life to live

PIET HEIN

An Invitation

I'd shrivel up and become plant food if I didn't entertain. It's how I've always connected myself to the world and made sense of it (even back in the days when I was dressing my little brother up with a tea cozy on his head to be my maître d').

I'm fond of the term "host" and its suggestion of benevolent leadership. A host is someone who steps forward and takes charge, almost always of things pleasing and good; his or her aim is to create a world in which everyday life is happier, more civilized, and delightful and where cooking, making a home, and entertaining are engaging, uplifting, meaningful, and valued. In short, a good host makes a true vocation out of living what I call "the inviting life"—the kind of life one wants to wake up to and, in the words of Auntie Mame, "Live! Live! Live!"

To me, the inviting life means two things. It's a life that involves a lot of what we rather inadequately call entertaining—a social life, if you will. And it's a life in which we approach the ordinary with a desire and determination to turn it into something lovely. This is not a frivolous desire, and it needn't be an extravagant one. It has very much to do with everyday activities and encounters.

Ultimately, living an inviting life is about being open, curious, and caring. It's about being attuned to beauty, ideas, creativity, and delight, especially where these potential pleasures tend to hide away—under a pile of dirty laundry, for example—and when our souls need them most. ("Desperate times call for desperate pleasures," as television critic Emily Nussbaum once tweeted.)

This is not a book full of strict rules and magic formulas that will turn us into the next Palm Beach society sensation. In what I think is a rather hospitality-hungry era, we might focus, instead, on finding the inspiration to do whatever we can in everyday life to make the places where we live—wherever they may be—welcoming, restorative, and uplifting for ourselves and for anyone who enters into our sphere.

A Bit of Backstory

My family would tell you I was born to host. Since childhood, I've been obsessed with cooking and with feeding people. As soon as I could sit up by myself without tumbling sideways, I was on the counter beside my mother's mixing bowls, taking it all in. Once I could write, I went so far as to interview neighbours, taking a notebook whenever we went visiting and later transcribing the results of my investigations onto 1970s recipe cards (Linda's "slush" and Vida's "hole whit rolls" are still preserved in my wobbly scrawl).

There was the requisite whoopee-pie phase, but that soon evolved into masterpieces such as Chicken *à la Dijonnaise* and *Marquise au Chocolat*, racy recipes from the pages of *Gourmet* magazine and a *Reader's Digest* cookbook. Before long, elaborate dinners for the family became my specialty. And I hadn't just become ambitious about the food, either: by the time I was a teenager, I'd grown into a proper little tyrant when it came to table settings and etiquette (I'd discovered Emily Post and Amy Vanderbilt, to the despair of my two brothers).

In a way, all of this was innocent, theatrical play on my part, but at the same time, I was aware even then that there was power in feeding people, that on the occasions I took over from my mother to cook for fun, I was somehow helping to keep our household together and make everybody happy. That gave me purpose and satisfaction. I was also aware that the *way* we ate said something about who we were, and I was determined that everything should be more civilized, more elegant. I instinctively sensed that these things started at the table.

Civility really does begin at the table. It's a place not just where we learn how to eat, but also where we acquire social fluency, values, conversation skills, literacy, and knowledge about how the world works. It's a place where hostility is unwelcome. (It's just too dangerous, what with everyone holding weapons, which in large part explains all the etiquette around eating.) In business, where parties come to a table to negotiate, it's the very same concept; if it weren't, we would have given the negotiation table a separate word. All of this makes dinner so much more fascinating than simply food on a plate, which is no doubt why it has for so long captivated my imagination.

As life went on, I never abandoned my identity as a cook and host, nor my impulse to try to raise standards, but I did put them aside for a while for what I thought were more noble pursuits. My generation of women was taught that if you had any brain at all, you became a doctor, a lawyer, or a CEO, so I earned a few degrees, absorbed a few languages, and set my sights on becoming a diplomat.

It wasn't until I was in my first corporate job that I saw how far off track any form of office life was for me. I couldn't sit still. Nothing sparked my excitement or curiosity. For relief, I spent every free moment reading cookbooks and plotting parties. Clearly, my heart was elsewhere. So I quit my job and flew across the country to do a six-month culinary program in Vancouver, figuring that the worst that could happen was that I'd learn to host better dinners.

It is amazing how life can start to flow when we finally make the right move. After cooking school, doors swung open: first, I was offered a job in wine country, California, which then catapulted me to France, where I worked for one of the most influential food writers and teachers of the day, Anne Willan, whose esteemed École de Cuisine La Varenne was operating from a château in the Burgundian countryside.

Anne was a crucial mentor, the kind whose legacy stays with you long after you've slipped out from under their wing. I lived and worked at Château du Feÿ on and off for years, helping with the school in the summer and working on cookbooks the rest of the time. Mostly I was researching and writing in the library, a high-ceilinged room with pretty red wallpaper that housed some four thousand culinary volumes dating back to the sixteenth century. I also cooked a good deal, sometimes because recipes needed testing, but mostly because an endless stream of high-profile visitors needed entertaining. Although most of the time there was an in-house chef, very often everyone pitched in. It was a unique education in that way: you didn't learn restaurant-style food and service with Anne, but rather tip-top home cooking and hosting skills. I was in my element.

My time at Le Feÿ transformed me, but so did being in France. France changes everybody who spends any time there. Almost as soon as a visitor's feet touch the country's soil, he becomes aware that pleasure and beauty are not vain pursuits, but rather innate parts of the culture that everyone is expected to uphold.

In France, you never just went grocery shopping, you sought out the best purveyors for every ingredient, even if that meant walking an extra ten blocks; you never showed up for cocktails at Le Feÿ in a T-shirt or Anne would send you back upstairs to change (other people had to look at you, so you were expected to have some respect for their eyes); the dinner table was always delightfully set, guests or no guests. It dawned on me that this way of living was basically my childhood vision of how the world ought to be.

Le Feÿ was just about the most comfortable I've ever felt in my own skin—I particularly loved the combination of earthy rural life and sophistication—but I couldn't stay forever. I went on to write my own cookbooks and make television shows, living mostly in Paris and working project to project for about ten years. There was a lot of freedom and satisfaction in that. I travelled a lot too, studying languages and culture and hunting down recipes, hosting ideas, and tabletop items wherever I went. I loved it.

But, when it came to what you might call real life, I was constantly hopping back and forth across the Atlantic and drifting around North America, living in temporary housing (a condo while we shot that show, a rental while I researched that book, another apartment while I studied somewhere . . .). Ultimately my cooking suffered, and so did my sense of self (homelessness doesn't look so hot on a consummate homebody).

As a self-imposed cure, I decided to plant myself in Toronto, take six months off, and not leave town, not even for a weekend, until I'd found my feet. I took a tiny flat on the second floor of a Victorian house on a leafy street.

It was September, still warm, but with the crisp, autumnal scent of fresh starts in the air. The new place was bright with a large bay window that had tucked into it a round, pine table and four sort of ecclesiastical chairs. I immediately put one of the chairs in a closet and shoved two others against a wall. I'd obviously be the only one sitting at that table. This main room also included a sitting area with a love seat and a cushiony reading chair, as well as a strip of kitchen along one wall. ("Sorry about the old stove," the landlord said when I moved in. "We've never had anyone live here who actually cooked." I didn't tell him I'd probably be living off cashews and avocados anyway.) French doors led off the main room to a snug bedroom, and farther off that was a tiny bathroom with a tub wedged miraculously into a corner.

At first, my days were thumb-twiddlingly blank. I had no job and no social life. I did have a handful of unconnected friends in the city, but that didn't constitute a community. I'd see one friend one week, another the next, then more weeks would go by. There was no way, given my cramped living arrangements, that I could put everyone I knew in the same room at the same time, shake them up, and sit back with a martini basking in the glow of my hand-picked social circle. Entertainment meant I went out occasionally, but nobody came in.

Until I broke my foot.

You see, I'd been asked out once or twice by the friend of a friend. Lunch, a drink... No big deal. Then one night I arrived home late in the pouring rain and tried to open the front door of the house, which had a maddeningly sticky lock. It wouldn't budge. I tried and tried and failed and failed until I was so fed up that, four-lettering wildly, I kicked the door, toe front on with a violent thud, wearing ballerinas. The next time the man called, I had to decline his invitation to go out because I could barely stand up, let alone walk. He said, "Stay put. I'm coming over." I nearly froze on the spot. "What do you mean you're coming over?!" I panicked. "You mean *here*?!"

That's the moment it really struck home how far I'd allowed myself to get (yet again) from being and living like the person I'd always felt I was meant to be. A solo apartment I couldn't open to a guest without blushing? A woman hiding from the world? The next thing I knew, the doorbell was ringing. It was the man, Peter, delivering the basics: milk, tea, bread, butter, wine. He looked around and said, "Wow, this is small. What are *you* doing *here*?" What indeed. In that moment, what felt truly small was me.

It can't have bothered Peter that much, because within about six weeks, he'd practically moved in. One of the chairs came out from against the wall and joined the table, and suddenly I was cooking again. For the next six months, with Peter to-ing and fro-ing between his place and mine, together we'd whip up dinners, glasses of wine in hand, at my grand total of two feet of counter space: potato röstis with smoked salmon and crème fraîche, chicken tagines, Spanish omelettes, pork roasts that turned into office-lunch sandwiches... My days, even though I was home alone, suddenly had purpose: shopping for food became fun again, fluffing up the house every day pleased me. I went real, live domestic goddess overnight!

The crux of it, in retrospect, was that having another mouth to feed and a piece of terra firma, however small, reminded me of who I was, what makes me happiest, and how I'm best at contributing to the world. It's a wonder something that has been so obvious my entire life should ever have escaped me: hosting and making home aren't just nice things to do for other people, they're essential to our own well-being. In my case, hosting, for lack of a better word, is what makes me thrive. Now that I'd been reminded, the only problem was my HQ.

Or *was* it a real problem? I'd made a new friend during that era, a French woman, and once, as I fretted to her over the inadequacy of my space for entertaining, she said, "It's completely irrelevant how grand the place where you're living is. All that matters is ambiance. Ambiance and you." (Just the kind of thing I'd preach myself and then hypocritically not put into practice.) Immediately I decided that if I was stuck living in this box for the time being, then I was going to tie a bow on it. The next thing I knew, I was entertaining several nights a week. I'd invite anyone and everyone over and we'd squeeze in around the pine table in the bay window and feast forth. My friend was right: nobody cares. The right people come for the right reasons.

Sometimes they even stay. As soon as my lease was up, Peter and I found a bigger and better place together, but by then I'd learned the crucial lesson once and for all: that with the right spirit, people can make a home and host no matter where they find themselves.

ONE

Make a Welcome Home

Here they come sailing up the gravel avenue lined with gently swaying, one-hundred-year-old elms. The swirly wrought-iron gates sit already open, and your guests whiz through in their snappy vintage convertible, the intoxicating scent of lilacs enveloping them as they purr to a halt. Immediately, the front door flings open and out you fly offering ice-frosted glasses of minty lemonade from a brass-handled butler's tray and shooing the guests' bags upstairs with the blue-eyed houseboy. The cool, wide veranda wraps around the house as effortlessly as a loosely flung-on shawl, and upon it is scattered that charming wicker furniture these same guests so admired last summer. ("Thank you, Granny," you mutter, eyes heavenwards, "for leaving it to me!")

The assembled company sink into a cluster of chintz-cushioned chairs and you pick up right where you left off. "How was Istanbul?" "Did you hear that Roddy's horse won the triple crown?!" As the conversation meanders, the afternoon sun sears its way across a cloudless sky, and just as it tilts to begin its descent over the hills, you insist your guests take a refreshing plunge in the turquoise pool before settling in and dressing for dinner. "Please take the yellow rose room at the end of the hall that overlooks the labyrinth," you tell them, adding in a singsong voice over your shoulder, "I thought quail with grapes might be suitable for tonight." You breeze toward the kitchen in vintage Pucci for a word with cook and . . .

Pop!

Forgive me for bursting the bubble before we even got our hands on a Champagne cocktail, but earth was calling. Of course, such scenarios do take place (and I begrudge no one such pleasures; if that's your world, seize the day), but the reality is that most of us host in much humbler conditions and without paid help at our beck and call. Never mind; this is no reason to allow our own parades to be rained out. There is room in this world for all kinds of hosting, and just as every host is different, so is (and should be) every host's home; otherwise, the business of entertaining would get very dull very fast.

There is no single ideal hosting home anyway. A five-year-old might say it's the jungle gym at McDonald's. A teenager might argue it's a shack on the beach. A hedge-fund executive might say it's half a floor at the Ritz. Personally, I envision a country house surrounded in heritage rose bushes—and I reserve the right to change my mind next week (though I won't). Anything is fair game to become the kind of place with a metaphorically open door and pleasant vibes that people feel good in, so the first step toward creating a welcome home is to embrace what we've got, whether it's a condo, a farmhouse, a houseboat, or a room. Once we're at one with our place, we can start to think about comfort and about filling it with as much of our own aura and personality as we can. This, to a significant degree, is what people come for.

It doesn't have to happen overnight. It's one thing to have a house, but home we all must make, and we have to make it every day. Making home is the spaghetti pot boiling, the laundry on the line, the phone ringing, the baseboards that need painting, the jasmine suddenly coming into bloom, that half-completed crossword on the coffee table ... We needn't be too hasty to "arrive," then, to do a massive expensive renovation all in one swoop and try to trick ourselves into believing we're done. We're not. Making home—a welcome home—is a journey, the best part of which, naturally, is the perpetual getting there.

And while it's in progress (which, as I've said, is always), there's no need to apologize. It's an honour to allow people into our private spaces. One of the reasons we do it is to show people we trust them and to reveal to them more of who we are. The American decorator Dorothy Draper famously said, "Decorating and entertaining are two halves of the same apple." I can see why.

A seldom-appreciated bonus of inviting people in is that it actually helps with getting our home into a welcome state faster and keeping it there. It's all too easy to become accustomed to so-so living arrangements when we never let anybody see them. Routine can breed blindness, whereas inviting people over has a remarkable way of making us suddenly realize that the front door is about to fall off its hinges and the floors need sweeping. (It's a sad truth that we tend to put up with far more ourselves than we'd expect anyone else to.)

One might argue that regular entertaining is the secret to keeping ourselves civilized in our private lives, rather than reverting to cavemen. It's an interesting perspective, because it suggests that our homes may not exist solely for the selfish reasons we like to think they do (i.e., just for us). Yes, they are retreats, yes they are private worlds away from the fray, but they are also (potentially, anyway) welcoming places that the outside world can come into and be transformed by, for the better.

If you lack faith in your current residence, let me share a little tale about one of mine. I lived in a number of different flats during my Paris years, but one in particular, at 16 rue Rambuteau, which I shared with a roommate, Camille, was a perfect example of how even a humble apartment can rise to the status of social hub. The front door to that apartment opened onto a short, pokey hallway that offered the only two ways into the rest of the flat: via the bathroom or via my bedroom. The receiving space consisted of one common room with a defunct fireplace, a round dining table with flea-market chairs, one sofa, one reading chair, and a few side tables. A tiny kitchen off that living room boasted no more than two square feet of counter space, along with a gas range that had a broken temperature gauge.

A far cry from Versailles, as you can see, but the amount of entertaining we did in that place (so much that I can't remember us ever dining alone, although presumably that did happen) made it legendary.

Despite its awkward layout, No. 16 offered amusing touches like colourful Alexander Calder-like mobiles (no relation, *hélas*), a few eye-catching mirrors, and coloured tissue-paper lights dangling into corners from the ceiling. The result was an air of kooky enchantment that drew people in like a flame and held them in thrall well into the early hours. The other thing, of course, is that we cooked all the time. People were lured in by our delicate and enthusiastic culinary experiments: stuffed zucchini flowers, steak *au poivre*, tarragon eggs, salad with fois gras . . . That broom closet of a kitchen didn't hold us back one bit. (Once we even built a two-foot-high *croquembouche* in it, which we carried to a party up the street on a makeshift stretcher.) In short, the place, despite its considerable drawbacks, had spirit and vibe. So, I suppose, did we.

It's a good thing those Paris days educated me in the art of bohemian living, because I'm sort of still at it, if not quite to the same offbeat degree. What can I say? At some stage, I subconsciously chose to lead an artistic (and until recently nomadic) sort of life. I craved experience, I wanted to see the world, I wanted to delve into my interests full on, rather than hobby style. And so, I let my passions lead the way rather than choosing a steady and conventional career set on the pursuit of the almighty dollar and the perks that come with it. The ride has been rich in other ways, to be sure, but not without consequences.

For one thing, when you're travelling and moving about all the time, you can carry only so much with you. The odd *coups de coeur* I had picked up along the way had been so long in storage by the time I met Peter that I couldn't even remember what most of them were. Peter wasn't exactly loaded down with stuff, either. He came with things like a sofa, a table, chairs, a bed, and a controversial black-and-white photograph of Bob Dylan. My collection, meanwhile, turned out to include some paintings, plenty of kitchen equipment and tabletop playthings, a pine chest, a moose antler (surely an essential, no?), an antique butter-making basin, and a mirror whose ornate white frame required considerable gluing after the move.

We cobbled our belongings together and set up base in a Victorian house, which, at the time of writing, is where we still are. The place is not huge, but it has wonderfully high ceilings, which give the interior an airy lift. It has also been gutted on the ground floor to create an almost loft-like space, so we entertain in a big, open rectangle, geometrically speaking. There's a dining table in the front bay window, and from there you can see all the way back to the kitchen, where I do my banging around. In between, there's a fairly roomy sitting space, another smaller dining area/office, and a corner devoted to being a bar. In short, it's modest. All I could think about in the beginning was what was lacking, but somehow, in no time, the place seemed to take on a life of its own and morph into one harmonious, host-ready whole.

House & Garden have yet to call (I can't for the life of me . . .), but we're happy with our place for now because it's unique and it's true to the stage of our lives we're in at the moment. Also, it's not a place that looks as though we went out and bought things to fill it in a single weekend. For two people starting out fresh, miraculously it seems already as though it has a long history, and personally that's how I want home to feel. In fact, that's partly what I think home *is*: a story, and the possibility for more stories after that.

Temporary Housing

Having grown up in a house that's been in the same family for five generations, I know what an anchor feels like and how nice it is to be able to depend on one. There is enormous security in a long-standing family house: it has had the luxury of evolving over time, it feels palpably safe, its history and identity are givens, and it will have developed natural character—all the kinds of qualities I adore and crave. I've always tried to recreate that sort of aura in my living spaces, but it's often not easy, particularly in a part of the world where so much is relatively new.

Contemporary places need extra attention to feel permanent and personal, and temporary places need more help than any, because either they'll have soaked up the vibes of others who've passed through (possible fumigation required) or they'll be so generic and sterile in an attempt to offend no one that they end up with all the aesthetic appeal of an airport.

It's the latter I'm concerned about here, because so many of us— almost all of us at some point or other in our lives—will need to live somewhere short term, even if it's a holiday rental. The trouble is, when we know we won't be living somewhere for long, it's all too easy to convince ourselves that it's not worth the bother of trying to put our own stamp on the place. This is a mistake. Over my long history of moving about, I've learned it's crucial to morale, no matter how fleeting our stay, to make whatever place we're calling home as much of an extension of ourselves as we possibly can. Besides, all housing is ultimately temporary, when you think about it.

All the world's a stage. The sets go up and the sets come down. We want to make sure our various sets are fit for the roles we hope to play while we're in them.

How to Make Ultra-Temporary Housing Feel Homey

In furnished, decorated places, ask to have anything offensive or obtrusive removed for the duration of your stay. The William Morris philosophy, "Have nothing in your house that you do not know to be useful, or believe to be beautiful," holds true even if you're in a place only briefly. (Once, during a television shoot, I was put up in a unit so jammed with bad hotel art and oversized furniture I thought I'd rip my eyes out. One quick phone call and half of it was carted off. This was a three-month stay, and not cheap, so I felt justified. In any case, management understood and was very obliging.)

⫶ If there isn't one already in place, bring (or buy) a handsome throw and fling it over the bed for colour (temporary places tend to be palaces of beige). A throw is also nice to cozy up with in a roomy reading chair.

⫶ Add potted plants, not just cut flowers, for a greater sense of permanence.

⫶ Fill the bathroom with all manner of gorgeously scented potions, scrubs, and elixirs so that it smells and feels inviting and luxurious. This is not frou-frou. Feeling footloose can wear down your morale to a thread. Being able to pamper yourself like a chatelaine helps restore dignity.

⫶ If you haven't brought an old favourite from home, buy a unique mug that feels good in your hands and on your lips for your hot morning drink. Morning is a time of ritual and you want yours to be a nice, familiar one.

⫶ Stock the bar with your favourite drinks and buy at least two good glasses so you're not stuck with the fat-rimmed stock stuff from the cupboard.

⫶ Sprawl. Place bits of yourself everywhere: a book here, a magazine there, a notebook somewhere else, your own dressing gown on the back of a door—in short, signs of life.

- Candles, candles, candles . . .

- Stick photographs, magazine clippings, postcards, and other ephemera on the fridge to make the place feel more active and personal. Every time you reach for the milk, the fridge door will have something affirming to say to you.

- Don't let the place feel hollow. Instead, open the windows, invite some people over, sit on the balcony, put your feet up, breathe life into the place, and be present where you are.

A Blank Canvas

Many of the challenges presented by temporary housing are similar to those found in generic modern-day spaces such as condos. If you've just moved into a white square and are finding it depressingly anonymous, think of artists and take heart. You could give ten artists the same four-by four-foot blank canvas and let them loose, and you'd get ten completely different paintings. There's no reason why a few square white rooms can't have the same potential.

Six Ways to Turn a Cookie Cutter into a One-of-a-Kind

SHOW YOUR TRUE COLOURS.

Colours are highly personal, so add a splash or two that speak to you, either right on the walls or with furniture and objects.

ADD CONVERSATION PIECES WITH REAL MEANING.

Decorative pieces brought back from travels, antique finds, or a few pieces handed down from family help tell your story. You can also use objects for a purpose they weren't intended for, such as turning a wooden shoe into a pen holder (I did that when I was about seven and it still sits full of Bics in my parents' house) or turning a tiny, antique metal lunch pail into a holder for tobacco pipes, as Peter has done.

PUT SOME GROOVY IN THE DETAILS.

We tend not to put care or personality into practical things like garbage cans and soap dishes, yet these are the very sorts of objects that we come into contact with most every day, and that therefore have the greatest potential for giving us comfort or delight.

PUT EXTRA THOUGHT INTO THE GATHERING SPACE.

You can entertain, one way or another, virtually anywhere, as long as you group furniture in a sociable way and have good lighting. It's nice to add a few thoughtful touches too, such as a pile of shawls for cold nights or a bouquet of cheap fans from Chinatown for relief on hot evenings. Comfort is key if you want people to stick around.

DISPLAY YOUR FAVOURITE BOOKS.

Bookshelves are a window to the mind of the person who owns them, and guests love the privilege of being able to peek in. With so much reading material available online these days, I know many are keen not to accumulate books in bulk, but a choice collection in full view is nourishing for the mind, even if we only wander over and read a sentence or two from our favourite authors now and again.

FILL YOUR SPACE WITH INVITING ENERGY.

Vibe is the most elusive thing on this list, but the most important—certainly it's the single most commented-upon feature of our house right now. The feeling a place gives people is always inimitably unique, so forget following décor trends and be true to yourself in everything you do. The more comfortable a space makes you feel, the more alluring your energy will be, and, in turn, the more inviting your house.

A Good Match

Ultra-temporary is the last thing Peter and I were looking for when we decided to move in together. We swore that wherever we landed would have to do us for a solid three years, which isn't exactly long-long-term, I realize, but we figured it would be long enough for us to sort out where we'd ultimately like to end up. In the meantime, I wanted to focus on getting my career back on track and Peter just wanted some calm.

It's no mean feat finding a place that feels right, let me tell you, especially for someone like me who's hypersensitive to her environments. Way back when, I allowed a university roommate-to-be, Dan, to travel ahead of me to the city where we'd be studying and pick out an apartment. Dan was *not*, at least back then, a person hypersensitive to his environments. I remember he telephoned and said, "I found a faaaabulous place! It's huge!" It *was* huge. It was also hideous, low-ceilinged, and in a basement. I lasted a month, and then, rather than do something like take a lot of pills in one gulp, moved out. The relief I felt was like that of someone who'd just dug herself out of a maximum-security prison with a teaspoon. Dan, meanwhile, stayed in the place, very pleased with himself, for three years.

Luckily, Peter and I, for the most part, have similar tastes. Staying in our neighbourhood was important, because it's leafy and central enough to be walkable to almost anywhere, plus so many of our friends live nearby. The place had, of course, to be respectable for entertaining, and we were both keen on having at least some space outside. We couldn't move until May, but nonetheless we started looking in the winter. Ugh. It was an especially freezing season that year and the side-walks were positively arctic. I got on the Internet and found every available place in range, and we trudged around determinedly for a few weeks in search of paradise.

The unloved look is extremely popular in the rental sphere. I can't remember how many places we looked at—many—but one after another we left shaking our heads and increasingly discouraged. ("Who lives like that?" they made us wonder.) Toward the end, we found one place that, at last, bordered on marvellous: a sprawling old-world apartment in a period building. It had hardwood floors; bright bay windows; a kitchen that was way out of date, but in a charming way (including black-and-white floor tiles, which I like); a litter of bedrooms; and grand, wide rooms for entertaining. Ideal, except that there was no access to the outdoors and no air conditioning (which we'd regret in summer), plus the fireplace was blocked off, which was a sin. So close, yet so not quite right.

Well, that was it. We'd seen every place on my list, except for one, and it hadn't looked all that hot in the pictures anyway. Peter said, "Forget it. Let's just wait until spring. In any case, anything we have to take now will mean paying three different rents for three months, which is ridiculous." He was right. It was the last on the list and the sun was setting so we should just forget it and go drown our sorrows in a couple of martinis.

On the other hand, it was only a block away and exactly in the neighbourhood we wanted, so maybe we should just go look instead of cancelling the appointment this late. ("Let's not bother . . ." "Come on, one more . . .") So we slipped up the street against the wind and stopped in front of a tall Victorian house. Peering through the front window, we could see that the place looked tastefully decorated, bathed in golden light, and entirely too good to be true. ("Make that a double round of martinis" is what I could see coming.)

A landlord let us into a light, airy space—high ceilings, white walls covered in art, hardwood floors, cozy furnishing—and introduced us to the tenants of the moment, who were busy making a giant pot of meatballs. (Oh sure, torture us with homey scents too.) We were taken on a tour, but I, who had already mentally moved us in (and was also mentally boiling spaghetti), didn't register so much as a doorknob because my brain was too busy calculating how we could justify paying three separate rents for three months while waiting for this place to be liberated. I had no idea what Peter was thinking because he was being so quiet. At last he asked the landlord when it would be available, and I just about passed out cold. "May," he said, which was when both our leases were up. It was meant to be.

Moving House

Judging by the number of times Peter and I have both done it in our lives, you'd think we had some sick fetish for moving, but truly we don't. Moving sucks. Even when I've been completely organized and the movers have been angels, it is still one of the most stressful things a person can do.

The first thing you should know before packing so much as an envelope is that moving companies can be completely unreliable and their insurance companies sheer evil. Also, no matter how friendly they may sound on the telephone, some do not ultimately care about your stuff and just want your money. (This is true in all spheres of life, of course, but with moving, somehow, the sting feels worse.)

I was gun-shy this time because of a move a few years earlier that had involved a number of my most prized possessions, including two large paintings that I had made sure to have professionally wrapped with bubble wrap, wood frames, and the works. Those paintings, just to give you an idea of the kind of handling things can get, arrived at their destination not only packaging- and frame-free, but with forklift holes through both of them. In that same move, my dining table arrived with just one leg, five out of six dining chairs were shattered beyond repair, and two boxes never arrived at all. This was a major moving company, one you'd think you could trust, but they and their insurance henchpeople argued it was my tough luck and that they were not taking responsibility for any damages.

Hardened from that experience, I was vigilant as a hawk this time, even though we were moving only streets away. First of all, I did serious research, getting names of local movers from friends who'd used them before making a single call. Before I hired a company, I met the actual owner and looked him in the eye. Then, during the move, I stayed present the whole time. This company was fantastic: they were careful and pleasant and even completed the job under budget. (Later, when Peter and I had to move quite a bit of loot from Montreal, we hired another small operator—in fact a one-man mover. He too was honest and reliable. Next time we move, unless it involves crossing an ocean, you can guess the kind of outfit I intend to track down.)

Interior Influences

All my life, I have taken a huge interest in houses. As a child, I constantly requested house-plan magazines from the hardware store, which were full of sketches of the exterior of houses with floor plans beneath. I'd study them closely and then draw my own floor plans, including all the closets and door openings, for what I thought the perfect house would be (i.e., back then, the opposite of the house I was growing up in).

Our house was not decorated by anyone apart from my mother, although "decorate" is a term that would never have crossed her lips. Since it was an old house, it was (still is) full of a great many things that were never chosen by my parents but that had been part of the house for over a hundred years. When you live in a house like that, there's no such thing as decorating from scratch; what you do is rearrange things and find new and ingenious uses for old items. I understand that now, but it used to drive me crazy as a child. I could see very well how life appeared in the home décor magazines, and clearly we were not living like anybody normal. It was an outrage: "Why don't we have a breakfast nook!?" "Can't we get our living room sunken?"

Much as it maddened me in my youth, looking back now I can see how strong an influence that house had, and still has, on my aesthetic. It was full of quirks, as I said, furniture and objects alike: a single room might have in it a two-hundred-year-old sea captain's chest, a collection of carvings brought back from travels in Botswana, upended antique crocks serving as stands for ferns . . . The arrangement of the rooms was also wacky: a garage off the kitchen accommodating everything from freezers to a woodpile (never any cars in that particular spot); a greenhouse attached to the front living room so that potting soil was constantly being tracked back through the house as sprouting things were transferred outside to gardens; a balcony off an upstairs bathroom with a heavy wooden door (that nobody ever opened) embellished by a stained-glass window...

It was a house as far away as you could get from the pristine examples of how to live promoted in magazines, but it was wonderfully full of character. And it didn't look like anyone else's because it was a genuine reflection of the lives going on within it: ours.

Anne Willan and Mark Cherniavsky's house, Château du Feÿ in Burgundy, where I lived for several years, was also a formative place in terms of shaping my idea of a perfect house and how it should be. Anne was a natural administrator, and she ran her house with the same sharp eye and efficiency as she did her cooking school. But she also (being British perhaps explains it) instinctively knew that a house should be welcoming and relaxed, even when it's relatively grand. So while Le Feÿ had a fountain outside, an impressive entrance hall, and fifteen bedrooms, you were still allowed to charge through the place in rubber boots with the dogs, over the Persian rugs, past the dining table that regularly sat twelve on a weeknight, past the grand piano and the statue of Marianne on one of the marble fireplaces... The house had a certain formality about it, but at the same time it was comfortable and truly lived in, not precious, stiff, or self-conscious (something difficult to say about many a humbler house than that one).

Those two very different properties—the house of my youth and Le Feÿ—in fact had quite a lot in common. Both houses were in the country with a lot of movement between indoors and out; both were old houses

with a mixture of different styles in them and a keen sense of history; both were warm and welcoming with a constant flow of people of all ages and walks of life coming through them. Clearly I absorbed those values and aesthetics, because that's the vibe I wanted to recreate in our new place, even though it was small and in a city. We had only so much to work with, but I held close to my heart the words of Deborah Needleman in her book *The Perfectly Imperfect Home*: "An element of quirkiness in your décor shows that you do not take decorating or, by extension, yourself too seriously." This gave me courage, because quirky would be hard to avoid.

"Playing Lady"

We're not all reincarnations of Sister Parish, exactly, but we are all decorators, for better or for worse, to some degree. Some people have a real feel for this sort of thing and some have none whatsoever, but we all participate in creating the places in which we live and host, and there's always something about how we make our houses or allow them to be that is an expression of who we are. As the late American actress and interior designer Elsie de Wolfe once said, "A house is a dead giveaway."

I like the idea of approaching decorating in the same way often attributed to how French women dress, which is to say with apparently effortless, unselfconscious, individual flair. That effect doesn't come from appealing to the brain so much as it does the heart, and it requires us to be ruthlessly honest and true to ourselves. Contrivance is a deadly sin in any art, and we root it out like sniffer dogs. Even when we can't quite put our finger on why a room feels wrong, we sense it.

I carry in my mind one example of a beautiful disaster. It was an apartment in London that looked quite stunning, in a rather minimalist way: white walls, exposed beams and stone, a beautiful grey pew beneath a window, a rippling leather chaise, and so on. I'd always admired it, until, by accident, I found myself staying in the place for a few weeks. About halfway through the first day, my admiration had flown right out the window and I couldn't wait to get out of there. In that whole ethereal space, I discovered, there was not a single comfortable place to sit. The pew was rock hard and off in a lonely corner by itself. To negotiate one's way into the chaise resulted in a permanent backbend position that only Gumby could hold for longer than half a minute. Furthermore, the elegant colour scheme of greys and browns (which ultimately I love) turned out all to be hard surfaces and no soft textures, making the place feel monastically punishing and hollow.

In short, the apartment had been decorated to look chic and sophisticated (which it was), but I found it completely unlivable. In the end, all you could do in the place was walk in circles wringing your hands until you gave up and went out to take refuge in a café.

That place (I thought about it for a long time afterward) hadn't gone through enough function-and-feeling filters, so I had that on my mind when I tackled our place. It seemed to me that two questions would steer an amateur like me away from any pitfalls—namely, "What am I going to do in this room?" (sleep? jumping jacks? write?) and "How do I want to feel in here?" (grand? cozy? efficient? young?). If you know you want a room to read in, then you'll imagine yourself reading and realize you need better light than you might if the room were for watching television. If you want to feel cozy in a room, you might want to rethink the Scandinavian trend and scrap the all-white walls idea. And so on.

The British decorator Nina Campbell talks about "playing lady," a trick she says she learned from another great decorator, John Fowler. The idea is that if you want to see what works or is missing in a room, you act out various activities on the spot, serving drinks or belly dancing or whatever. By acting out, you realize what flaws need to be fixed.

Not that every flaw can be.

For example, in this rented house, I may have the power to paint a wall, but I can't take one down. I can't move the staircase or cut a hole in the room at the back for another door. Then there's the question of possessions that aren't necessarily negotiable. We've got a pine diamond-point armoire that was passed down from Peter's dad that we're expected to keep until it goes down to the next generation. If you are donated a dining-room set by your grandmother, she'd better not spot it at an auction or you'll be toast. We're not just owners of things in life; we're custodians sometimes too, and that comes with responsibility.

The bottom line is that we can't always go charging around forcing our environments and circumstances to adapt to us; it's for us to adapt ourselves to them too. The upside, I suppose, of not having everything exactly as we want it right from the get-go is that it forces us to be clever and creative.

Another Useful Trick: The Scan

Remember that trusty relaxation technique where you lie on your back with your eyes closed and start scanning your body from head to toe? First you make yourself aware of the top of your head—just the top of your head—then you move down to your ears, then your eyes, your mouth, your neck ... One body part at a time, down the body you go in your mind, noticing any tension and deliberately relaxing it, all the way down to your pinky toes. Perhaps some spots will be relaxed already, but some, you discover, aren't at all. You get to the mouth and suddenly realize your jaw is clenched like a sprung trap. Or you get to your feet and realize they're flexed so stiffly backward they're like two snowshoes sticking out of a snowbank. What can it all mean? It's worth figuring out and attending to, because your body is telling you something important.

The same exercise works with houses, or any living space. Just as our bodies alert us to threats to our well-being, so too do the rooms we inhabit and the things we keep in them for our use. The difference is that you have to scan your house and your own emotional reactions to it simultaneously, as if the house were your own body. When your senses react to a part of the house making you irritated or glum, that's a part that needs fixing. For example, if you hate getting your coat on in the morning, is it the coat's fault or is it because the closet door sticks and you've never bothered to fix it? Is there a room nobody ever wants to sit in? (So many houses have these!) What's the reason? Are the chairs uncomfortable? Is the wallpaper eye-watering? Does it have all the ambiance of a refrigerator?

I was big into scanning when we first moved into our place. Every time I sat down anywhere, I'd analyze how I felt and ask whether or not things pleased me and how I could improve them. What was making me feel uncomfortable wasn't always immediately obvious. For instance, early on in that apartment I realized I found cooking a bit depressing. For me, that's not normal, so I sleuthed the kitchen trying to put my finger on the trouble, but found nothing that made any sense. It was big enough, it was well laid out, I had all the tools I needed . . . Then one day while I was peeling potatoes at the sink and looking across through the house and out the door into the vestibule—my direct eye line—it struck me: a gloomy view.

The door to the vestibule was open because I like getting the light through the windowed front door. In a cold climate, however, light is a precious commodity much of the year, and even when you do get it, it can often be dull and grey, not helped by a dull white vestibule with grey floors. What I really wanted, I realized, was to look up from the kitchen at blue sky, all year long, even if I was being hoodwinked. Next day, I marched out first thing and bought a tin of palest blue paint. By noon I'd transformed that gloomy little entry room into a distant heavenly view to cook by. It worked.

A more obvious problem was a bathroom in the back that had three doors: one into the room itself, another into a closet, and the third opening onto laundry machines. Why did I want to scream and punch walls every time I went in there? Because every time I opened one of those doors, it would bang into another one, with me caught in the middle. Absurd design. I made it more livable by ripping a door out and chucking it into storage, then replacing it with a yellow velvet curtain. It made the room less maddening from a practical point of view, but at the same time it softened and brightened the space considerably. I no longer wanted to tear my hair out every time I went in there. Now the room actually cheered me up.

Those are just two examples. I could find many more, and will, but you have to take breaks from all this scanning every once in a while, because it's impossible to solve every problem at once. That said, regular scanning, or at least taking note of moments when you lose it with a drawer or a window, is essential if you want to avoid getting too comfortable with discomfort. We went for a few months keeping five folding chairs in the closet with all our jackets, even though every attempt to put a coat on resulted in a crash. The day it finally dawned on us to put them somewhere else, a particularly heavy straw was lifted from this camel's back.

The Grand Tour

It took a good year to get our house to feel like grown-ups lived in it, and even then, with all its charms, it still felt like a bit of a starter, especially compared to how our friends live: most in our circle are established, with houses plural, sleek cars, and high-powered jobs from which half of them are already dreaming of retiring. Meanwhile, here we are, like a couple of twenty-somethings, just starting out.

Oh well. There was no way we weren't going to entertain, including inviting people we barely knew (which, in the beginning, meant most of the time). Sometimes it takes guts, but I stand firm by the conviction that if we want friends in life then we have to be prepared to let people see our true colours. Anyway, even if this isn't our dream home, it's still pretty dreamy in its bobo way. Until we have one of those aha moments people talk about—where you walk past a strange house or miss a turn on holiday and drive into a town of unknown name and suddenly think, "This is it! This is home!"—then we'll content ourselves with what we've got. For now, then, you'll just have to take us as we are like everybody else does. On that note, come on in and I'll give you a tour.

THE ENTRANCE

What I yearn for is a whole large room dedicated entirely to comings and goings, a big airy space in which you could truly make an entrance. It would be fully equipped with full-length mirror; a long bench for sitting down or setting packages on; an umbrella stand; a console for keys, mail, metro tokens, sunglasses, pens, and other little things that tend to get dropped as soon as you're in a place; a nice lamp to leave on for anyone getting home after bedtime; and a gigantic vase of flowers, of course.

While I'm on a roll, I should add that off this grand space, perhaps behind a high panel door that reaches the ceiling, would be a gigantic cedar-lined cloakroom or, failing that, a cloakroom with hidden pouches of lavender all over (lavender and cedar both offer protection against moths) and, of course, a glamorous powder room. Because I'm greedy, I'd also love a second casual entrance with a boot room and a wall of hats, but I'm getting ahead of myself, because the reality is far from any such bower of roses.

What we in fact have here is a small vestibule that irritates me to distraction because it's so pokey you feel like a letter being slipped through a mail slot whenever you come through the door. Plunk. You can't land properly, in other words, which is the case in a lot of places and a serious design flaw. What seems to be overlooked is that a huge amount of activity goes on in an entrance. It's where we collect ourselves before leaving the house, making sure we're not forgetting our wallets and that we don't have parsley in our teeth. It's where we land when we get home, dropping whatever is in our hands (bags, mail, shopping . . .), and where we take off our boots, set down our umbrellas, and hang our coats (except for here, where I have to cross half the apartment to get to the nearest hanger—rant). It's a place, too, where we open up to strangers (or not) who've come to remind us to vote or to get us to buy chocolate bars for charity.

Perhaps most importantly, it's where we greet and bid farewell to the people we love most in life. Sometimes these arrivals and departures can be quite emotional, everything from saying goodbye to a friend we may never see again to waiting with open arms for Johnny to come marching home. Surely these moments, along with all our other door-related business, deserve proper space.

GATHERING

It's pretty difficult to create a welcome home without having places to sit. While cocktail parties can be stand-up affairs, most of the time when we want to see people it's so we can have a good long visit, which means sitting down. One elite circle in long-ago France (Les Précieuses) used to refer to chairs as *les indispensables de la conversation*, which I've always liked because it's a reminder that decent seats aren't just about giving our legs a rest, but also about allowing our upper halves, notably from the neck up, to function effectively.

From the perspective of entertaining, a living room is essentially a place to sit and talk (although a games table is useful, too, if you can fit one, allowing things like jigsaw puzzles to remain in progress for a few days), so for it to work it needs not only comfortable seats and enough of them, but also a comfortable arrangement of those seats. The late decorator Mark Hampton wisely warned, "All rooms look their best if they are used by the people they belong to. Unless a room is arranged in a way that allows it to function comfortably, it will never be used."

Consider, for example, these common user-unfriendly faux pas:

- Furniture that's too big and bulky for the space (and too much of it). How many times have you stepped into a living room so full of giant leather blocks that you had nowhere to go but directly onto one? It's like being all set for a nice dip in a pool and finding it bumper to bumper with floating loungers.

- All the furniture braced against three walls, facing a fourth blank wall, usually containing an enormous television set. Death to social interaction is what this is (especially if said TV is on). If you want people to interact, they must, more or less, face one another or at least be angled toward one another, which begins by having the furniture do the same.

- Furniture placed in one giant circle around a large room, rather than broken into a few smaller groupings. This makes talking to anyone opposite like screaming across a lake, plus it lacks intimacy, which makes people squirmy and self-protective, like it's about to be their turn next to speak at an AA meeting.

Even the most skillfully arranged furniture won't keep anyone in it for long if it's uncomfortable, which makes you wonder if most designers don't resent company. The world is knee-deep in terrible seats that warp your posture, punish your backside, and practically require a tow truck to get out of or a call to ground support to climb down from. A lot of these chairs, sofas, stools, etc. *look* deceitfully cool, which is presumably why people buy them, but they're impossible to sit on for longer than three minutes without needing to see a chiropractor, and therefore not remotely conducive to an inviting life.

Remember, too, that part of the job of a good seat is to make the person sitting in it look good, something not a lot of modern furniture takes into consideration. A deep, soft sofa may be wonderful for diving into with your whole body and a book on the weekend, but anyone elegantly dressed who tries to sit in one will immediately be made to look like a discarded bath towel. (Don't get me started on bar stools without backs.)

By contrast, I have a friend who recently inherited two large and rather regal German chairs with upholstered bases and carved armrests and feet. At first I dismissed them as being too serious, but then I sat in one. Well! It was so comfortable and gave me such fantastic posture, I felt as though I should have been wearing a tiara on my head.

Our living room *du jour* consists mainly of two sofas, two comfy armchairs, and a big coffee table. It is hardly the drawing room at Chatsworth, but it works, although the coffee table is a bit of an enemy of mine because I've discovered that you can't set food and drinks in the middle of something the size of a tennis court and expect people to be able to reach them. Furthermore, it's too low, so I'd like to replace it with something smaller and then compensate with various side tables of a better height within reach of every chair so that nobody has to stretch as though they have a puppy on a leash in a park full of pigeons every time they want to set down their glass or get their fingers into a bowl of tamari almonds.

We can seat a maximum of ten comfortably, but that's with bringing in two extra chairs from elsewhere. Whenever I invite more people than this, I end up on the floor gazing up at my guests like the family golden retriever, so I really ought to learn to tailor my entertaining to the space we've got. I've at least been wise enough to put the cocktail party for one hundred on the back burner.

DINING

The family I grew up in ate every meal together at the dining-room table. (We did homework at the same table and my mother always wrote there, so the room was forever in active use.) It's said that friends and families sitting down to share home-cooked meals is rare these days and that most people eat on the run. I'm willing to believe this, but I have to say I never see evidence of it. Apparently, I keep the company of people who take eating as seriously as I do.

Right now, I have no actual dining room because the common space in this house is one big room into which, fortunately, living-room and dining-room furniture both fit fine. However, if it were smaller I wouldn't give up. I recall a clever way to combine the two that I saw long ago in Munich in a small ground-floor apartment on der Kaiserstrasse. The owner had placed an elegant settee with pretty cushions along one wall and two or three comfortable upholstered chairs opposite—i.e., living-room style. Instead of a coffee table at the centre of this cluster, however, there was a small round dining table with a tablecloth that reached the floor like a ball gown. When ladies came for afternoon *Kaffee* and *Kuchen*, they sat there. When the family gathered for braised venison and egg noodles at *Mittagessen*, they sat there. And when you just wanted to write a letter or sit for a chat, you sat there too. Living-room décor with a dining table at its heart worked like a charm.

Another inspirational décor moment I had was at a Persian rug exhibit at the Arab World Institute in Paris years ago. I find Persian rugs exquisite to begin with, but what really captured my imagination was the notion that a rug could have the power of walls. It's not for nothing that desert cultures—nomadic ones at that—are the world experts in the art of the carpet: a desert is a vast, seemingly limitless, colourless space. Talk about neutrals! But as soon as you lay a carpet down on the sand, you've created a room. The demarcation of space has the power to claim and define turf for specific purposes. (Owners of wide-open lofts, take note.) That's another way to make a dining room if you don't actually have room for one.

Even in a place so small that a table can't be left up at all times, it's still possible to create a stylish, dignified dining atmosphere simply by erecting, say, a card table and throwing over a nice cloth. Heck, you could do it in a field! It takes less than a minute, and the very minor effort pays back in spades when it comes to morale. (I've always believed that without calm, social, sensuous, civilized dining, the rest of life quickly plummets into the abyss.) Even if you have a vast house with a gigantic dining room, this can still be useful to remember, in case you get bored eating in the same room all the time. How about dinner in the front hall or in a sunroom? Yes please!

And, going back to carpets for a second, friends of mine in Paris once threw a dinner party for a crowd that outnumbered places at the table by moving all furniture out of the way and spreading out on blankets on the floor. Indoor *pique-nique*! Why not?

I've started with the worst-case scenario of having no dining room proper, but a far more common problem seems to be having a dining room but not using it. An unused dining room is a giant hole at the centre of social life, because whereas a living room can be a place where people gather for various purposes (one might read while another knits while another plays Sudoku), the dining room—the dining table, to be precise—is *the* location in a house where everyone comes together for the same reason and partakes of the same activity at the same time. This is positively sacred, and therefore it is essential that a dining area, wherever it is, be made as alluring and unifying as possible, like a good campfire.

A few things can make or break a dining room. The first is lighting, the aim of which, as with a campfire, is to gather people around a central focus. Full-blast ceiling lights completely defeat this purpose, giving the room all the ambiance of an operating room. Lamps placed around the room can fail too, certainly if they're too bright, because they distract from the table. What works best is lighting directly on the table—the most obvious being candlelight—or lighting directly above it. The latter can be tricky because it's important to have any hanging light at precisely the right height: too low and it blocks eyes and communication; too high and the light is overly diffused. The experts say that thirty to thirty-four inches above the table is right. I have yet to test this theory, but certainly intend to before installing any crystal chandeliers.

The second key factor is, of course, chairs. I don't love the ones we have at the moment because they're too hard, which is punishing for people who spend so many hours sitting on them. What I'd like to do is sneak over to our neighbour's house in the middle of the night and steal his, because he has the most derrière-friendly chairs you could imagine (by Marcel Breuer, if you must know). His have a cane base, which has natural give, leather backs, which provide superb support, arm rests, and, because the seat rests on a sort of metal base, a bit of spring. Five-hour lunches, here I come! Meanwhile, ours are oak and too country for my taste, but I'm holding on to them until I find exactly the chairs I'm looking for. I'm not sure what those will be yet, but I trust I'll know them as soon as I sit on them.

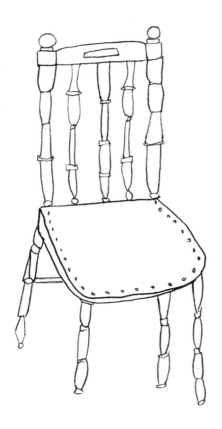

A table is perhaps not quite as crucial—any flat surface you can get your legs under can suffice. But if you're going to invest in something you want to last, it's important to give it thought before splurging. You have to decide if you want your table round or square, oblong or rectangular. Will it have legs or a pedestal? Will it be heavy or light; one piece or flexible? Is it wide enough; too wide? And so on.

The most charming round table I ever saw was tucked into a long-windowed nook in a house in Paris, permanently decked in a floor-length tablecloth, and set with stunning Royal Crown Derby. It sat four, no more, which was ideal for intimate and glamorous proper late-night town suppers of a bygone age. I'm keeping that in storage in my mental palace until I can find one just like it and have a romantic alcove to set it in.

A word of warning: Round tables are preferred for many events, the main reason being—as King Arthur worked out—that they waive the problem of seating protocol. Unfortunately, they're usually too big to allow for conversation, which is one reason why events can be such a bore. It's my opinion that a round table should never seat more than eight, otherwise all you get is a lonely crowd. (Also, if you get one dominant talker, which is so often the case, he traps the whole table, rather than just the few people closest him.) At home, this is no doubt less of a problem, but it is something to keep in mind if you're in the market for a table, enjoy putting on feasts for twelve, and have been wondering what shape to buy.

Another table I've coveted was also French, but in Montreal. It was a strong rectangular piece, antique, with a handsome patina and magnificently thick yet elegantly turned legs. Closed, it measured roughly three by four and a half feet, which seems average until you realize that to open the table, you pull from the long sides, not the short ones, resulting in a palatial rectangular table four and a half feet wide and long enough to seat twenty-four (in gowns). Swoon!

I torture myself with these reminiscences because the table upon which I am writing this minute—and at which we dine every night (until I can hire vandals to come destroy it)—is a clunker. "Why are you living with it?" you wonder! Well, because Peter's children are so attached to it that my life is under threat if I ever throw it out. This is the table they grew up with, the table at which they dined every night and learned their multiplication tables. It wobbles and has clumsy legs that are always in the way, but for his children it is highly charged with memories and emotions. What wonderful energy for a piece of furniture to have, really.

Now if only one of them would take all this positive energy to go live at *their* house, so I could buy a replacement . . .

KITCHEN CONFIDENCE

At last we arrive at everybody's favourite room, and the room so many have strong and opposing feelings about. I do love a romantic country kitchen, the kind with a sofa in it for naps and a table for having break-fast and reading the paper. The trouble with such a kitchen, however, is that it can be so alluring that you end up living your whole life in that room alone while completely neglecting the rest of the house. Unused rooms feel cold and lifeless and nobody wants to go in them, as we know, so in the interest of keeping the rest of the house alive and well, ultimately I prefer a kitchen that acts as just that: primarily a place in which to cook. (Not, mind you, to the degree that it's anti-social. It's nice if people can gather on the opposite side of a counter while we cook. Children, for example, can learn a good deal about healthy cooking and eating this way, almost by osmosis.)

For this reason, I quite like the kitchen I'm working in right now (although it would be improved by a pantry with an additional fridge). It's basically a modest-sized horseshoe, which I find to be one of the best kitchen shapes, because you can spin around in it, swooshity whoop, from chopping board to sauté pan, from fridge to sink, from dishwasher to dish cupboard. It's a truism that where there's a vacuum, it will be filled, which is why a gigantic kitchen would not necessarily be a bonus. A vast expanse of counter space rarely lasts; before you know it, it's piled sky-high with appliances you never use, magazines, plants, decorative chunks of this and that. A smaller kitchen often forces us to be more efficient and organized, with "a place for everything, and everything in its place."

I had a few problems with this kitchen in the beginning. For one thing, it came equipped with mammoth chrome appliances. What is it about the stainless-steel look that people find so appealing? Perhaps they think it's cleaner somehow? Or maybe it's meant to make home cooks feel more professional? (I don't know why anyone would want to replicate a sweaty, stressed-out place on the line at home.) I couldn't do anything about the stove, but the fridge, which didn't even have the courtesy of being magnetic, I simply couldn't suffer. I wrote to every friend we know in every corner of the globe and asked them to send us a postcard; then, as the mail began pouring in, I taped them all over the refrigerator, turning it into a patchwork coat of many colours. (One friend referred to her postcard as a *cache-misère*. Quite.)

Another aspect of the kitchen that bothered me was the all-whiteness of it. The bias toward white kitchens may stem from a notion that white is somehow cleaner than, say, green or yellow, but to me this one—like most of them—just felt bleak and sterile, like going through Customs. My solution was to paint the longest wall of the kitchen very pale pink (Farrow & Ball Pink Ground, to be precise). It's not girly, if you were worried: it's balancing, a perfect foil for the rack of copper, cast-iron, and steel pots that's set against it. (I'm not anti-white, incidentally, but I am anti-cold, clinical white. A wonderful way to avoid this effect, if you really want an all-white room, is to layer a few different hues of white and cream in the same room [in different textures even, if you can], which will add warmth, interest, and romance.)

It's mystifying how many books on décor leave kitchens out altogether. As someone who spends a lot of time in one, I don't think there's a room in which it is more important to feel calm and carefree. Just because the primary purpose of a space is function doesn't mean it's not a living space too and that furnishings and décor don't matter. Obviously nobody wants a ton of flounce getting in their way, but a kitchen does have to have allure or we'd never want to go in there and make supper, which would put a serious damper on inviting. (On that note, do consider a dimmer switch in the kitchen. You need proper light when you're working, but the rest of the time, such as when you're sneaking in late at night or early in the morning for a hot mug of cocoa, the room benefits from a quieter ambiance.)

In addition to the paint job, I put a striped curtain instead of a cupboard door over the toothless space left by a removed wine fridge, hung a romantic mirror on the wall next to the rack of pots and pans, and added a bay tree (a wedding present from a friend). In all, I didn't do much (and what I did cost peanuts), but the result is a kitchen that feels like part of the house rather than some sort of cockpit, aesthetically cut off from the rest.

ZZZZZZ

Upstairs, Peter and I have a loft-like bedroom oasis with a bathroom en suite and a room-sized balcony off the side. Correction: it *would* be an oasis (and should be), except that we also keep our clothes up there, because somebody, somewhere, once upon a time, decided that getting dressed and sleeping belonged in the same space. For someone like me who tends to drape things all over everywhere, it's a curse. A place to sleep should be cozy, safe, airy, cool, dark at night, and restful, something very difficult to achieve if you have a bedroom doing double duty as a walk-in closet. (I know it's considered a luxury, but a separate dressing room makes all the sense in the world, and the next time we move I want one.)

It has always puzzled me why rooms in which people spend so few waking hours get the kind of real estate they do in most houses. I can see why vast hotel rooms appeal, because they act as entire homes away from home, but surely a domestic bedroom is primarily about the activities that go on in a bed itself: sleep, sex, sickness, and the odd bit of sulking (as a matter of interest, the French word "boudoir" comes from "bouder": to sulk). Any other occupation that modern design has shoehorned in there, I'd rather shoo to another part of the house. (Teenagers may disagree, because bedrooms tend to be their personal kingdoms, but ultimately, for me, most of the room in a bedroom that's not actual bed feels like a waste of space.)

However, we basically like it, even though the décor of that bedroom has thus far been relatively neglected, apart from the installation of a couple of closets. From a hosting point of view, you'd think "Who cares?" because generally a bedroom is the most private space in a house. But we sort of do care, because so many people come tramping through in summer to get out to our balcony.

One of the best things about our bedroom is the sheets. Peter went away for a few weeks once, and when he came back he discovered that I'd nearly bankrupted us with a greedy order of excellent linen bedclothes. I defended my sleight of hand by arguing that they're an investment, not an extravagance. Peter protested, but luckily, within a week, he was as sold on them as I was. You might expect linen to be rough, but in fact these sheets have the texture and substance of deep luxury. Furthermore, they have the miraculous ability to be both cool in summer and warm in winter.

I can see myself getting interested in sheets, blankets, and bed coverings in quite a serious way, because just as a dining table can become a micro-decorating playground, so too can a bed be changed up in a way that transforms the look and feel of the whole room, which is a heck of a lot easier than launching into a full-blown bedroom renovation every time you get bored.

A Few Ways to Make a Bedroom Better, Even When It Is Also a Closet

⊹ Get the bed height that's right (for you). There are at least two schools of thought when it comes to bed height. One says we sleep better the closer we are to the ground (I have not thoroughly tested this, unless camping in my youth counts, in which case I disagree). Another says that better is a bed of such a height that if you're sick and someone sits in a chair beside you, you can talk eye to eye rather than having to strain up at them. Ultra-high beds can be fun, but generally I like to be able to sit down easily on a bed without having to climb up or collapse down.

+ Invest in a high-quality mattress cover. A good one makes a bed more comfortable and will extend the life of your mattress. They're also easy to clean (a mattress is not).

+ Have bedside tables at bed height or slightly higher so your herbal tea and water are easy to reach. Also, make sure the tables are roomy enough to hold all the things you like to keep on them.

+ Have a respectable bedside lamp, preferably with a dimmer switch so it can be used for reading but then lowered to a gentler setting for, say, checking the clock in the middle of the night.

+ Invest in an alarm clock that's beautiful to look at, has a nice wake-up sound (i.e., not like a recess bell going off at the local school), and is easy to set, rather than being covered in a zillion confusing buttons.

+ For good air, keep a plant or two in the room. Alternatively, try a diffuser with essential oils or a spritz of lavender. For good cheer, keep a bouquet of flowers (which is another easy way to toy with décor).

+ Try to keep clothes out of sight. (Incidentally, if you have a room that might become a dressing room but no budget for installing rue Royale–boutique- style cupboards, remember rolling garment racks.)

- Even if you don't iron bedclothes, at least iron the pillow cases so they're fresh and crisp.

- Depending on your climate, use a humidifier or dehumidifier to improve the quality of your sleep.

- Ban, as a rule, the following: television, computers, phones, food, and arguments.

THE GUEST BEDROOM

We don't often have overnight guests, so the bedroom that's supposed to be in guest-ready shape is in fact more of a place where we put everything we don't otherwise have room for. I'm ashamed of this and promise to fix it, because it really should be a part of a house that any guest can fully lay claim to and use as a retreat any time of day. A guest room needs all the basic accoutrements that any other bedroom would call for (including flowers and water), along with a few extras:

- A suitable, sturdy place, such as a chest, on which to set a large suitcase

- Plenty of hooks and clothes hangers (empty except for one with a dressing gown on it)

- A (completely empty) chest of drawers

- A nightlight for navigating in the dark on unfamiliar turf

→ A selection of books and magazines you deem of interest to your guest

→ If possible, a desk, with paper and pens at the ready. (Writer's bias, perhaps, but you never know when a person might have to jot down a Nobel-prize-worthy idea in the dead of night.)

A BIT ABOUT SLEEP

While we're here in the slumber chamber, I thought I might share some things I've recently learned about sleep. My own became infinitely healthier a few years ago when I learned about the medieval notions of first sleep (or dead sleep) and second sleep (in French, *dorveille,* which is a marvellous word describing that particular in-and-out state between sleep and wakefulness). The terms describe a latter-day notion of what once was considered to constitute a good night's sleep: a night divided naturally into two parts, one deep sleep and one light, in that order, with about an hour of wakefulness between.

For me, this is how sleep always seemed to progress anyway. I'd conk out for a few hours, then later come to and lie awake for a stretch, then drift in and out before finally falling asleep again. This is not what I had ever learned a good night's sleep was meant to be (the word on the street being that we're supposed to have a solid eight hours of shut-eye, no peeking!), and so whenever I woke in the night, I'd panic. My mind would start to race and I'd thrash and stress myself to exhaustion, eyes wide open. Once I discovered that old-time language of sleep (first sleep, second sleep, etc.), I could finally relax and actually enjoy being awake in the night, quietly resting and waiting to drift off again. (Around the same time, incidentally, I was told that a solid eight hours without waking is virtually impossible anyway, at least without sleeping tablets.)

Strangely enough, at the same time as we've been brainwashed with the idea of needing a solid eight hours' sleep, so too have we come to hold in awe anyone who claims to manage on only five hours or less. I don't know if this is corporate machismo or some weird religion of deprivation, but either way, the implication that it's meant to indicate some sort of moral superiority is a bit much.

The bottom line is that we all look better, feel better, and function better when we're well rested, so, far from being a lazy indulgence, a good night's sleep (possibly even napping, although I'm not into that—yet) is key to living a good life and being able to contribute the maximum we can. "Early to bed, early to rise, makes you healthy, wealthy, and wise," as my late grandfather used to chant.

A Few Ways to Get a Better Sleep

- Get the most comfortable bed you can afford and make it up with good-quality, season-appropriate, natural-fibre sheets and bedcovers. (Synthetic fibres don't breathe.)

- Keep your bedroom uncluttered and peacefully decorated.

- Arrange for your room to be dark at night (without channeling a coal mine). This sounds obvious, but so many live in glass high-rises these days that it can be difficult to keep light out.

- Let the room be quiet and restful, protected from noise as much as possible. (If that's a challenge, keep earplugs close by.)

- Keep your bedroom cool. Open a window when it makes sense for fresh air. (But have fine screens to keep the mosquitoes out if you live in a bog.)

- No television, phone, electronics . . .

- Try to stick to the same bedtime every night. That sounds a bit toddler, I know, but it works.

- Be grateful for three things in your day before you shut your eyes.

- If you wake up in the night, try to rest and enjoy the fact that you don't have to get out of bed any time soon. If you're restless, practise listening to every sound: the person breathing beside you, a siren in the distance, birdsong, wind in the trees . . . It's incredibly relaxing and much more effective than counting sheep.

- When the alarm goes, get up. Get up! Don't loll around or you'll become lethargic and want to stay there all day.

- Be disciplined about making your bed every morning so that it's ready to welcome you when you return to it at night (and so the sight of a giant wad of bedclothes doesn't communicate to you all day what a slob you are).

PRIMPING

Back to the house, and to another of my pet peeves. Why are bathrooms so often the smallest and darkest rooms, with barely enough space to turn around in or set down a glass of water? Is this not *the* room in which we're meant to take care of our bodies and gussy up for our guests? Well then, it would help to be able to see said bodies, stretch them out a bit, and pamper them in style. (I've read that the best place for a vanity, for example, is right in front of a window so we can see ourselves. I'm dying to test the theory.)

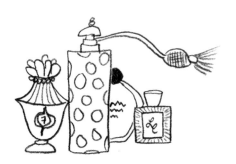

In my ideal world, this important room would always be given the Elsie de Wolfe "bath salon" treatment: in other words, decorated like a living room rather than a telephone booth. So splendid was her Paris bathroom, apparently, that she'd go so far as to serve coffee to guests in there!

Meanwhile, I have three duds to contend with here: dark, pokey, gloomy closets with nowhere to set down so much as a box of dental floss. Even the largest of the three desperately needed shelving, but there was nowhere to put it, so I inserted an Ikea CD tower, removing some shelves so that those remaining could accommodate shampoo bottles and glasses for toothbrushes. It works great, although I consider it makeshift.

The upstairs loo I'm still trying to figure out (one thing it needs is a close-up mirror with a light), but I keep in mind a "bathroom" that my friend, Rebeca, installed once in the *chambre de bonne* in the attic above her Paris apartment: the essentials, in somewhat Lilliputian form, fitted sleekly into a sort of silo, all shiny, bright cherry red.

Another second downstairs WC took me some time to get around to because it needed thinking about in a different way. You see, a washroom is often for guests and often used in the evening. Whereas in the daytime you want a bathroom to be bright (so you don't end up accidentally shaving off an eyebrow or putting lipstick across your cheek), at night there's no reason it can't be dark and dramatic. You might think of dim lighting, a glamorous mirror, maybe bold wallpaper or a striking paint colour—something to make it a bit of a fun place to go to get away from the fray at a party for a moment.

Also, it occurs to me that people don't dash off to the loo just for the obvious reasons, but also for when they have little emergencies like a sneezing fit or a broken fingernail or an encounter with an ex-lover they need to flee from. I plan sometime soon to stock the cabinet in there not only with the usual suspects, but also with a nail file, clear nail polish for stopping snags in stockings, anti-static spray, feminine supplies, room scent, lip balm, toothpicks, aspirin, mouthwash, and Kleenex (in case anyone has to bawl). None of these things ever need be mentioned; they just have to be there.

Before I leave the topic, a couple of tips: The first I got from Peter's mother for what to do if you have only one loo and several people from several different bedrooms relying on it, which is the case upstairs in her summer house. Rather than have everyone heap their toiletries around the same countertop, what you do is put a square basket per person in each bedroom into which guests can put their toothbrushes, face cleanser, razors, etc., to be carted to the bathroom only when needed and then carried back to each bedroom and out of everybody else's way.

Another fine tip, from a friend of mine in New York, is to have rolled-up washcloths in the washroom, say in a basket, for drying hands, instead of a single hand towel on a hook. They are excellent for lending tone to a party, so long as you don't forget to have a basket for tossing the used ones into. It's cheap luxury, and with the money you save you can perhaps buy a gorgeously scented trio of hand soap, exfoliant, and cream.

A ROOM IN THE OPEN AIR

This house has no back garden, sadly, but it does have a balcony and I was determined to make a summer "room" out of it so we'd be compelled to spend more time outside. It took a year to decide how to achieve this—actually, it took five minutes, but that was after a year of sitting on it whining about the dreary brown wood stain, the searing heat, and the nasty view to one side of a laneway of cars.

It was never going to be sophisticated (and since we don't own the place, our options were limited), so we decided to work with what it was: rustic. We got a tin of white outdoor paint, watered it down, and slicked it all over the brown stain to cover it. Much more heavenly! Two different friends were casting off deck umbrellas, so we inherited those (and want a third), which, once erected, provided shady nooks of intimacy like on a restaurant terrace. Finally, I went out and bought about an acre of plants, green and white only, which I lined along the edges of the deck to block the bad view spots.

In the end, we hardly did anything—and nothing wildly original—but it sure made a difference. Now we love to sit up there among the

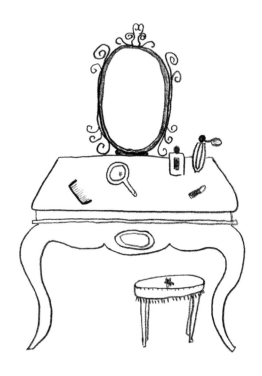

jasmines and the ferns, gazing out through the treetops, watching jets draw chalk marks through the blue sky, watching the sun descend the steps of another day...

So there you have it. End of tour. Not exactly Buckingham Palace, but I'm cooperating with the place and learning to love it as long as we're living in it. I accept that there's a lot we don't have the power to change, but that's OK. This place has been a wonderful practice ground for us. It has definitely helped me to develop a better eye for the things I do have the power to change, and I'll be that much better when we tackle our next place, whenever that time comes and wherever it may be.

The All-Important Ambiance

Getting your four walls and your furniture to where you want them is only half the battle of making a home welcome. The next step, and one that requires sensitivity, is ambiance, which is, of course, something you may want to change from one day to the next, even from one time of day to the next. Obviously the bricks and mortar of a room come into play too, but intangibles can often have even greater impact.

LIGHTING

When it comes to the hardware of lamps and lights, it takes a real pro to get a room right. I've read about lining shades with tobacco-coloured fabric and using translucent shades, never dead white in colour—that sort of decorator's trick. For the novice, this delicate business can be a minefield. Alas, most of us *are* novices and we're not about to race out and hire an interior decorator just because we happen to be having six people for dinner on Friday.

Fortunately, the most glaring party-lighting faux pas are easy for even the most block-headed of us to identify: you don't want people stumbling around in the pitch dark and neither do you want them exposed under a cold glare, as though they were inmates just about to sneak out the gates of a prison when the tower spotlight swivels around and lands bang on them. Light, like salt, is one of those details that we don't seem to notice unless there's too much of it or not enough. We know we've got it right when everybody in our place looks stunning and is happily at ease.

If you are trying to create a cozy atmosphere, avoid fluorescent and halogen bulbs and any bright or white overhead lights. Some people say not to use overhead lights at all, but as long as you have a dimmer switch and can turn them down to the lowest level, I find they can be useful for setting a base tone for other light sources in the room, a bit like the makeup artist's foundation before the drama is applied on top.

In our dining room, we always eat by candlelight—even on a Tuesday. The trouble, for me at least, is that because I always serve family style, the platters leave only so much room for anything else. The candles I can fit on the table itself don't alone provide quite enough illumination, which leads to more than one problem: first of all, while people can look fabulous in candlelight, insufficient quantities of it can have the same spooky effect as holding a flashlight under the chin; also, people need to see what they're eating and be able to appreciate the lovely table you've set. There's no point using your best crystal if diners are just going to knock it flying, and there's no point serving a gloriously garnished platter of snapper if everybody's just going to choke on the bones.

This is where the softest and dimmest possible overhead lighting comes in. It leaves the room dark, but not like the inside of a coffin, and, combined with the glow of candles, seems just right.

The living room is a different story, because usually the focus of action isn't all in one place, unless you're two people cuddled up in front of a fireplace. In this case, I prefer light from a variety of different sources, at various heights, to add depth to a room. My uncle Freeman has a large living room with at least three separate sitting areas. He wouldn't let an overhead light get as close as the foot of his driveway, let alone into the house; lamps only, and with low bulbs, are his mantra. In his living room, lamps are scattered all over the place, and I love how they cast different shadows around the room and create nooks of mystery. With overhead lights alone, exposing the whole room like a hockey rink, all that would be lost.

Twinkly hanging lights don't suit every room, but I have a penchant for them. Where they fit—including outside—they can be nicely playful and whimsical. We have a cord of them running around our front window, which I plug in at night. We have a similar cord, only with colourful round woven balls around each light, hanging in the living room. The lights are dim and mostly decorative, but they have a fairy-tale quality that adds a pinch of magic to a room. Especially in winter, the lights in the front window give the house an allure that makes passersby yearn to come in. ("Oh, you're the people with the lights who always have candles on the table," some detective from several houses down once said to us at a street party.) With a gentle snow falling and the world all a-hush, peering into a house with warm, beckoning light is all rather enchantingly *"Au Clair de la Lune."*

P.S. Now that we've moved outside, I might mention that a friend of mine always sets a huge lantern outside her front door to welcome guests. It's enough to turn any passerby instantly into a moth.

CANDLE CONNOISSEURSHIP

I'd love to make a bit of a study of candle making, because creating truly good ones is an art—or so one assumes, because they're certainly not easy to come by, nor are they cheap. Mind you, in the long run, more expensive candles can cost less than the cheaper ones because they burn longer, especially if you take good care of them.

Tall, slender tapered candles are quite straightforward, as long as the wicks are trimmed to about a quarter inch before every burn or whenever a candle starts to smoke. It's the wider type of candle, often sold in glass containers, that can be tricky, because if you don't let the wax pool to the very edges on the first burn, you can end up with tunnelling. It takes about an hour per inch in diameter to allow wax to melt all the way out to the edges, so the first burn requires a bit of a time commitment. (Some say that with wider candles, not trimming the wick on the first burn will make a bigger flame that melts the wax faster.)

A useful trick in the case of tunnelling is to wrap foil around the top of a candle, slightly turned inward at the top to create a bit of a funnel, and to burn it this way for a while until it rights itself. Setting a candle in a hurricane glass does that job as well.

I recently acquired two candle accessories that I now couldn't live without. The first is Mr. Mole's Sticky Wax, which is soft wax in a

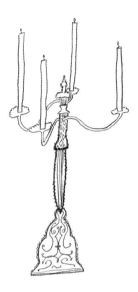

container that looks like a pot of lip gloss into which you turn the base of tall candles before inserting them in their holders for extra stability. The second is a candle sharpener, which works exactly like a pencil sharpener for trimming the base of candles that don't quite fit into their sticks.

Candle wax on table linen is a bit of a pain, but setting an ice cube on the spill will make it easy to chip off, and then a hot iron generally takes care of the rest. On hard surfaces, a blow-dryer is useful once you've pried any serious pieces off with a plastic pastry scraper.

THE SOUND AND MUSIC

Hearing may well be the most neglected and abused of all the senses at this particular juncture in history. You can't smoke a cigar within twenty-eight feet of a tobacco shop (not that I'd want to, but I'm making a point), but you can blast as much banging and screeching as you like from out your shop front or your car windows. Few things are more obnoxious and anti-social than that, but because there's apparently no proof that this sort of cacophony can make us fatally ill or harm the children in our wombs, it's allowed. We live in an era of sound tyranny, when you think about it. (Some say the same about light.) I have been known to complain on more than one occasion—once famously at a bar whose stylish waterfall wall was so thunderous it was like trying to have a conversation standing beneath Victoria Falls.

For a host, once you get enough people in a room gabbing away, there's really no need for music at all, certainly not in a dining room. It's one of those things people *think* they need or that perhaps does the initial job of drawing people into a place and shedding inhibitions, but once they're in there and talking, music is often barely noticed, unless it's so loud as to be deafening, in which case so much for any chit-chat.

When it's not for dancing or for entertainment, the point of music is to create ambiance and unite people, but for some reason people often misuse it and end up killing exactly that which they're trying to generate. Put on overly loud music of any kind and you'll find me crawling out the nearest window and making my escape across the lawn.

I have a friend, John D. S. Adams, who is a sound-recording engineer. On the side, he offers services to restaurants to improve their sound. (Restaurants are notorious these days for having such bad acoustics and blaring music that nobody over the age of forty-five feels safe crossing their thresholds without being armed with a tin ear. Do let us hosts at home set a better example.) According to John, what gives a room bad acoustics is having too many smooth, flat, reflective surfaces (windows being especially terrible), because they cause a high degree of resonance, which creates a sound environment that rings with echo and overwhelms.

So if you want glorious sound (mellifluous voices and lovely music) you must reduce the reflectivity of the room, which can be done by adding soft, not-so-flat surfaces like curtains, rugs, cushions, and curves. Apparently, really serious soundies sometimes even install special panels: two-inch Corning semi-rigid fibreglass insulation in a wood frame, covered with acoustically transparent fabric, according to John. If I ever get a living room the size of a concert hall, I'm going to look into this.

A WHIFF OF SOMETHING

I'll keep this short, but it's worth mentioning scent because if it's off, it can slay any sense of welcome in no time flat. A house should smell clean and fresh, above all. There's a reason why Diptyque has never used the aroma of stale cigarette smoke, mould, dead mouse, wet dog, closed air, rotting compost, or ancient shag carpet in its scented candles or room sprays. If your house is guilty of being a lab for such fragrances, get on to it, and not by trying to mask them with taxicab-style air "fresheners," which are often so overpowering and off-putting that stench might actually be preferred. Instead, race into the arms of Mother Nature and be saved. By the way, don't forget an old real-estate trick when you're entertaining: a high-end scented candle in the hallway makes a delightful first impression on arriving guests. Diffusers with high-quality essential oils will do the same trick, and often at a better price.

BEAUTIFUL SCENTS
TO HAVE IN A HOUSE

Fresh air

The scent of rain in trees
(so do sometimes open the windows as it falls)

Woodsmoke

Blossoms

Onions frying in butter

Cookies baking

A good-quality candle burning
(not cheap scented candles, which can be sickening)

A diffuser emitting a mist of essential oil,
such as lavender or geranium

A sparing amount of luxury room spray

Conversation Pieces

I like eclecticism and originality and am put off by too much sameness, of which, out in the world, there is a lot. *Zeitgeist* is one thing, harmony another—both acceptable—but lazy, insecure copycattiness is a bore. There's a strange tug-of-war that goes on in people between wanting to fit in (and therefore conforming) and wanting to stand out (and therefore daring to be unique). Striking a balance is key. There's a place for certain kinds of standardization. Nobody wants buildings fashioned after skulls, or cars on square wheels, or, unless they're a lifeguard, chairs on stilts. But dashes of style, which require originality, are the spice of life. Without them in a house, visiting people can become like driving around to multiple outlets of Pottery Barn.

It's the touches of difference that stand out in a home and really tell the people we invite in (and ourselves) who we are, so we should feel free—obliged, almost—to be fearless when it comes to scattering them around. Things like:

PIECES OF THE PAST

Even people who make home from scratch, getting all their furniture fresh from a box store and every appliance new, still usually have the impulse to add some pieces of their own story, whether it's a few family photographs, or a fishing-rod collection, or some African baskets brought back from safari. Hopefully, too, there's at least something passed down from a family member or other relevant force in one's life: Aunt Agatha's day bed, or Grandmother's Chinese urn, or Mother's vanity . . . something to act as a marker on the path that led us from our beginnings to where we are today.

But there are also people who want nothing old. I understand not wanting to live in a museum, knee-deep in antiques. On the other hand, a house full of entirely new things can feel rather like being on a spaceship, with no tie to any familiar origins. It's tricky, because we live in a bit of an Ikea world and people resist hand-me-downs these days. My older brother, who has a big house and two little children, refused a piano, which I could not understand, for example. I notice at auctions all the time that it's the big pieces—sleigh beds, mahogany wardrobes—that are hardest to sell.

I've learned not to be hasty with my rejections because even things that go into boxes for ages and are forgotten can have a funny way of resurfacing and sometimes wiggling their way right back into our daily lives. For example, teacups. I inherited enough for an army, but by that time was drinking tea from mugs, so I didn't want them. Into storage they went, until Peter came across them and started using them (sans

saucers) as coffee cups with his Nespresso machine. Suddenly they seemed cool and desirable again. It made me realize that a lot of what puts us off old things is when they're left in their past tense and not encouraged to join the present through a clever modern usage or by being mixed with new things.

Nobody wants to live in a time warp, but a single piece of solid, old furniture can really anchor an otherwise modern room. I find rooms that are 100 per cent modern can feel ungrounded. We have that diamond-point pine armoire from Quebec, which I mentioned, in our otherwise fairly contemporary living room. There was a debate over whether or not we'd take it when it came up for grabs, but now we're grateful, because it totally makes the room, pins it down like a tent peg, and makes us feel like we won't be rolling up the carpet and fleeing in the night quite yet.

ART, ETC.

I left home for university at the age of eighteen, and on the last Christmas before I did so, my parents gave me what I felt was my first truly grown-up present: the artist's proof of a delicate lithograph of golden pears hanging from a leafy branch against a sky of almost imperceptible blue. "This can be the beginning of your art collection," they said, and I felt like the next Peggy Guggenheim.

The second piece of art I owned was one I bought during my first Christmas *after* university, when I was living in Munich all on my own. I got it at the *Weihnachtsmarkt* in Schwabing, the glorious Christmas market in my part of town, where artists and craftspeople displayed jaw-droppingly quality wares. (In case you've never witnessed them, German Christmas markets are the best!) The work I chose, on thick, handmade paper, was a boxy, earthy, and golden abstract that I still find as beautiful as the first day I saw it. Both this and the pears are hanging in my direct line of view right now, as it happens, and if I turn my head, my eyes fall upon other pictures that are not just decorative, but also secret whispers to me about a particular period of my life.

My parents loved art. I remember once when we really needed a new car (i.e., as soon as possible, or we'd be like Fred and Wilma Flintstone, rolling down the road with our bare feet racing along out the bottom), and at a gallery we always visited in the city, the painting of a favourite artist suddenly appeared for sale. A frenzied debate ensued: Car? Painting? Car! Painting! Car? Painting! And that was that. I had to suffer a few more years of humiliation being delivered to school dances in a lemon, but at least that spot of wall above the mantel in the dining room finally had some class and soul.

Something to think about, if you happen to live in a remote place or in a low-rent part of town, is that you probably have the great luck of being surrounded by artists, whether you know it or not. It's a well-known fact that 99 per cent of artists live off the smell of an oily rag, which is why they tend to gravitate toward un-rich areas, not only under-developed urban spaces, but also rural areas where they can buy a whole farm on the river for a third the price of a studio downtown. Furthermore, any art they sell locally goes for a fraction of the price it would fetch in an urban gallery. This is not art that's cheaper because it's less good; it's cheaper because the artist's cost of living is lower, and sometimes because there's no middleman involved. I mention this for anyone who dreams of buying art but lives in a major centre where so much of it seems unapproachable: look farther afield.

Matters of taste are a tricky topic. Everyone has a right to their taste and nobody agrees entirely on what's good and what's bad. "The great sadness, really, is that there is no leadership," the British decorator David Hicks once bemoaned. This isn't strictly true, although reliable authority does tend to get watered down in our Internet age, when everyone is a so-called expert or guru. When it comes to the arts, the way to develop good taste is of course to expose oneself to as much greatness as possible. This is fairly democratic, because public galleries are open to everyone, so even if we can't own certain works, we can look at them, feed our souls, and, over time, cultivate our own aesthetic.

Some people buy art as an investment. Fair enough, but I can't fathom living with even great art if it didn't truly speak to me. In a house, art has a lot of power over how we feel when we look at it every day. It's worth remembering the personal influence, then, before investing a few mil in a painting of, say, a saint that makes you feel judged every time you walk past it, or a black stripe just because it's fashionable and fetching a high price on the market (for now, that is; keep in mind that value is influenced by fashion, not just quality).

Peter and I have yet to buy a piece of art together, but I can't wait for the day. The closest we've come—and this to fill a giant, empty wall—was to buy a very long string of fairy lights with coloured balls on them from a shop in Montreal and then shape them into a giant heart. It might have cost fifty bucks, but it is as beautiful and meaningful and gets at least as many comments as any "real" art in the house. "That's so you," my friend Stephan commented when he saw it, and I know what he means. I read a line on the back of a Marguerite Yourcenar novel decades ago, and identified with it completely: *"Une touche de folie sur une base structurée."* The heart of lights is exactly that.

HOUSEPLANTS

One day, Peter and I will move to the country, and when the day comes we may very well acquire a cat (i.e., a mouser) and a dog (security system and walking buddy that we intend to call Eiffel). Until then, we're a pet-free zone, but I make up for it with my houseplant addiction.

This is an obsession that struck me out of nowhere as soon as we moved in. Once the furniture was in place, I expected the house to come alive and feel like home. It didn't. I'm the one who works out of here and I didn't like the empty feeling that crept over the place when Peter went out the door every morning. (But as I said, until that dreamed-about move to the country, pets are out of the question.)

My mother has always been a green thumb (if she put her mind to it, I swear she could make a pair of chopsticks sprout). She has jungles of houseplants all over the house, which she dotes over constantly, upstairs and down. My father, meanwhile, who's an outdoor gardener, has taken over the greenhouse, which by early spring is all a-sprout with hope. So keen is he on this hobby that offshoots of the greenhouse tend to appear all over the house. You'll innocently sit in a rocking chair in the living room to read a book and find yourself surrounded by trays of next year's crop of tomatoes and basil. This chummy cohabitation with future ratatouilles and batches of pesto may not be for everyone, but rural types seem unfazed, and I like that style.

In any case, it explains why I'd have taken plants for granted. They were a constant when I was growing up, and the subconscious memory of their effect on the psyche must have stayed with me, because I immediately realized that that's what was missing here. The next time I went home to visit my parents, I made off with slips from geraniums, a finger of cactus, a wad of purple shamrock, and a meandering hoya in a pot.

I started the geranium slips rooting in glasses of water on a windowsill, which was thrilling. In about a week they were ready to go into pots, and from there they grew and blossomed like miracles, which made me feel like God. The purple shamrock looked like a dehydrated weed when I first got it home, but once I'd set it in a light spot in the kitchen, it went gangbusters, producing a new sprout by the day. The cactus has grown so fast, I'm slightly terrified of it. It was no bigger than my index finger when I first poked it into its earth; now it's the size of a baseball bat.

Someone covered in tattoos once warned me never to get one. "You get one tattoo and you stop seeing the tattoo," he explained. "All you notice is the blank space beside it. Then you get another tattoo to fill that blank space, and that only makes you see the next blank space that needs filling. The next thing you know, you're completely covered in ink." He looked more than a little regretful.

Well, that is *not* how I feel about houseplants, but it is houseplants that made me understand the tattooed man's predicament. No sooner had I filled my front window with plants than suddenly all I could see were all the other spots around the house lacking the same burst of life. This explains the arrival of the orange tree, the palm tree, the jade, the twin stephanotises, the two ivies, the three ferns, the parade of orchids... We're a motley gaggle at this point, but we've also become a rather tight clique.

You wouldn't think so, but houseplant life is full of surprises. I initially got the plants for the simple reason of wanting to cheer up the house a bit, give it fresher air and some personality, and keep me company. The plants have done all that, but they've also affected me in a way I didn't expect. A mysterious thing happens the minute you start to take care of something regularly. Even when it's "just" a plant, you actually start to bond with it. It's impossible not to, because you become engaged in its life and start to notice when it needs things—a drink of water, a turn to face the sun, a little attention and appreciation from your eyes—and you genuinely begin to care, just like you would about a pet.

Plants, you discover, are responsive beings, like any other form of life. They don't just sit there being green, they actually react to the energy that people bring into the house and they feel it when the house is empty for unusual lengths of time. If you think I've gone crackers, start living with plants yourself and you'll soon see what I mean. You get attached and start to depend on each other.

If you aren't stealing clippings and pots from your mother's house, then the obvious place to buy plants is in a garden centre in summertime. Garden centres have the best variety as well as experts milling about who can tell you what's what and how to look after your purchases. The trouble is that these outfits are open only about four months a year (where I live, anyway). Luckily, grocery stores and hardware stores also carry plants (and potting soil). They don't generally offer what's nicest in the world of flora, but they do tend to sell hardy varieties, which is good for beginners. I've bought a few plants from gigantic box stores in my time too, partly because I always think the poor creatures look so miserable under all those fluorescent lights that I have to rescue them. It never ceases to amaze me, incidentally, how much happier they look once they're home. Instant, visible relief getting out of those malls.

Anything in a plastic pot I transfer to terra cotta to restore it to dignity. If I don't know what something is, I try to find out, then I google to see how it likes to be cared for. From there, it's trial and error, but that's how we learn about each other and, over time, how mutual adoration blooms.

P.S. Houseplants in overly large numbers can look freakish. (Ditto cut flowers, particularly of the dried variety, so some of us might be well advised to curb our enthusiasm.)

CUT FLOWERS

The best cut flower arrangements look like you just stepped out to the garden with a pair of clippers, a gentle breeze teasing your hair, snipped an assortment, brought them in, and plunked them into a vase, resulting in a bouquet of such effortless perfection it might have been made by Mother Nature's own hand. At least that's the look I like, and of course it's hardest to achieve, even for professional florists.

I spy on a few top florists on Instagram because they cheer me up on a gloomy day. It's not surprising that the English are among the best, given their great tradition of gardening; however, it's fun to see what's going on elsewhere too. Right now I'm keeping my eye on the work of an Australian and a Korean. It's amazing how fashion differs from one country to the next, even in the floral world. (A quick Google search on "best florists to follow" will lead you to some gems.)

The marvellous thing about cut flowers, in addition to their ability to cheer up a house, is of course how every bouquet can be unique. You can transform the whole look and feel of a room simply by replacing the bouquets, which of course has to happen regularly because they're as fleeting as clouds. In cities like London and Paris, it is very easy to have glorious cut flowers at home because florists abound and the markets sell wonderful bunches at reasonable prices. I never used to go to the market in Europe for food without coming home with a handful of pretty blossoms too. It reminds me of a funny line a French friend of mine once came out with: "Even when I didn't have a penny to my name, I never deprived myself of three things: *les taxis, le Champagne, et les fleurs.*"

Canada is not exactly a botanical garden, at least not most of the year, so access to beautiful cut flowers is challenging in most parts of the country. Also, because traditionally we're more forestry than floristry, proper flower shops are few and far between, with most people resorting to year-round tulips from the local 7-Eleven. When you do visit a proper florist, the bouquets can be frightfully expensive, and there's the problem that great florists are as rare as great hairdressers. So it's a conundrum.

We live not far from a strange little strip of flower shops in our city. They aren't florists, per se, or maybe one is, but the rest just sell flowers, which is different. So I go pick and choose from what's available and construct my own bouquets at home. If you're going to get into doing your own bouquets, I recommend having a pair of clippers on hand for more twig-like stems. Cheap, plain glass vases are available all over and I have a few in various sizes. I have also started saving any interesting empties from Peter's bar; for example, a dark brown stoneware Riga Black Balsam bottle holds a single stem beautifully, and I'm waiting for a third grenade-shaped whisky empty so I can put white poppies in them for peace!

I've acquired some coloured glass bowls and vases too, which are great fun, and soon I'll branch out (no pun intended), because an interesting and appropriate vase, I'm learning, really is part of the artistry, even if it's just a Mason jar or the faux-copper container of a one-time scented candle.

A Few Floral Pointers

- All flowers in an arrangement don't die at the same time, so don't just plunk bouquets into a vase and forget about them. After a few days, check to see if anything needs weeding out. If necessary, change the vase to fit what's left.

- Refresh the water in a vase daily to keep flowers alive longer.

- Make about a one-inch incision in the base of flower stems to allow them to absorb more water. With woody branches, bruise the ends by giving a light bang of a hammer for the same effect.

- Strip off excess leaves to help bouquets last longer.

- Fill your vase with warm water if you want to make closed flowers open more quickly.

- Try what the late British florist Constance Spry swore by, and that is "swimming" flowers in a bath of cool water (basically putting them in a giant bucket of water) and keeping them overnight in a cool place before arranging.

⸓ If fresh flowers are just too expensive to become a habit, buy a bouquet or two that dry nicely, such as Japanese lanterns, strawflowers, dahlias, everlastings, or silver dollars (there are many more). You never want too many, because they can make a house start to feel a bit cobwebby and Miss Havisham, but one or two dried bouquets in a house can add a lovely burst of colour and texture.

The Open-Door Policy

For years, my living arrangements repeatedly cut me off from the world. I'd rent lovely-looking Parisian apartments online, for example, only to arrive and find that their only views were of a courtyard or a bunch of rooftops rather than a street where I could look down and see people and action. It was the strangest thing how it kept happening to me—and in Canada too. I once rented a loft that ended up having windows all so high up that I couldn't see out of them unless I stood on a chair. The last time I found myself in a beautiful place that completely cut me off, in Paris again, I thought I must truly be jinxed. In fact, it was that last blow that finally drove me to Toronto.

I remember being very clear, arriving back from France that last time, that my number-one criterion for the stay was not to feel like some sort of crazy person being kept in an attic. I wanted to live in a place where I would look out my window and have a clear view of things and feel connected, a place where I could see what other people had on before I got dressed or, even better, step outside and get a feel for the weather myself.

That first Toronto apartment, the one in the big house where I lived when I met Peter, was exactly that. So comfortable was I there that I always left my door into the main house open (hmm . . . as I now do here as well). My landlords, who lived below, used to wander up the stairs occasionally and stick their heads in for a bit of gossip. So did the other two people living in the building, perhaps to check about the heating or swap a bit of neighbourhood news. Nobody was intrusive, just appropriately social, and in any case, if I wanted privacy I could always shut the door.

Feeling so lucky with this arrangement, I was struck by the strangeness of the world we've created, with so many single people, young and old, living in little compartments like so many cuckoos trapped in dark clocks, waiting for those precise moments when they get to pop out, briefly, and announce their existence to the world. We've come to accept this as a normal way of living. We've to a large extent lost our sense of tribe. An inviting life is surely one way to start reclaiming it.

Our Face to the Outside World

It's important to remember that what we (and others) see as we're coming up the walk toward home can affect us in the same ways as our walls and furniture. Having grown up on land—four hundred acres of it—I had drummed into me from the earliest age what it means to be the custodian of outdoor spaces and, in fact, was raised to consider the land as much home as the roof over our heads. The view of hills across the river, the cry of coyotes in the night, the explosion of dandelions to usher in summer, the eagles overhead, the particular muting of colour in November and brightening scent in April . . . all that was and is as much home as any bricks and mortar.

When I lived in the French countryside, I felt the same strong link to the land, almost more than to the house. Home in Burgundy was the fields of poppies blowing in the breeze, the hourly gong of the clock that could be heard across the fields of wheat, the figure eight of the herb garden, the crunch of the gravel in the driveway, the stretches of colza in the valley below, and the train clickety-clacking through on its way south.

When we moved into this house, that fortunate first May, it was just as everyone else on the street was ripping out their front gardens—well, not everyone, actually, just the thoughtful people, which didn't include us. You see, initially our logic was "We don't own the house or the patch of garden, so why should *we* have to take care of it?" Then, after a few weeks, another perspective dawned on me: "Why are we putting up with this overgrown stamp of ugliness that we see every single time we arrive home and that greets our guests like a dishevelled concierge?"

I got my hands on a shovel and dug the whole thing up, scattered wildflower seeds over it, and stood back waiting for Sissinghurst Castle Garden to blossom forth. Weeks passed, squirrels invaded, and before long we had the ugliest garden in the street: the Garden of Weed-dom. I was depressed. Then one day I looked out the front window and espied our neighbour, Eden (that's really her name), on hands and knees ripping the whole thing out again. She came in with proper plants, and the next thing we knew, we had one of the happiest front patches in the street. People stopped and admired it as they went past, pointing out little blooms, taking photographs on their cell phones. Once our garden was shipshape, I started to get a bit huffy about anyone on the street who didn't tend to theirs. Having made the same mistake myself, I realized that our front garden is not just about us and our morale, it's about the morale of the whole street, which gets an instant lift when everyone does their bit.

"One knows the mind of a hostess just by stepping over her doorstep," Balzac said. I'd say it's sooner than that. Our gardens, lawns, front porches, front doors: these are all opportunities where we can get creative, express our individuality, and make the world a more inviting place even for those who may never cross our thresholds.

FRONT-OF-HOUSE CHECKLIST

An easy-to-see house number

A clearly labelled mailbox

A safe walk and/or drive

A nice lawn/garden/window box

Safe front steps

Garbage bins out of view

A front porch that looks nice to sit on

A doorbell that works (or a knocker)

A door that's nicely painted and sturdy

An awning, so people don't get soaked
waiting for the door to open

A light

Clean windows

A welcome mat

An Even Wider View

I recall an animated cartoon I saw sometime in the late Bronze Age that was my youth. A little boy stands in front of his house with a picket fence. He says, "This is my house." Then the camera pulls back to reveal the houses of neighbours on both sides. "On my street," continues the boy. The camera pulls back again to reveal several streets. "In my town," he expands. On and on it goes with the boy getting smaller with every change of slide and his world getting bigger around him. I can't remember if it ended with "in my country" or "in the universe," but it doesn't matter because I'd got the message: home doesn't stop at the front door.

We're not really wired to think this way. Every wad of gum stuck to the sidewalk, every explosion of foul language in the street, every creepy, damp wind tunnel—each of these is another small reminder of how easily and carelessly we can let standards slide in the places we call home. We can't, as individuals, rush out and try to fix every single problem around us (although some we can), but we do at least have the power to start with ourselves. "Be the change you want to see in the world," to paraphrase Gandhi.

When I lived in France, I learned an interesting nuance of the term "anti-social." In English, we think of it as a descriptor for anyone who's not particularly outgoing or friendly. In French, the meaning is different, or at least broader. It's considered *anti-sociale* to be badly dressed (you're not just you, you're someone else's view); it's *anti-sociale* not to observe respectable table manners (you might put someone else off their appetite); it's *anti-sociale* not to keep your front yard tidy (you'll destroy the ambiance of the neighbour's lovely garden alongside); it's *anti-sociale* to blast music so loudly it comes out your earphones. And so on. It's a refreshing shift in perspective, particularly for anyone brought up in a culture that teaches that life's all about me, me, me—and me's right to do whatever me wants. It forces us to remember that the way we are in the world is part of what makes our world what it is. It also forces us to be aware that we don't own the whole road.

Another way to approach the wider world as an extension of ourselves and, indeed, of our homes proper is to be more consciously aware of how we build our metaphorical nests out of all the scraps and twigs that are the places we frequent outside our houses. I live in a huge city, but most of it will remain as foreign to me as a faraway country because, like most people, I tend to beat a similar path every day: the drycleaner, the butcher, my yoga studio, the grocery . . .

It reminds me of a funny habit I had as a child, back when I was still attached to my baby blanket. I used to gather up all my favourite toys in the blanket, sling it over my shoulder, trudge to my grandmother's, and spread it out in her living room. Then I'd sit down in the middle of it and arrange all my toys around me in a ring. When I did that, it wasn't because I wanted to play with those toys; I just wanted to sit there in the middle, looking at them and feeling safe at the centre of all my stuff.

We have a similar way of establishing our place in the world in adult life. Anyone who has ever moved house, especially any great distance, will immediately relate: along with having to unpack our books and clothes and move furniture endlessly around until it feels right, we also have to find a new dentist, seek out the best place for fish, discover hidden spots where we can go to find peace, choose the restaurants and cafés where we'll become regulars... A new place to live can be intimidating, but breaking our surroundings into these smaller pieces that we eventually can consider ours—and arranging them in a circle in our minds with ourselves at the centre—can help make even the most sprawling city feel more like a cozy den.

Remember, all of this activity of ours, out in the wider world, is essentially a form of homemaking too. And because we're constantly interacting with other people as we go about it, we're basically hosts or guests at every moment of our lives.

TWO

Hug Your House

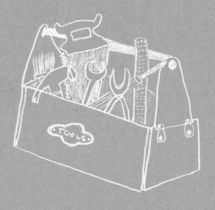

If we're having a dinner party, I don't leave laundry hanging all over the place. But nor do I start hiding dirty coffee mugs behind plants if someone pops by unannounced. As Roseanne Barr once put it, "Excuse the mess, but we live here."

There is an honesty about the state of our living spaces (not to mention the state of ourselves) when we're not in hosting mode proper. It takes trust and confidence to let people see our true colours, and that can be intimidating, but a lot less so if we remember that we're all human and that just as everyone's family is drooling mad, so is everyone's house a true living space and not a booth at an interior design show.

There's nothing nice about neglect in any sphere of life. We all know what it feels like to be in that down-and-out state of mind that makes us not want to bother combing our hair or getting dressed; but notice how if we threaten ourselves with the possibility of being seen in this condition, we can generally pull ourselves together, drag a comb through the tangled locks, and tuck in our shirts. This is part of what makes an inviting life not just a fun way to live, but also healthy: it prompts us to look after ourselves better and not slump into tramp mode the moment we're home from the office and nobody's looking.

Apply that psychology to home surroundings and you'll find it's quite motivating. In those moments when the idea of vacuuming is about as appealing as getting a root canal, even though the living-room rug looks as though a tornado just went through carrying a pack of Afghan hounds, the niggling fear that our mother-in-law might float in any minute for a cup of tea can be just the kick in the butt we need to plug in that machine and deal with the debris. Once we've done it, of course, we benefit more than anyone.

For some, especially women, there is a stigma attached to housekeeping. (Erma Bombeck once said, "My idea of housework is to sweep the place with a glance.") The mass post-war exodus of women from the home sphere was an important advancement. Women were sick of not having their hard work valued, so they went out and proved that they could do what men could do and took a more equal place in society.

That's all fine. The trouble is that while it did give women a greater sense of value as people, it at the same time even further diminished the apparent worth of any occupation traditionally considered female, everything from fixing dinner, to volunteering, to looking after children and old people, to things like polishing glasses and washing floors. Essentially, it affirmed what the establishment had been saying all along, which was "Damn straight that domestic stuff has no value. It's all cotton in the wind and we're proud at long last to be done with it."

Part of me understands, but then there's reality: I find I'm not done with that domestic stuff at all. In fact, making sure the house feels good, so that anyone entering (myself included) doesn't turn on their heels at the front door and flee, has come to be one of my biggest jobs. It's hardly making me rich (total earnings this lifetime: zero), so that's not a great selling point, but I do feel this area of life deserves some affirmation.

Apart from the fact that housework can be quite satisfying, small-seeming jobs like polishing mirrors, getting gunk out of shower tiles, and making sure herds of ants aren't parading across the kitchen have a significant impact on keeping the world on an even keel. Especially in these unpredictable times, whenever we water the plants or get a stain out of a sofa, we are reinforcing that we do, in fact, have some control over our lives and that by taking that control, we can, little by little, make the world a more secure, beautiful, and loving place. It's not, then, just about picking up wayward socks and sweeping out the cobwebs, but about establishing and maintaining solid and reliable foundations, without which everything on top collapses—without which nothing else has a hope in hell. To me, that's not fluff.

In general, the mental categorizing we do of work can use a healthy dose of perspective. In the normal run of things, anything manual is meant to be "downstairs" and anything vaguely cerebral gets to be "upstairs." This is silly. I once knew of a symphony orchestra cellist who had an admirable way of sticking it to this kind of attitude: he took a day job collecting garbage. In the pre-dawn hours, while the rest of us were reaching out to slap our snooze buttons, there he was hanging off the back of a truck in overalls, leaping up and down dragging bins to the back and dumping them in. He was fighting fit, making lots of money, and (read it and weep) *done* by breakfast. That left him with whole, wide, airy days for living life and practising cello before slipping into a tux and heading off to the concert hall. As far as he was concerned, he had it made.

Funnily enough, right off the top of my head I can think of two friends, both of whom have buckets of money, who are cleaning fanatics (although they don't broadcast it). One has a housekeeper who comes every day, but she nonetheless relishes every chance she gets to dive into a cupboard with a wet sponge because it's a way she burns off steam. My other friend, who has a very big house and no housekeeper at all, likes to do the cleaning herself to make sure it's done to her high standards. Neither of these two glamourpusses attaches a mental stigma to scrubbing down the front steps or loading a dishwasher; instead, they seem to treat cleaning in the same way others might treat rose gardening, which is refreshing.

I must admit, although I always had to help out with housekeeping at home in childhood, in my adult life I've done precious little because there has usually been help. Being off the hook does free up time, which I suppose is a luxury, but only if one's doing something better with it.

As it happens, I had too much time on my hands when Peter and I first moved in together, so that's when I decided I would be our *Hausfrau*. I was writing at the same time, but a person can only do so much of that in a day, and I found it rather a relief to have excuses to get up, take a mental break, and move the body about, say, by throwing in some laundry or cleaning a sink. It dawned on me that people who most avoid housework tend to be the sedentary and cerebral types, because I can't think of anyone who could benefit from it more. I did. In fact, I became rather interested in the subject. *What's the most hassle-free way to clean a bathtub? What's the most sensible way to organize the fridge? Is there* ANY *way to get red wine stains out of white linen the morning after the night before?* It wasn't always just me cleaning, I hasten to add. On Saturday mornings,

Peter and I used to take on the place together for an hour or so to give it a good scrubbing (a rather bonding as well as energetic experience), and we fancied ourselves pretty good cleaners. (So thorough was Peter, in fact, that I used to joke he'd missed his calling as a janitor.)

Then, not quite a year into this jolly routine, I broke my arm and found myself in a cast for over a month. This is how Maria entered our lives and made us realize we weren't the hotshot housekeepers we'd thought. The first day she came, she spent hours, upstairs and down, and when she left she said, "I'll be back. I haven't got this place to where I want it yet." Huh? We looked around and, indeed, it did seem different. It was as though we'd been peering at the place through foggy specs for a year and suddenly someone had slipped a clean pair onto our noses: the place gleamed. That gave me a whole new respect for the housekeeping role. There's such a thing as being really good at it, which is why, even once my cast came off, Maria stayed on. Now she does the regular overhauls and I maintain in between.

It is fascinating, considering the low esteem in which our society holds jobs such as cleaning houses, that one of the best-selling books of the last decade was an ode to the joys of precisely this type of work. Marie Kondo, in her book *The Life-Changing Magic of Tidying Up*, comes at cleaning and organizing as a kind of practice, suggesting that examining the state of our housekeeping is the same as peering into our own souls. With lines like "Visible mess helps distract from the true source of the disorder," she no doubt had half the world about to check themselves into mental institutions. Then she'd return us from the brink with reassuring statements like "From the moment you start tidying, you will be compelled to reset your life." Really? We all ripped the tea towels from our kitchen drawers, refolded them like maki rolls, and put them back. We fell to our knees with buckets of soapy water and brushes, lifting our eyes heavenward and muttering yogic chants as our arms drew purifying, sudsy circles over our sin-black floors.

Can housekeeping really be a spiritual act? I'm not sure how many young mothers would buy into the theory and claim to feel overcome by a rush of holiness every time they race around trying to corral armies of Fisher-Price toys and keep up with the hummus-caked carpets and smelly diapers. However, there is something to be said for the fact that there is a lot of good and potential happiness to be found in domestic duties. Besides, few of us can avoid them, so we might as well focus on the bright side, as I've been learning to do.

The Unmagical Facts About Keeping House

... because, let's face it, even rose-coloured glasses can fog up

✦ It's time consuming.

✦ Virtually all tools of the trade (appliances, hardware, and products) are ugly, industrial-looking, toxic, and a total downer for all five senses.

- It often goes unappreciated, sometimes even unnoticed.

- It doesn't pay (unless we do it for someone else).

- It never ends.

However . . .

HOUSEKEEPING IS EXERCISE

If you're a person whose life involves a lot of sitting, then diverse activities around the house are a great way to get your body moving without having to commit to a triathlon. Don't think of washing windows as cleaning, then. Consider such pursuits as a variation on Tai Chi.

HOUSEKEEPING IS EMPOWERMENT

You may be a resentful pawn in your day job with an arrogant, demanding boss, but at home you are in command position, queen of the castle (or king, as the case may be). Furthermore, by looking after your house, you're learning valuable practical skills that will ensure you don't have to pay somebody else every time you need to change a light bulb.

HOUSEKEEPING IS CATHARTIC

The world is full of mirrors disguised as other things. People, situations, and, yes, our houses are often reflections of the state we're in ourselves. If you look around your place and it makes you feel like a crumpled-up piece of old newspaper blowing around a back alley, that's a sign it's time to tackle things head-on. Take a Saturday (or two) and really shovel out your living space. Throw out the junk, fix anything broken, pull out furniture and clean behind it ... The process will automatically give your psyche the long-overdue scouring it needs too, and by the time you're done, you'll have a new perspective on yourself and a shinier ego.

HOUSEKEEPING IS SATISFYING

We all have great to-do lists that build up and topple over in our cluttered brains. They contain big to-dos like "write term paper on Heidegger" or "put a new roof on the house," and they contain little to-dos such as "screw hook into back of bathroom door" or "change bedlinens." For the most part, housekeeping consists of a great many little to-dos, plenty of which take only minutes to tick off the list but somehow pay back disproportionately with a sense of accomplishment. So, feeling in need of a pick-me-up? Dust that bookshelf! Sweep those front steps! It actually works.

HOUSEKEEPING IS MEDITATIVE

Many believe that to find peace of mind, they must hop on an airplane, fly to Goa, and track down a guru. How Hollywood. There are plenty of ways to calm an anxious spirit without going anywhere or spending a cent, and housekeeping is one of them. Gentle, repetitive activities, like washing floorboards or ironing, are excellent ways to zone out and relax. We're too quick to dismiss these chores as mundane, when in fact it's thanks to their very mundane nature that they have the power to still our anxious minds. As William Morris said, "The true secret of happiness lies in taking a genuine interest in all the details of daily life."

HOUSEKEEPING CREATES INTIMACY

Even if we have household help, it can be healthy to take on at least a few tasks occasionally ourselves, because without that kind of intimate interaction with our surroundings, it's very easy to become disconnected from them. Engaging with things, as with any relationship, brings us closer and helps us notice details.

A CLEAN AND TIDY HOUSE HELPS US BE MORE PRODUCTIVE IN OTHER AREAS

There are those who claim to thrive in a mess; I'm not one of them. If my desk is cluttered, I can't write; if the kitchen counter is a shambles, I can't cook. An upside-down house blocks my productivity in other areas completely and I can't carry on until the mountains of mess are moved. This is not to say that I always need things to be pristine (on the contrary, I like a lived-in look), but when things really get out of hand, I become anxious, restless, and distracted to the point that it's impossible to accomplish anything beyond fetal position.

A CLEAN AND TIDY HOUSE IS A SOURCE OF PRIDE

You don't want to look like those men with fancy cars and motorcycles who love nothing more than to park them right in front of their houses and, neighbourhood agog, polish away until they gleam; however, there's nothing wrong with taking care of the things you love. Besides, a nicely kept house is one that others will like to come into, and that's always flattering.

CLEANING OUR HOUSE IS A REMINDER
THAT WE ACTUALLY HAVE ONE

With the world in the state it's in, if we're in a position to be puttering around with a soft cloth and a bottle of furniture polish, we're damned lucky.

Seven Ways to Put the Magic into Housekeeping

- Don't wear scruffy clothes; instead, dress with dignity for the job. (I don't mean you should hop into a designer gown, but avoid the grunge look for the sake of morale.)

- Play spirit-lifting music while you clean.

- Team up with another person for the task (or at least do it when others are around, for company).

- When possible, schedule housework so you can achieve something else simultaneously, such as keeping an eye on a braise in the oven or waiting for a delivery to show up.

- Try to find at least some tools and cleaning products that you like the look, touch, and smell of—and that work.

- Keep in mind the many positives of housekeeping (see above).

- When the job is done, reward yourself with a pretty bouquet of flowers, a hot bubbly bath, or a cold glass of bubbly.

Right then, let's get on with it.

For the Love of Lists

Actually, just *before* we get on with it, indulge me for a moment on the subject of lists—of which, in this chapter, there are rather a lot and with which I'm having a bit of a love affair.

Not long ago, I'd finished a big project and found my schedule blank once again. This is one of the hazards of my style of working: there are times of great creative intensity, inevitably followed by the dreaded "black hole" periods, during which a sort of post-partum depression can creep in and has to be fought off like a snarling dragon. I've learned to recognize its footsteps coming up behind me and a weapon I've found to be very effective for slaying the beast is: the list.

During that stretch when I felt I was doing nothing useful and was therefore unworthy of taking up space on the planet, I started, as an ego-boosting tactic, to write down everything that I did accomplish, even if it was only stuff like picking up the dry cleaning or making a batch of granola. What I discovered, very happily, is that days I'd normally have written off as blank ("I didn't do a thing!"), in fact had been full of all sorts of achievements and contributions. The list as solid evidence was a savior to my morale.

Once the pace of life started picking up again (it always does), I no longer needed lists to prove to myself I was accomplishing things. But as writing things down had turned into such a useful and positive habit, I stuck with it—except, I began instead to jot down everything that I *wanted* to get done, the *next* day. Before bed, I'd make a list (with tick boxes) of whatever it was I wanted to achieve, big and small, which meant I always woke up to a purpose and a mission. Used this way, lists act like a motivating boss who steers us away from procrastination. It always amazes me how much gets done as a result.

I bring up lists here because we tend to drag our feet towards domestic duties with our heads hung low (although, as I've been arguing, I'm not sure we should). Lists are useful tools in other areas of life for helping us to avoid feeling overwhelmed (or underwhelmed, as the case may be). In addition to my daily to-do lists, I always, for instance, have a list on the kitchen counter when we do dinner parties to remind me of finishing touches that dishes need before I serve them. (This is how I avoid mishaps such as serving a pudding and completely forgetting its sauce.) I've discovered that collections of petty errands can be turned into a satisfying mass of accomplishment when listed together—things such as "buy stamps, check air in tires, clean candlesticks, pay Amex..." Seeing all those checkmarks in a row makes your chest puff right out like a frigatebird. And so on.

The more I think about it, I'm not sure why "live by lists" isn't considered one of the "seven habits of highly effective people." If you're not already a convert, you might want to introduce them into your life (especially as you read on, because things are about to get a bit, um, realistic).

There. *Now* let's get on with it.

Everyday Housekeeping

Breaking my right arm was what made me aware of just how much housework I normally squeeze into various tight time slots throughout a day. In my two-armed life, I get tons done without it even registering:

the dishwasher gets emptied and the recycling taken out in the time it takes for the tea kettle to boil in the morning, the downstairs gets dusted and laundry is tossed into the machine while I await a taxi, and so on. If we always hold out for picture windows of time before braving the slightest household job, the few insignificant molehills we've ignored suddenly turn into as many Mount Etnas. Seizing the moment (and it really is only moments) to polish that streaky mirror or rearrange books keeps us on a turf of gentle knolls.

Everyday housekeeping is a question of quick and relatively easy tasks, as we all know. The trouble is simply that there happen to be a lot of them, everything from bed making to dishwashing to oven cleaning, and on it goes. *C'est la vie.* The trick is staying on top of the tasks, which begins by keeping our eyes open and noticing things, not living like zombies. I also think it starts with adopting the attitude that our houses are extensions of ourselves, so looking after them is like any other form of grooming, like washing our faces or polishing our shoes.

This list is bound to evolve, but right now the items below constitute the components of my household cleaning kit. Everything is available in most hardware or grocery stores. I keep the kitchen stuff under the kitchen sink, bathroom stuff in the bathrooms, and anything else in a cupboard. How you organize depends on where you live, but whether it's a bachelor apartment or a manor house, you'll no doubt want these basics:

- Dust cloths and duster

- Cleaning cloths (wash separately in the washing machine after every cleaning session)

+ Sponges

+ A toothbrush for getting into tricky crevices

+ All-purpose soap (with a natural scent, if any)

+ A squirt bottle of white vinegar solution (½ cup vinegar per 4 cups of water)

+ A box of baking soda

+ A broom and dustpan

+ A floor duster

+ A mop and a bucket

+ A vacuum (one that's easy to lift)

+ A toilet brush in every loo

+ Paper towel

+ Rubber gloves

Pride

It's difficult to be critical of anything a person does with conviction. Say we're snooty about belly dancing, for example, and then one evening find ourselves in the company of someone who brilliantly personifies a hula hoop. Who looks the fool? The dancer? Or us? What about if we have a bit of a block when it comes to rockwork. "Grunt job," we think, and then we stumble upon someone who's made a stone wall as intricate as lace yet as sturdy as Stonehenge. Suddenly we're awe-struck. Sometimes we forget that admirable excellence can be found where we least expect it.

This is all leading up to a recent encounter with Mercedes, the lady in her eighties who lives up the street. As soon as you set foot on her walk you realize you're on the turf of someone exceptional. The garden, the steps, the porch all are as neat as a pin. You could practically eat off her welcome mat. "You think I'd let someone else clean my house?" she said to me the other day, rolling her eyes. "They don't clean. They pretend to clean." (Mercedes would be merciless on a competition show if there were one pitting homemakers against one another.) "You want a clean house," she went on, "You start at the front door and you go all the way to the back, but you don't move one inch until the spot where you're standing is spic and span."

That put the fear of God into me. (Note to self: only invite Mercedes into the house after dark.) It's not realistic for most of us, especially anyone with children, to keep a house as pristine as a dental clinic at all times, and I don't believe guilt has a place here. On the other hand, just as those of us who couldn't run a bath might admire a marathoner, we can also learn something from the Olympian housekeepers among us to help improve our game. The next time I spy Mercedes sweeping the sidewalk in front of her house, I'm going do what any start-raving masochist would do: ask her to come to my house and give me a cleaning consultation before springtime. I'm not just looking for a clean house any more, I want an education.

Pick a Job, Any Job, Any Old Time

- Air the house out
- Dust
- Wash the floors
- Clean toilets
- Clean the shower or tub
- Make mirrors and glass surfaces sparkle
- Fluff things up
- Make a bed
- Clean the Oven
- Clean a sink
- Clean doorknobs and light switches
- Empty garbage cans
- Shake out small rugs
- Wipe kitchen surfaces
- Tackle a small appliance
- Clean salt and pepper vessels
- Clean out the cleaning cupboard

Ode to Baking Soda and Vinegar

I don't know how many will be old enough to remember Cow Brand baking soda, but if you ever knew it, perhaps you felt as deflated as I did about the rebranding. The powder used to come in a dreamy pastoral blue box with the picture of a cow (outstanding in its field, as they say) on the front. It was calming to look at and to reach for, whether to add a spoonful to gingerbread batter or to blizzard into a porcelain sink for scrubbing. And then Cow Brand was rebranded, whereupon the soda box suddenly appeared on the shelves in a raging protest orange and bearing the logo of a rolled-up work shirt ready to pound something with a hammer. Grim.

I love baking soda and believe that a thing of such beauty should be packaged as such. Ditto plain white vinegar, which, hand in hand with soda, makes for a cleaning dream team: non-toxic, disinfecting, fragrance-free, effective, and cheap. No household should be without this pair because between the two of them, they practically do everything, from sinks to toilets to refrigerators to garbage bins.

I especially like to keep a bottle of vinegar solution in a squirt bottle for doing mirrors and windows. A good spray over the surface and all you need is a wad or two of newspaper to rub them squeaky clean and streak-free. (Peter and I have fights about this on Saturday mornings because I always try to grab the paper while he's still reading it. The general rule is that I can take the travel section and not get hollered at; otherwise, I have to wait through a couple of cups of coffee before I can rub the faces of politicians over my rain-splattered panes.)

Baking soda, meanwhile, is my best friend for things like the bathtub and—a new trick I learned from Maria—the oven. One day, I pointed out to her that a scouring was badly called for and I set out the cleaner for the job. Maria promptly opened the lid of the garbage can and dropped the cleaner into it with a frown. "You have to treat your oven like any pot or pan," she scolded. "You eat what comes out of there. Do you want to eat poisonous foam?"

While she turned on the oven to warm it briefly, she prepared a paste of soda and vinegar. Then, oven off and shelves removed, she rubbed the paste all over the warm inside of the oven and its door. Next, she attacked with a cooper cloth (I'm sure other scrub clothes would do fine, too) and finally rinsed it out with water and a cloth. (While she did that, I went to the sink and scoured the metal shelves. A tedious job but a necessary one, unless you fancy being in a constant shouting match with your fire alarm.)

I won't exhaust you with the entire curriculum vitae of white vinegar and soda, but if you happen to be bankrupting yourself with an over-abundance of diverse cleaning products, or perhaps provoking your allergies with them, do read up on vinegar and soda and give them a go. They may not sound sexy, but they absolutely work for the majority of jobs around the house, and the price is right.

Laundry

A late friend of mine used to wax nostalgic about a Mrs. Somebody who, in the big house of his childhood, "looked after all our clothes." What a lovely Downtonesque image: someone whose full-time job it was to wash delicates, hem skirts, darn mittens, sew on buttons, get the grass stains out of sports gear... I would *kill* to have a Mrs. Somebody! (Instead, like most people, we have a washer, a dryer, an iron, an ironing board, and me.)

There is no question that washing machines changed history. We're just two people in this house and I seem to throw in at least a load a day, so I can't imagine how much time it would gobble up if it were just me, a cold brook, and a bar of soap. What we have is not an ideal set-up, because the machines are stacked and in a closet, which doesn't give me much room to manoeuvre. Still, it's better than down in a basement, stuck in a damp, dark corner designed for socks to go missing among the cobwebs. (Even if I had one of those magical chutes, down which undies and jeans could slide to their destination amusement-park style, I wouldn't like that. Too dungeon-like.)

If I had my dream laundry room, it would be relatively large and full of sunshine and have access to the outside so I could dry things like linen sheets in the sunny, summer-scented air. In addition to a *gemütlich* ironing/steaming station, I'd include a roomy table for bou-tique-worthy folding. And I'd have plenty of space for hang-drying things, which takes so much less toil on clothes than a dryer. I'm remembering now an apartment building I lived in long ago in Germany that had a communal *Trockenraum* (drying room): a giant room strung with clotheslines where everyone took their clothes and pinned them up to dry. (So admirably eco-minded, those Germans— and how convenient it was.) My parents' house in the country has not only a clotheslines outside, but also a long beam on a pulley above a wood stove inside, which serves the same purpose in winter and from which my mother, quaintly, hangs summer savory to dry for soups. A nice long bar along a wall would be good too.

I do not love laundry, I admit, but the whole business is not entirely without its positives. For one thing, I can't think of anything closer to a hug than pulling fresh, warm laundry out of the dryer on a dreary day.

The Laundry List

+ Soap powder that works and smells delicious

+ Borax

+ Bar soap

+ Soap for handwashing delicates

+ Serious stain remover

+ A soft brush

+ A clothes-hanging rack

+ A flat-drying rack

- An ironing board and a high-performance iron

- A basin

- A laundry bin

- Laundry baskets

- Hangers

- A sewing kit

- A lint brush

- Static spray

Stain, Stain, Go Away . . .

I've bought no end of stain removers, especially for red wine, but the most effective method I've discovered has been to pour boiling water through any such stains as soon as possible after they appear, and then to wash immediately. (Clearly you can't do this if people are still eating, so just try to keep the spot damp until the party's over.) If the stain isn't gone after that, never put the item in the dryer or you risk setting it forever-more. Instead, mix lemon juice and baking soda into a paste and rub it all over the stain, then set it in the sun to dry and bleach. This procedure may need to be repeated more than once. For red wine stains on linen, you may need to resort to actual bleach. (Note, this is a *last* resort.) Put on an apron so you don't ruin your favourite shirt. Fill a large bowl with a litre of cold water and add to it about ½ cup of bleach. Dip the stain spot into the bleach, rubbing your rubber-gloved hand over it until it disappears. Then wash the linen in the machine on the cold-water setting.

Storing Table, Bed, and Bath Linens

A woman I know keeps all her tablecloths at the ready on hangers in a cupboard off the dining room. Think of a carpet showroom: you walk through and they're all hanging down with their pretty patterns so you pick one that fits the scene. That's what she does choosing a tablecloth for an evening: "Ah, tonight that blue Ottoman thing with the red circles . . . Today, the burlap-coloured linen, unironed, for the rustic effect . . ." I'm quite jealous of that arrangement, but not quite organized to follow suit just yet. (If ever I do, I've noted that fat, round hangers are the trick to avoiding creases.)

For now, because I haven't all that many linens, I keep them folded in a cupboard along with dishes that we use every day. I don't always lay a cloth (most of the time, though not religiously), but we definitely use cloth napkins at every meal and consider them as indispensable as cutlery. Some people think this is crazy, but I don't; I think it makes everyday dining more civilized, and it's eco-friendly. Napkins just get chucked in the laundry along with everything else (not necessarily after every use, which is where napkin rings come in), and, as ironing goes, they're the easiest thing in the basket.

Bed linens present their own challenges. Nothing is more aggravating than digging through a chest full of folded sheets, hauling a few

out, shaking them out over a bed, and realizing they're the wrong size. If you have beds of different sizes, mark those sheets or store them in the bedroom they belong with. Find some way, in any case, not to get them confused, because making beds is labour intensive enough—downright athletic!—without any added confusion or effort.

I have read about folding sheets and keeping them inside their matching pillowcase (with the second pillowcase inside with them), but this is not a practice I'm keen to take up for the simple reason that it can be fun to mix and match, so I don't want everything hidden away in pillow cases. It's nice to be able to play around to keep bedroom décor from becoming dull. This is even truer when it comes to blankets, bedspreads, throws, and the like. I went through a phase a few years back of collecting shawls on travels; my plan now is to do the same with table linens and bedspreads, because they're so much fun.

There's not a lot to say about storing bath towels, except that I find it really makes a difference when they're all folded exactly alike and can be piled into a neat, fluffy stack, like a roll of Lifesavers. The most enticing storage system I've ever come across in the bath-towel department was in a bathroom with a long bench upon which were placed generous stacks of towels, no two alike. There was a sort of candy-shop effect to that storage décor: every time you went for a shower, there before you lay an array of patterns and colours, so you could pick just the right towel to suit your mood.

Washing Dishes

Nobody on the planet agrees with me, but I find handwashing dishes much easier and far more pleasurable than battling with a dishwasher every day. For a start, the machine is a complete nightmare to load for my personality type (Type Z, I think). Unless you practically wash the dirty dishes before putting them in the machine in the first place, half the time they won't clean properly, leaving you with plates caked with egg and glasses half full of brown water in the morning. Machines are death to silver, crystal, and proper china, and I'm too much of a tabletop fanatic to live a "dishwasher safe" sort of life.

The other trouble with dishwashers is that they too easily become a place to pitch things, like a ladle or a zester, that you end up needing half an hour later and have to dig out again, dirty, and handwash anyway. All things considered, the dishwasher may well be the single most over-rated appliance in the modern house. This, I trust, shall make anyone who doesn't own one feel much better about his lot.

Having grown up in a house without a dishwasher, I don't think twice about filling a sink with warm suds and plunging my hands in. I like the feeling, actually, and since progress is immediately visible, the job is rather gratifying. Above all, washing dishes by hand gets things done right the first time; when you're done, you're done, and you don't have to come back in a couple of hours or the next morning to finish Part B, the dreaded unloading.

Perhaps washing dishes isn't a job that holds a great deal of allure immediately after a dinner party. In moments like that I groan and whine, but Peter always insists we get the dishes out of the way before we go to bed. He's right. There's nothing worse than coming into the kitchen the morning after the night before, serenely floating toward the first cup of tea, only to stumble onto a demolition site. The late-night washing sessions give us a chance to unwind and have a post-mortem before we tuck ourselves in for some hard-earned, post-party zzzs. (And on the rare occasion when we decide "Sod it," at the very least we rinse and stack everything so that the next morning the job's a breeze.)

How to Handwash Dishes Like an Expert

ORGANIZE THE MESS

Scrape, empty, and rinse the dishes. Stack by category to the left of the sink. Put utensils in a container of warm, soapy water, making sure knife joints are above the water line.

SET UP STATIONS

If you don't have a double sink, buy a basin to act as sink number two. Fill sink number one with warm, soapy water and sink number two with hot, soap-free water. To the right of the second sink, lay an absorbent drying pad or dish rack (I use the former, the latter being too presumptuous about what dishes you'll be washing). Have absorbent towels at the ready for drying.

WASH, DRY, PUT AWAY

When we were kids, we rotated the jobs of washer, dryer, and putter awayer. Now I'm all three, or Peter and I split the tasks. Always start with the cleanest dishes and work toward the dirtiest, changing the water as necessary. Glasses first, followed by plates and bowls, then cutlery, next serving dishes, and, lastly, pots and pans. Dry as you go, and put away. (P.S. Don't soak knives with joints or anything wooden. Never put cast iron in soapy water.)

TACKLE THE TOUGH STUFF

If you've made a serious mess of the bottom of a pot, don't let it sit. Put in a few rounded tablespoons of baking soda and ½ cup or so of white vinegar, then bring to a boil, remove from the heat, and set aside to soak for an hour or so, or overnight. If the goop still hasn't lifted, repeat once more, then drain and scrape clean with a pot scraper, followed by a scrubber cloth.

TIDY UP

Drain the sinks, rinse, and dry. Wipe the countertops. Hang wet cloths and towels to dry if you're not tossing them straight into the laundry room. Check that the floor beneath the sink is dry; if not, give it a swipe so that you don't go skidding across the room and land in a heap on your tush.

Dishwashing Kit

- Lovely-smelling dish soap that cuts grease. An increasing number of organic brands are on the market these days, with natural scents that make you want to hop right into the sink yourself. If the bottle is ugly, decant it into one you like.

- A jar of baking soda for the tough jobs

- A giant stack of dishcloths (always hang wet cloths on the tap or elsewhere to dry; never leave them in a wet wad to go sour)

- An even more giant stack of tea towels (there is no such thing as enough) in cotton and linen (including linen glass cloths, so you're not trying to do glasses with some white, furry thing that leaves lint)

- A plastic pot scraper with a thin lip (thick ones are less effective)

- A flat copper "cloth" or other scrub cloth. If you use cast iron, you might like a chain-mail cleaning cloth too (such as one called the Ringer).

- Polident for soaking wine carafes or other water-stained vessels

- Silver polish and accoutrements, if appropriate. I polish every few months, putting in the required elbow grease. In the interim, I use Hagerty gloves, which take off tarnish in a snap, and I store silver in silver-friendly cloth away from heat and humidity.

- A nail brush, body exfoliant in a tube (Aesop's geranium is divine for hands), and hand cream (my favourite being L'Occitane). Your busy hands deserve them.

Division of Labour

Maybe we're just lucky or maybe it's like this for most households, but the workload for keeping our house running seemed to divide itself quite naturally from early on. We never discussed it; it just happened. I found myself doing things such as laundry, tidying, and taking care of plants, while Peter changed lightbulbs, fixed computer problems, dragged out the garbage, and so on. An arrangement right out of *Leave it to Beaver*. Sorry, but it works for us.

It doesn't really matter who takes on what jobs in a house (my mother was always the one to check air in the tires; my father made the cookies), but if you don't want to become resentful towards the person or people you live with, it's important to have some kind of balance. Everyone should participate to a reasonable degree or you risk the outbreak of WWIII.

As a way to get teenagers involved, some families keep a sort of cardboard wheel on the fridge with the regular duties in various sections around it and the names of household members on a second circle within it. Every day (or week), the wheel gets turned and the jobs each person is responsible for change. It's a fair system—and being confronted with your chores every time you go for a glass of juice or a piece of cheese is one way to help ensure they get done. (This is also a good solution for people who share housing, such as students.)

What a Load of Rubbish

Thousands of years from now, when our landfill sites get discovered like ancient tombs, the people of the future will be writing very unflattering academic papers about us and our way of life. We are junko-philes, lovers of all things disposable, indifferent to anything promising to last a lifetime (precious little is made to anyway), and shameless about the tons we toss out wastefully every day. (How's that for giving our culture's wrist a slap?)

Having been brought up in the country, surrounded by people whom the Second World War had taught to do things like wash out plastic bags for reuse, I am aware of and shocked by my own shameful consumption. I suppose it's easier in the country to save things (condo dwellers can't exactly resort to their barns for storage), but even in the sticks, garbage has increased tenfold. And it's not easy to get rid of either! With all the various categories of rubbish these days, you practically need a Ph.D. to be sure how to dispose of so much as a Kleenex.

An environmentally activated friend of mine always used to repeat the mantra "reduce, reuse, recycle," complaining that people tend to over-congratulate themselves on their recycling efforts while ignoring the arguably even more important first two steps. It's not so easy. As a constant (and grateful!) reuser of flimsy plastic grocery bags, I get very annoyed when I'm given paper ones that I can do nothing with *except* recycle. (The light plastic ones at least are ideal for lining garbage bins and occasionally for wrapping things, such as shoes when travelling (when you run out of shoe bags), or paint tins, and—ironically—for carrying out recycling.)

Worse is being forced to buy special sturdy, padded, plastic so-called eco-bags every time you shop. Of course we're supposed to remember to bring our old ones back with us over and over again, but we never do, resulting in a closet crammed with so many of them, we eventually end up throwing them out anyway.

Reducing at home is as challenging as reusing, because packagers of food, beauty, and household products don't appear to be controlled by any restrictions. I once bought a toothbrush that came in a box large enough for a pair of men's shoes. Whenever I buy butter lettuce, I have no choice but to bring each head home in its individual plastic greenhouse. Who's winning with this it's hard to say, but it sure isn't the average household. We're just two and we throw out a full carton of recycling every day. The shocker is that this is presumably far less than most people do, because we eat very little packaged food.

This leads me to composting, which our city also requires to be separated. We toss out a full bag of that every day too, but with less guilt, because it's testimony to a good diet and to the fact that a lot of cooking goes on around here. I'd love to have my very own compost operation someday so I could use the resulting soil for gardening. My father does this and also has in his cellar a whole perforated box of earthworms in potting soil who dine biweekly on coffee grounds and vegetable peelings and leaves. "I have thousands of dependents," he likes to boast.

Once I called my mother complaining that the leaves on my geraniums were turning red. "Oh," she said, "I wish I could send you some worm poop! It makes plants go gangbusters." I'm sure this all sounds terribly barnyard, but even my friend Camille has a miniature earthworm farm in her Paris apartment. As house pets go, surely they must be about as low maintenance as you can get.

Spring Into Action

I usually dread the prospect of spring cleaning, but something in the season itself—in the first few days that spring blows into town—seems to have a tonic effect that suddenly unbridles a galloping desire and energy to do things like flip mattresses, shovel out closets, and set unwanted bits of furniture onto the curb.

I remember the very Saturday it happened to me that first year we moved in. It was the day before Peter's birthday and the extended family was coming for dinner. Chicken was brining, the cake was made, wine was chilling—all by early afternoon—and the house was calm. We had just returned from a shopping expedition (done on foot, in bright sunshine, our jackets flapping open in the breeze). We set down our grocery bags on the kitchen floor and suddenly, about to put away a bag of beluga lentils, I found myself on all fours flinging every last bit of foodstuff out of the cupboard and onto the countertop.

The bottom of the empty cupboard was littered with wayward bits of pasta and droppings of basmati rice. I swept it clear. Then, with the newly bought ingredients intermingled with the old, I combed through

the wreckage. Try this yourself and, mark my words, here's the sort of situation you'll find: a giant jar with three tablespoons of oats at the bottom, several unidentified jars of white powder (baking powder? icing sugar? cream of tartar?), popcorn, popcorn, popcorn (we almost never eat popcorn) ... And then *poof*: there you are right in the thick of spring cleaning before you can even say "forsythia."

I got that cupboard organized, amalgamating like ingredients and chucking anything past its date, and then, driven by some invisible force, I found myself diving into the cupboard under the kitchen sink. It's always a war zone under there, all cleaning-product goo and garbage bags. After fifteen minutes, that cupboard too was pristine and its contents miraculously minimalist. Peter had disappeared by this point; however, it wasn't to avoid participating, as I discovered. I found him in the back of the house in a mesmerized state, running a soft, wet cloth over a dust-thick venetian blind.

It's a form of madness, really, this spring-cleaning business. What amazes me is that we live quite placidly with . . . let's be diplomatic and call them "cold-weather conditions" all winter, barely noticing if a raccoon takes up residence in the living room, and then, one thawed-out day in April, we promptly spy a streak of grease above the stovetop or a smudge on a windowpane and start foaming at the mouth. I recommend not fighting this sudden urge to deep clean, because, as we all know, the feeling will eventually pass and what doesn't get tackled in the brief off-season will only sit around unattended for another year. Otherwise put: it's not called summer cleaning for a very good, big, hot reason.

Springtime Cleaning Projects to Cherry-Pick

- Open windows and air out the house.

- Change from cool-weather to warm-weather bedding (dry clean, where appropriate, before storing, and clean any mattress covers).

- Wash windows, inside and out.

- Check for cobwebs in all corners low and high.

- Wash baseboards and walls.

- Empty every closet and cupboard and reorganize. Get things like winter coats dry cleaned and pack them away until they're needed again.

- Wash doorknobs and around doors and light switches.

- Dust paintings.

- Wash the tops of cupboards, especially in the kitchen.

- Deal with the dungeon effect of basements and attics.

- Sweep front steps and walkways.

- Set any unwanted objects (as long as they're operational and in good condition) on the curb for passersby to take as they like.

- Donate unwanted clothes.

- Wash cushion covers (possibly even change from winter to summer fabric).

- Get upholstery and curtains cleaned.

- Wipe down all lights and lamps, especially any hanging from the ceiling.

- Defrost the fridge.

- Clean the oven.

- Wash shower curtains.

- Rinse garbage cans and recycling bins, indoors and out.

- Tackle bathroom tiles.

- Get chimney cleaned.

- Clean carpets (or beat them out).

- Polish furniture, copper, and silver.

- Oil cutting boards.

- Get kitchen knives sharpened (this is good to do if you're going away for a few days; pick them up when you get back and you won't have missed them).

- Get cars, bicycles, etc. inspected and oiled.

- Repot plants that need it and move them outside, as appropriate.

- Attend to outdoor trees and shrubs.

- Fill any potholes in the driveway and make sure the steps and walk are safe.

- Check the status of household umbrellas. Replace as needed.

- Make a list of everything broken and determine whether to replace or repair.

- Replenish bar with gin, Lillet, rosé, tonic water . . .

P.S. Many of the above jobs are fall-cleaning appropriate too, although obviously things like the plants and bedding operations work in reverse. Specific to fall, you'll want to add the following: store outdoor furniture, drain hoses, clean air vents and chimneys, check fire alarms, clean gutters and spouts, and store warm-weather clothing.

P.P.S. Get out in the sunshine and enjoy the weather. You can't do everything and sometimes you just have to let stuff go.

How to Make Spring Cleaning More Manageable

Just reading a list like that is enough to drive a person to drink. Realistically, few of us could even begin to check off half the spring-cleaning boxes, but as I argued earlier, a list is at least a start.

Before we had Maria in our life, Peter and I once hired a small team for a day to come sort us out. Three strong women descended upon the place, carrying everything from ladders to buckets to vacuums. We made ourselves scarce for the better part of the day and when we got back everything from ceiling fans to chair rungs to windowpanes to fridge drawers were clean as whistles. It's an expense, but one well-worth splurging on once or twice a year, if you can.

When at last we did have Maria, her regular schedule wouldn't accommodate the extra work, so Peter and I decided to join her on her rounds for a day. Six hands are certainly better than two (and a lot less lonely and dull). With all three of us in action, we burned through our list in no time.

I won't pretend it was any picnic, but there's definitely something about looking after your nest that makes you feel well looked after yourself. Somehow, clearing junk out of an attic, garage, or even just a drawer immediately becomes mirrored psychologically. It's therapy, really, and who doesn't want to start off spring with a light heart?

The Electronics Drawer

"What is in here anyway?" I asked Peter one day, pulling open the black hole we refer to as the electronics drawer. "Oh gawd," he answered. "Wires I'm not courageous enough to get rid of, earphones I never use . . . overall an embarrassing reflection of the inside of our heads."

Whattaya mean "our" heads, Batman?

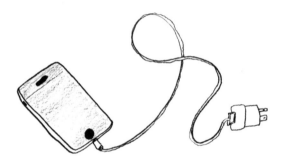

The electronics drawer is my least favourite drawer in the house and I generally have nothing to do with it, but if I'm honest, I must admit it would be risky not to have one; our world is simply too wired up with things waiting to go wrong not to be prepared.

When I was growing up, the guru in these matters was my mother. She still knew how to—and was equipped to—bring old ways back to life whenever necessary. For example, if the power went out, she had a standby woodstove to fire up where she could bake a loaf of bread and have a pot of soup going in no time. She also had an attic full of useful, if archaic, items such as kerosene lamps, which were titillating and haunting to have on at night; large pots for water; cupboards gleaming with preserves... Come hell or high water, we weren't going to freeze or starve.

I'm not sure this has anything to do with an electronics drawer, because what's in that would be hopeless in an ice storm, but there is something about being prepared for emergencies that makes it a very reassuring thing to have. To keep it efficient and functional, be sure to replace anything you remove from it immediately and go through it every six months to get rid of any junk, such as outdated phone cords or an old VHS machine you were telling yourself might one day be a valuable antique.

ELECTRONIC DRAWER ESSENTIALS

Light bulbs to replace any currently in the house

Batteries for everything from flashlights
to cameras to kitchen scales

An extension cord

A multi-plug electric cord

Any charger, cord, or plug associated
with any household electronic device

A USB key to back up computer

A flashlight

A cheap backup cell phone that
a visitor might need to borrow

Adapters for foreign travel

Manuals for all electronic items

The Toolbox

Once again, not my department, although I have been known to raid that mysterious little case hidden away in the closet where the water heater is. A million years ago, I actually had my own toolbox, a metal one in fire-engine red, but it was full of kitchen equipment: potato peelers, pastry bag tips, a butane torch, etc. It's possible I took it with me to France, because I seem to remember emptying it out to give to someone who found it exotic (such are the dangers of being a shirt-off-your-back type). I don't miss it, really, although it was snazzier than what Peter's got, which is plastic (shudder). Oh well, it's the contents that count.

Even if you're someone who wouldn't know an Allen key from a juice-box straw, if you ever want a towel rack hung or a piano carried through a door, you'll want the basic tools so that whoever you harangue into doing these things for you doesn't throw up his hands. (P.S. A toolbox makes an excellent gift for someone moving into their first house or apartment.)

TOOLBOX BASICS

A standard hammer, preferably with
a shock-absorbing handle

Standard-size pliers

Needle-nose pliers

An adjustable wrench

A Phillips screwdriver

A few flat-head screwdrivers of various sizes

An Allen key (i.e., the Ikea tool)

A level

A tape measure

A utility knife

A sharpened carpenter's pencil (plus sharpener)

Various nails and screws, packaged according
to type and size in anything from zip-lock bags
to small jars or metal containers

Various picture hooks

A cordless power drill, if you're really serious

An old-style bottle opener for opening paint tins

Backup paint-stirring sticks

Duct tape

The Medicine Cabinet

While we're on the theme, putting together a cabinet of healing supplies for emergencies is another good way to make a house feel ready for anything, whether we need a Band-Aid or cough medicine in the moment or not. It makes a good rainy-day or I've-got-the-blues project too.

Ice packs

Sunscreen and after-sun lotion

Aspirin

Band-Aids of various sizes

Polysporin

Disinfectant

Cotton swabs

A thermometer

Eyedrops

Anti-itch cream

Epsom salts

Calamine lotion

A magnifying glass

A hot water bottle

Throat lozenges

Earplugs

An eye pillow

Very precise tweezers

FOR WHAT AILS YOU

Let's take a moment here to think about *us*. When the body is truly worn down because we haven't taken care of it, sometimes a walloping head cold is just what we need to force ourselves into temporary retirement. One March, just before yet another house move and when I was stressed about a zillion other things at the same time, my body suddenly collapsed in protest. I can't remember the last time I was that sick. I spent a whole week in bed sleeping, living off nothing but lemons, and not seeing a soul. Apart from the fact that I felt like simmering hell, it was heaven.

The thing with getting sick is that suddenly we don't need to make excuses to get people to leave us alone; our excuse is written all over us, in fact it's being audibly hacked up and blown out of us (forgive the imagery). There is no fortress like the flu: people keep their distance. And, to compare them more to storms, we can't really fight colds and flus, we have to weather them, so it pays to be prepared.

As soon as I feel illness coming on, straightaway I gather the sickie supplies: hot water bottle, tissues, herbal teas, lemons, honey, zinc tablets, vitamin C, chicken soup, rice... It's always smart to change the bed so it's fresh and cozy (we could end up spending a week in it), take a bath (we may not have another for days), stockpile any reading we've been wanting to catch up on (knowing that we may not have the energy for so much as *Hello!* magazine in the beginning), and hop into some linen pyjamas, if you can get them (linen is the perfect fabric for keeping us warm when we're cold and cool when we're hot). There, now we're ready to rest and let our body do its thing.

BONUS: A RHYMING REMEDY

My brother's father-in-law, a retired Norwegian sea captain whose name, not surprisingly, is Tor, once gave me a recipe for tackling colds. He delivered it in his booming, thickly accented voice, which is ideal for the menacing recital of nursery rhymes (of the Fee-Fi-Fo-Fum variety), and for this:

> *One of sour*
> *Two of sweet*
> *Three of strong*
> *And four of weak*

Eeek! You picture the evil troll in a fairy tale concocting this in a vial to poison his innocent rival, but actually it's a very pleasant and comforting elixir to sip on. You might translate it this way: sour = lemon, sweet = honey, strong = rum or whisky, and weak = hot water. Tor swears that taken before bed, this will knock any invalid out for a good, long, revitalizing night. (Not suitable for children, needless to say.)

P.S. My mother also has an excellent remedy for colds: herbal tea made from steeping handfuls of herbs, such as fresh rosemary, sage, summer savoury and oregano in boiling water. It will be strong and slightly bitter tasting, in a pleasant way, and it really seems to do the trick. If it gets too strong, just dilute it.

The Economics of Housekeeping

Running a house is not much different from running a business: income must be balanced against "outgo," taxes must be filed, bills paid, help hired and fired . . . They didn't call this "home economics" for nothing. What with all the easy ways to spend (Peter just taps card machines with his wristwatch, and "bing"), perhaps never before in history has it been easier to wake up and discover that one's household finances are in a state of capsize. If they're not dealt with, there might soon be no house to keep at all.

    I'd never managed my home accounts with particular aplomb (all my moving around made it tricky, excuses, excuses . . .), although I was relatively good at staying on top of those associated with business. At about the same time that Peter and I got married, I decided it was time I start applying the same principles I'd been using in business to home.

It began with saving every receipt for every single thing I bought (and I made Peter do it too). For everything from cars to chocolate bars, I decreed, a receipt would have to be produced or I'd go on the rampage. Every bottle of water, every magazine, every toothpick . . .

Is it a pain in the neck to do that? Not really. It's a habit you get into, like any other, and it's an essential first step to getting financial affairs at home in order (i.e., knowing exactly what you spend on what).

I allowed a month's worth of collected receipts to accumulate on a tray near the front door. (A drawer is more sensible, if you have one, but the place for them should be somewhere easy for unloading as soon as you get home.) On the last day of the month of January, I drew the receipts to my bosom like an armful of daisies (not!), carried them to the dining-room table, and sat down with them.

Perhaps more sensible people hire out jobs like these (sorting, compiling, adding, etc.), but I was determined to tackle it myself, at least in the early stages. The reason is that money is emotional. I figured that if someone else was doing my accounts, they would do them with a cold heart, and my own mind would remain delusionally detached and never truly register the potential consequences of not getting a grip. The grown-up thing to do, I realized, was to face the music myself, including however that might make me feel.

My method for working out our spending was to divide all our receipts into categories. Everyone's categories will differ slightly, but as a rough example, these were mine:

Rent or mortgage

Utilities (heat, water, etc.)

Communications (Internet, phone, etc.)

Insurance(s)

Clothes (including dry cleaning and repairs)

Health and body (medical appointments,
yoga membership, toothpaste, facials, etc.)

Household (hardware, paint, flowerpots,
pots and pans, art, chairs, etc.)

Travel and transportation (planes, taxis, etc.)

Home office (stamps, paper, computers,
greeting cards, subscriptions, etc.)

Professional development
(courses, seminars, conferences, etc.)

Legal and other professional services

Food

Restaurants and bars (divided into personal and business)

Bar and cellar

Entertainment

Savings (if you're smart, you must
always save at least a small percentage)

Charity

Gifts

Some people prefer to deal with accounting on a computer using spreadsheets; I find it much less stressful to do everything manually on paper, and it seems simpler. I even have a bit of a game: I write "place cards" for each category, set them in different spots on the table, and place the appropriate pile of receipts at each setting. Then I move from chair to chair, adding everything up on a calculator, spot by spot, and writing down the totals. At last, I type up a single page that lays out how much was spent in each category plus the total figure of household expenses that month. Then I go show the monthly expense sheet to Peter.

The first time I did this, he just about fainted.

It turned out we'd spent twice the amount he thought we'd spent. We couldn't go on doing that if we were ever to live within our means, so Peter swiftly drew up a strict budget and the next day marched me to the bank, where I was handed a wad of cash that would have to do me for the week. (Sigh, so old school.) I'll tell you something, though: it worked. We both immediately became much more careful about spending. Instead of automatically jumping on Amazon to buy books for research, I actually went to the library for the first time since university. (It turned out that half the books I was going to order were useless for what I needed anyway.) I got a lot more creative about turning dinner leftovers into lunches. Peter resumed running instead of joining a gym.

Was it daunting always trying to figure out how not to spend money when we were just about to spend it? Well, sort of, but once you get into the groove, it can become almost fun to find solutions. Plus, by December 31, having already done the math for the whole year, taxes are basically done and ready to file at the snap of our fingers. No scrambling in spring. That's always motivating.

We continue with our system, occasionally getting slack and having to wag our fingers at ourselves. It's sticking with the program that's challenging, but also essential. Otherwise, I've found it heartening to discover that I'm not too dense to handle household accounts (even though I'm no Warren Buffett) and that it is possible to get things on track if a person puts his mind to it. Eventually I'll hand the job over to a proper bookkeeper, but by then I'll be intimate enough with our finances to keep a sharp eye on affairs. As I've said, running a household is like running a business, and I figure if I want to become a good CEO, it can't hurt for me to start, as I am, in the mailroom.

First Steps to Solid Home Economics

- Figure out how much money, exactly, you can rely on coming in every month. Think conservatively.

- If you can, put 5 to 25 per cent of that amount into savings and just pretend it doesn't exist. Live off what's left.

- Have every household member save all receipts and know their spending.

- On the last day of every month (or at least every quarter), categorize the receipts, add them up, type the results on a single page, and save it in a file.

- Do the household finances yourself, at least once. Your emotional reactions to the results will keep you more on track with your goals all month long. You'll also be able to talk the talk if you do eventually hire someone to do the job for you.

- Pay with cash as often as possible.

- Avoid debt at all costs.

- Treat the first of every month or quarter as a clean slate, a fresh start, and a chance to do even better. Don't beat yourself up if you've fallen off track; just get back on.

- Never buy anything because it's cheap; only buy something because you need it or because you love it so much you can't live without it.

- If things are going to hell, don't throw your hands up and go out on the town for Champagne. Go to bed. Wake up tomorrow. Take back control.

- When you get a grand idea, figure out a cheaper version that will come off equally grandly. For example, instead of making the crown roast of beef for a party, braise a cheaper cut that will be equally delicious. Instead of buying pricey tickets for a hockey game, invite friends over to watch the game on TV with buttered pot-popped popcorn. (See page 224.)

Ten Tips For Entertaining on a Tight Budget

This may seem an odd place to put this, but we are on the topic of finances. If Peter and I ever go bankrupt, the reason will come as no surprise. We spend untold fortunes on wining and dining our friends. In fact, Peter jokes that we run a soup kitchen for millionaires, which, as exaggerations go, is relatively slight. But entertaining gives us enormous pleasure, so we don't resent what we spend in this category. In any case, most people have some sort of sieve of passion into which they recklessly pour cash: vinyl records, model airplanes, makeup, shoes,

golfing, whatever. Ours is what it is, and what we do is what we do. If we end up having to live off growing turnips and milking goats one of these days as a result, we'll carry on hosting, because being low on pennies should never stop people from celebrating life.

BYOB

You're obviously not going to throw a dinner party and have everyone sit with their own bottle like a circle of Dickensian down-and-outers around a fire in a back alley. One tricky aspect of the Bring Your Own Bottle principle at a party proper is that it very often results in a tableful of plonk. Keep this in mind if you're a guest; never show up with a bottle of wine that you yourself wouldn't drink with pleasure.

THE EVER-SO-RETRO POTLUCK

Once fashionable, the humble potluck has fallen out of favour. In case you're of a generation that's never even heard the term, a potluck is a gathering for a meal to which everyone contributes a dish. The dishes are arranged buffet style on a table and people help themselves, usually sitting around a room with plates in their laps rather than at a dining table. When you're the one playing host, it's good to plan on one anchoring dish (a pot of chili or pasta), tell people what it is, and let them bring things to flesh out the feast, such as salads, appetizers, or desserts. When you're playing guest, think of something as universally pleasing as you can, and make it nice (i.e., no showing up with a plastic tub of hummus from the grocery store and those so-called carrots that taste like pressed wood).

PICNICS

I had a friend in Paris who was a brilliant organizer of picnics. He set a very smart tone: no plastic, no packaged foods, no pizza, no pop ... He had rules. Everyone had to show up with a dish to share, plus china, cutlery, and glasses for themselves, as well as wine. These were (are still) legendary picnics, always set in a gorgeous location, such as overlooking the Seine, or in a Roman arena. If you really want to come off as host extraordinaire, you might organize some games; bring along some Frisbees perhaps, or a stick for playing limbo; bubbles for blowing, or boules or a croquet set.

CHEAP/CREATIVE CUTS

Just because we're having guests doesn't mean we have to pull out all the stops with lobster, a giant *côte de boeuf*, caviar, or what have you. When we're tight on pennies, it's time to remember the joys of legumes, the decadence of pork belly, the possibilities of tinned fish ... Having a lot of money to spend in life may make decision making easier, but it can also allow the muscles of our imagination to go slack for lack of challenge. We must never let the need to be frugal get us down; rather, let circumstances inspire originality.

GO MEAT-FREE

Especially in this day and age, vegetarian cooking is more than acceptable for entertaining. In fact, it's a useful way to cook all round because it sidesteps a lot of people's phobias and allergies. Vegetables aren't necessarily cheap (although you can whip up a coleslaw for not much), but starches and grains do tend to be, especially if you buy them in bulk from ethnic shops. A chickpea curry on rice, a meatless ragout, a platter of various baked potatoes with different toppings, a big lentil soup, omelettes—with a little thought out of the box, it's possible to feed quite a crowd for no more than you'd pay for a single main course in a mediocre restaurant.

SUNDAY BREAKFAST

You see what brunch costs in restaurants—and how full those restaurants routinely are—so obviously the idea of socializing over food in the morning is attractive to many people. Since that appears to be the case, why shouldn't we all feel fine about inviting a handful of friends over for breakfast *chez nous*, rather than organizing an elaborate evening? Breakfast can cost peanuts (no alcohol required, although I may be speaking for myself there, so perhaps be prepared, just in case, with some bubbles to add to the O.J....), but still makes us givers. You can serve only pancakes, or only oatmeal, or go full on and serve bacon and eggs with toast. (Friends of ours once added a board of French pastries—a much appreciated touch, but only if you have the budget.) It's sort of fun to be all rather truck stop about it, with a full pot of coffee ever at the ready.

FOCUS A MEAL ON AN ACTIVITY

There was an era of New Year's festivities during which my parents, as a way of including the teenagers, used to organize an afternoon hike, followed by a feast of lasagna, salad, and trifle before launching into an evening game of Dictionary to get us through to the fireworks. By planning a get-together around an activity—a baseball game, a treasure hunt, a barbershop quartet—pressure can be taken off the meal itself. Any food and drink is secondary and can be minimal, as long as it's nice: a corn boil, a cookie and lemonade stand, hot chocolate and cake—you get the idea.

CO-HOST

If you share mutual friends with another person, you can always team up and do a joint dinner, splitting the bill in two and at the same time seeing everyone you both want to see. Just be sure that the guests know it's a joint effort. That way the person whose house the hosting happens in doesn't get all the credit, which can happen. Also, be sure that you and your co-host agree completely on your spending limit, otherwise you may find yourself with a bill that makes you reach immediately for the smelling salts.

PEASANT NIGHT

Call it like it is. There is a vast repertoire of dishes from all around the globe that come from peasant traditions but that don't carry a negative stigma. Think of minestrone, burritos, corned beef and cabbage, baked beans, meatloaf... Just because they're inexpensive doesn't mean they aren't delicious. If you need to do a night on the cheap, why not work it right into your invitation and have fun with it? Tell guests to dress down (or maybe even in costume). Serve wine (or beer) out of tumblers.

TEA OR COFFEE

Ah, the democratic pleasures of tea and coffee, those universal drinks beloved of all the classes. They barely merit a mention and certainly don't require much explanation. Make a pot of either tea or coffee, set out a few cookies on a pretty plate, *et voilà!* See? Being broke doesn't mean we can't host.

And now, back to business.

HQ

Every house needs its headquarters, the "office" where everything to do with running a place can go and therefore be found when we need it. A room with a desk and filing cabinets would be nice—a sort of Jane Austenesque gentleman's "growlery" sort of space, or as Montaigne called his writing room, an *arrière boutique*—but for most of us, a chest of drawers, or some other suitable spot for important papers, is all we need.

Set aside, then, some spot in the house, preferably one that doesn't get a huge amount of traffic, where you can keep all the important papers in one place: files of receipts, contracts, passports, bills, licences, etc. It's useful, too, to have a calculator, a hole puncher, a stapler, and paperclips at hand, along with file folders, sticky notes, and markers for labelling.

Hired Help

Rare—if not non-existent—must be the house that never hires help at all—no electrician, no plumber, no roofer, no landscaper, no painter, no cleaner . . . Having been born without an ounce of Mister Fixit in my genes, any place I've ever lived would have been crumbling to the ground in no time if it hadn't been for outside experts coming in now and again to save the day.

The best way to find qualified people is through word of mouth. The trouble with just diving into Google (including looking at customer-review sites of the TripAdvisor ilk) is that you're basically volunteering to be a guinea pig. You have no idea what you'll get. Sometimes there's no choice, in which case you must rely on seeing work done for other clients or consulting references from people you have no real reason to trust, but the best is always to get names from a person you know personally (preferably someone who's valuable to the person you're about to employ) and whose standards you share. The best bookkeepers, travel agents, handymen, and so on that I've ever found have been through friends, and it's a favour I'm always pleased to pass on.

The sad truth is that people who do work of exceptional quality in any field (and who sincerely care and take pride in their craft) are few and far between. ("Good help is hard to find," said everybody.) My brothers, who have renovated a lot of houses, can tell no end of chilling stories about ripping down walls to expose electrical wiring millimetres from bursting into flames, thanks to an amateur job.

My parents once had windows replaced in a house only to have to redo them all again a year or so later because they'd been installed incorrectly. None of these jobs comes cheap, so it's maddening to discover you've been had by a quack or by someone who is sloppy and couldn't care less if, while plowing your driveway, they happen to take out a few prize fruit trees.

One moral of these sorts of stories is to do your homework first; another is not to assume that once the homework's done you can hire and walk away. I once had a guy come to tile a bathroom. I distinctly told him to put a stripe of different-coloured tiles three rows down from the top, then to carry on with the original colour. When I came back a few hours later, the tiles, by then set like stone, had been done to his liking rather than mine, the stripe two down from the top. I wanted to take a swing at him.

I should not have paid for that job, which I did, meaning that he got away with incompetence and I had to live with a bathtub wall I couldn't stand (not least of all because every time I looked at it I was reminded I'd been a pushover). Nobody likes to be micromanaged and nobody wants to have to micromanage, but without getting agreements in writing and without keeping an eye on things to make sure jobs are being carried out as agreed, we're asking for trouble.

I rather like to think that by insisting people live up to their commitments and do their jobs right, we make the world a better place. Allowing people to get away with shoddy work or to cheat us only means they'll rub their hands together and go off and do it to somebody else. The times in my life I've done a so-so job on something myself and been called out for it (my former boss, Anne Willan, was merciless), I've appreciated it, at least retrospectively, because it made me clean up my act and be better. There is such a thing as constructive criticism. We live in a time when too many people feel they deserve a happy-face sticker just for showing up. But why should we not be grateful to be pushed toward excellence? Besides, when praise and compensation are reserved for when they're truly deserved, they actually mean something to people.

Five Tips for Hiring and Holding onto Outside Help for the House

- Know what you expect to have done and know your standards. Communicate them clearly, in writing (with both parties signing off), where appropriate.

- Make sure the person you've hired has the right tools and conditions to do the work, including those that you're expected to supply yourself.

- Take an interest in the work being done and check in to make sure you're satisfied, without micromanaging, unless you need to (in which case, also recognize you've probably hired the wrong hands).

- Be pleasant, respectful, and friendly, but remain professional. (Don't try to be the best friend of people you hire; it doesn't work.)

- Pay only once a job is done to your satisfaction. Remuneration justifiably withheld is a great—and sometimes the only—motivator.

The Directory

The admirably organized Anne Willan, my former boss, used to keep a house directory for Château du Feÿ that was updated annually. At the front were all the emergency numbers: police, ambulance, etc.; next came professional services: travel agents, lawyers, the hairdresser; and finally, by category, came full contact information for anyone who had anything to do with the house: the village mayor, the plumber, the computer man, the baker, the postmistress, the gardener, and so on. Several copies of the directory were printed out and planted near various telephones around the house. We consulted them constantly.

A fascinating thing about putting a household directory together is that you realize the extent to which no house is an island. We all become woven into incredibly complex webs of relationships—relationships that play vital roles in our lives, even though they don't include family and friends, and that need to be maintained.

At Christmas, Anne used to order crates of sparkling wine, put bottles in decorative bags with personalized cards attached, and have them delivered to every person in the directory, from the cheesemonger to the tree-trimming man to the pool cleaner. This struck me as being unusually generous and rather a lot of work, but I learned that it paid off: during the rest of the year, whenever Anne needed a special order from the bakery, it was delivered; if a plumbing incident occurred on a Sunday, the repair man was there.

Emotional Housekeeping

Not to go all touchy-feely on you, but we've all been in those pristine houses, with lovely furniture all perfectly placed and mirrors gleaming, that nonetheless make us want to run for the hills. When misery is in the air, it's as penetrating as dampness.

I read an article not long ago by a mother who was talking about unrecognized women's work. The usual list was covered—laundry, cooking, helping with homework, booking dentist appointments—but the focus was on the truly invisible stuff: keeping the emotional well-being of a household balanced. Of course, this is not women's work alone (although perhaps women are more inclined to take it on); it's the responsibility of everyone in a household to look out for one another. Indeed, this is the basis of any well-functioning community.

Peter jokes that he and I should hire ourselves out as barometers to hang in people's houses to alert them whenever there's a change in emotional atmospheric conditions. We're both so sensitive to this sort of thing, it's almost a problem; the weight of a person's step on a stair, the robustness of a voice or lack thereof—we don't miss a beat.

Anyway, I'm no family counsellor, but it is worth keeping in mind that sometimes the most important piece of housekeeping to attend to is clearing the air. No matter how sparkling a place, it doesn't mean much if everybody living in it is under a mound of emotional grit.

THREE

Keep a Living Kitchen

These are confusing times in the world of food. On the one hand, there's the unsettling evidence that people are eating fewer home-cooked meals than ever before, and on the other, there's the fact that a great many have also rediscovered the pleasures of cooking, a lust for learning about it, and a pride in doing it (albeit perhaps only because food and cooking are desirable status symbols right now). At the very least, we seem to have moved away from the mistaken notion that when it comes to food, eating is the only pleasure and cooking the punishment. This is a good thing, because cooking and eating both are central to home life, essential ties that bind. No wonder the kitchen is considered the heart of the home.

You could in fact argue that home and food are nearly synonymous, ye olde hearth being symbolic of both. There's something about cooking that brings a house alive in a way that sleeping, taking a bath, or reading a book just don't do to the same degree. Houses can feel cavernous and lonely without cooking—and I don't just mean without the presence of food, I mean without actual cooking (which is why ordering in, as a rule, can't compete). It's as though the activity had an aura, an energy flowing out from it all through the house. There's certainly a very different feeling evoked by the smell of frying onions in butter when one comes through the front door than there is by a waft of steaming cardboard and Styrofoam (or worse, by the scent of nothing at all). Home cooking has a magic that nothing else can beat.

Personally, I've always loved being in the kitchen, because that's where so much of the action always is. No matter how big or small, inviting kitchens have buzz, and it's hard to stay out of them. I don't think I ever came home from school a day in my life when my mother wasn't already at the stove making dinner, usually with a woodstove crackling in the background and adding to the ambiance. On weekends, my dad took over and would turn the place upside down with bread making and cookie production. Even when you weren't in the kitchen with them, the scents and clattering emanating from the room were as reassuring as the aroma of my grandfather's puffing pipe at the end of a day. A happy kitchen is a sign that all is well.

That early model, I suppose, shaped my idea of what a kitchen is meant to be, and no matter where I've found myself living since, it has always been my instinct to set a still kitchen into motion and to keep it there, otherwise it's just too depressing. This requires being present, at least around mealtimes, which is controversial because the structure of our working lives makes this challenging for so many. We can't be in two places at once, yet perhaps we must be (unless we hire a full-time cook, which most can't).

I'm lucky to work from home for the most part, so it's easier for me to balance professional life with running the house. But it was a bit of a surprise to discover just how demanding running a house can be. Quite apart from laundry, cleaning, and those nuts and bolts, the kitchen alone presents a serious business. You need cupboards and fridge stocked at all times, a clean space to work, and dishes at the ready, and you have to be prepared to come up with at least one serious meal a day, if not three. This mostly falls on me, and sometimes it feels like a hassle, but I basically accept this as part of my role. Keeping on top of it makes home a better place to live for everyone, and besides, unless we're prepared to live on Kraft Dinner for the rest of our lives, the reality is that somebody has to do it.

It's work, but the job comes with a lot of joy too. Indeed, my favourite time of any day is when Peter gets home, bang on the cocktail hour. I'm always already in the kitchen getting any heavy lifting out of the way, but I like to save some jobs for him too—any steak or fish frying, for example, and sometimes mixing a sauce or setting the table. He likes helping and I love how social a joint effort makes the place. The whole house comes to life, like a wooden puppet suddenly turned to flesh, even more so when other people are joining us, which is usually several times a week.

Having dinner guests so often may sound outrageous, but spontaneous home entertaining is a habit I picked up in Paris and it has never left me. Because Paris is such a compact city, getting around is easy. That paired with the fact that people love to socialize over food (and the fact that food is easy to buy, what with butchers, bakers, greengrocers, etc. peppered all over the place) means people routinely tend to ask one another over last minute to share a meal.

One friend of mine—a man with a wife and three growing kids living in a chaotic apartment in the ninth arrondissement at the time—was notorious for this. You could get a call from him as late as 6 p.m. with an invitation for that night, and as many as twelve people would show up to dine on a Tuesday as though it were a Saturday night. He wasn't the only one, either. All my friends seemed to operate like that—as did I, of course—so you sort of went around on a circuit, which meant the variety of cooking styles and social mixing was quite dazzling.

Perhaps on this side of the ocean we tend to draw too firm a line between family cooking and entertaining. I don't myself, at least not anymore. My cooking style is maternal and homey no matter who shows up: a big platter of butter chicken with rice might get plunked into the middle of the table, or a slab of spiced salmon with fennel salad on the side. I simply don't do performing-arts-on-a-plate sort of stuff. I used to worry this would disappoint people, but I've grown comfortable with my cooking, not only because it feels true to who I am, but also because it finally dawned on me that this is actually the kind of food most people want when they come into a house (especially chefs, by the way).

No matter how much we appreciate restaurants, we never, any of us, lose our craving for the kind of easygoing, love-basted food that a mother might make and (very importantly) for the way that kind of food makes us feel: nourished, balanced, defined, included, safe. This is why it's vital for us home cooks to give ourselves permission to cook like home cooks and to understand the unique value of our contribution every day. It's one of a kind.

If it's any consolation, I have to give myself this same pep talk sometimes. I'm as vulnerable to the insecurities of the cooking host as anyone.

Most of the time I know what I'm doing in the kitchen, but I also have a tendency to try new things when people come over and occasionally they don't work out. Once I set a first course on the table and found myself asking, "Now then, would anyone like a nice, damp slice of lawn?" I forget what it was, some sort of spinach flan I think, but it looked as though I'd got it onto the platter with a cricket bat swung over an overgrown pitch after a downpour. Oh well. I sucked up my shame, served it forth, and, for once, didn't apologize.

(This is my new thing: do not, no matter how much you want to, apologize for food. If you really screw something up, make a joke of it, no more than once, and then shut up. Example: "One might call this little delicacy 'pasta confit,'" or "My 'chocolate mystery,' here, tastes especially good when you hide it under a lot of whipped cream and can't actually see it.")

Whenever anything goes not quite to plan with any aspect of a meal, I console myself with the idea that people actually like to be served the occasional slightly sub-par dish. It makes them feel comfortable because they know they're being fed by a human and not by a factory conveyor belt. It also makes guests more likely to return your invitation: hallelujah, you're not perfect, *ergo* they won't have to be either. I think this is especially important when we invite people we don't know particularly well and are hoping to become friendly with. Counterintuitively, it can be wise not to try to be overly impressive or we'll scare them away.

Test the hypothesis: invite acquaintances for spaghetti and see how long it takes to have your hospitality reciprocated. Now invite some others for stuffed woodcock on toast points with sauce Bordelaise and see how you make out. (It often pays in life to err on the side of simple.)

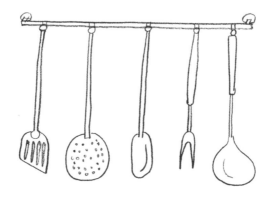

The Habit of Home Cooking

As a child, the fact that everything we ate was homemade used to make me cringe with embarrassment, because the other kids at school seemed to be allowed a lot of bought things: mini sips, Oreos, Cheese Whiz... My brothers and I were shipped off to school with sandwiches made on homemade brown bread (everybody else had grocery white bread, and my older brother sometimes traded his for that on the sly). Boxed cereal was so foreign to us that whenever my paternal grandparents came to visit, we'd gaffle onto their box of All-Bran, thinking it must be exotic since it came in a box. I remember begging to be allowed to make cake from a mix. No way, José, was my mother's stance. At last I managed to get my uncle's cook of the time to let me try one at his house. (The cake turned out to be little-girl pink, which I thought was the height of gastronomic bliss.)

Even though the idea of eating those bought foods appealed to us back then (oh the magnetic allure of forbidden fruit!), in the end barely any crossed our lips, and in any case bought foods weren't very useful to someone like me, because I wanted to cook. Without that, where was all the fun? I still feel that way, and I suppose this sense of adventure in the kitchen is what gave me an early habit of cooking that has stayed with me all my life.

Some people aren't terribly interested in preparing food. (Fair enough; fashion doesn't do much for me.) For this and other reasons, the ubiquitous availability of ready-made food products and restaurants is considered to be a luxurious advantage of our time. I suppose it is, but there is a downside, too. If you never cook, what are you to do when you actually *do* want to cook—for a family celebration, say, or a hot date? Then it's panic central, whereas if you just cook all the time anyway, it's not such a big deal.

That's one good reason for making a habit of home cooking: it reduces dinner parties essentially to sharing what you've got in the oven anyway. I acknowledge that this is relatively easy for me to say because I don't consider making dinner to be any more optional than I do getting dressed. I just do it. Still, that's a decision more than a privilege. We all learn by doing, so making a habit of home cooking is really a way of life that is available to anyone who wants it.

Peter tells me that, about two years before I met him, he decided to change the way he was eating for the sake of his physique. He'd been bacheloring for a spell and, as most of us know, there's nothing like the single life to drive people to the ramen boxes and pizza delivery. Thank goodness for vanity, really, because sometimes it's the only thing that saves us. Peter took a look in the mirror one morning and went straight out and bought a pair of running shoes and a sack of rice. Overnight, he went from takeout pulled pork and so-called sushi to making his own dinners religiously: vegetable stir-fries, grilled chicken, omelettes . . . He also started running a few mornings a week. In four months, he was down thirty pounds and fitting into the sleekest Italian suits. Needless to say, after that he stuck to his home-cooking lifestyle (and then he married me, which cemented the deal).

Though home cooking is not just about weight control, it sure makes a difference. If we want to know what's going into our bodies, we have to cook food ourselves, because even the best restaurants tend to use more fat and salt than are found in home cooking. It's also about learning how to taste and developing a sharp palate in our pursuit of pleasure. It's true of many things in life: rather than necessarily always setting our minds to what knowledge, taste, and opinions we might acquire, we simply soak things up. That's a good reason why, as soon as we're old enough to have any say in the matter, we must be careful what (and whom, for that matter) we let near us. Too much elbow-rubbing with ersatz butter and orange juice and we start to believe they're the real deal, then we wonder why we don't find eating or cooking terribly interesting.

If you were to give me a soapbox, I'd go on all afternoon. The benefits of making home cooking a habit are endless: it's unquestionably healthier, undeniably cheaper, educational and empowering, sophisticated and civilized, grounding and comforting, and often plain-old better tasting. If you're sold on all this and don't yet have a home-cooking diet, but think you'd like one, then here are some tips.

Eight Simple Ways to Get into the Home-Cooking Habit

- Taste with awareness, wherever and whatever you're eating, including when you dine out and including when you don't like something. Notice textures and temperatures, quantities and cuts, tastes and flavours. In short, start taking a true interest in what you eat.

- Keep the kitchen well stocked with raw ingredients (and low on prepared foods) so that when you're hungry, you're forced to prepare something rather than grab from a package, even if it only means cutting up an avocado and sprinkling on some lemon juice and salt. Buy flour instead of pancake mix, buy butter and icing sugar rather than ready-made frosting, etc. A bit of enforced discipline is a good thing.

4. Keep the kitchen clean. Personally, I cannot cook in chaos, and whenever I try, I do stupid things such as forget to add sugar to a cake or knock knives off the counter and nearly skewer myself. Even if you're a chaotic type of cook, when the kitchen is dirty, it's pretty off-putting (if not to you, then definitely to guests).

4. Prepare something from scratch every day, or at least most days. Maybe it's just a vinaigrette, a sandwich, or a piece of fish fried in a pan. However simple, it counts. (When I'm not in the mood, I often just start frying a chopped onion in butter, which creates ambiance and motivates me.)

4. Become a connoisseur of your "mother tongue"—in other words, of the cuisine of your culture. This will give you a core of tastes and techniques that will always act as a touchstone, no matter what other cuisines you cook from.

4. In tandem with that, or alternatively, depending on your circumstances, become a connoisseur of the ingredients that are native to the place where you live. Know the taste of your own *terroir*.

4. Develop and master a repertoire of basics, using cookbooks written by people who genuinely know what they're talking about. Eventually

you'll be able to cook many delicious things without looking at a book at all.

↲ In the words of Nike, "Just do it."

My Philosophy of Healthy Eating

While I'm breezing over the health benefits of home cooking, I thought I should perhaps lay bare my own philosophy, because healthy eating is always a hot topic in the press and we are constantly bombarded with dubious advice. It amazes me that people continue to believe the latest trend, because if one thing is certain, it's that the doctors and nutritionists will soon replace it with a new one. Eat more eggs! Don't eat eggs! Eat no fat! Eat fat! Eat more vegetables! Cool it with the juicing! The pendulum of healthy-eating contradictions swings like a trapeze artist at the circus.

A great many people strive to be very thin, because that's where the beauty ideal *du jour* seems to have settled, wisely or not. ("You can never be too rich or too thin," said Wallis, Duchess of Windsor.) I ignore this. I have a normal, healthy body and I can live with it as it is because it's basically low maintenance. I exercise, but not fanatically, and I eat normally, which I define as a balanced diet of real foods (i.e., as unprocessed as possible), mostly at home. I do eat meat, but not too often. I eat vegetables every day. I use butter, cream, and other fats to flavour things, along with salt. And I don't give house room to ready-made packaged food.

My friend Phil, who spends a lot of time flying around the world eating in the very best restaurants, started overdoing it at one point and put on weight fast. He went on a diet that went like this: Eat whatever you want and as much of it as you like, as long as you make it yourself. You want a burger, you make it. You want tacos, you make them. You want ice cream, you make it. Would you care for the results of that experiment? He lost thirty pounds in twelve weeks.

So that's a health regime I can approve of. Phil wasn't living on a diet of homemade junk food, by the way. Mostly he made good things such as steak and spinach or chicken and rice, but if he fancied something indulgent, he didn't deprive himself, which means the diet didn't require unusual willpower to stick to (apart from having to stay out of restaurants for a while). Many slimming programs are the opposite, based on self-righteous puritanical notions of deprivation and sometimes quite unsafe and/or ridiculous recommendations.

I see it this way: quite apart from the potential physical risks of such diets, any regime that messes with our minds and turns us obsessive and anxious surely defeats its own purpose. Losing weight if we're over may improve health to a degree, but not if we turn into a complete stress case in the process. Good real food, eaten at regular intervals in a pleasurable way: that's my idea of healthy eating.

We All Need a Repertoire

When I moved back to Canada from France after more than a decade, my repertoire of recipes was almost entirely *classique* and my identity had

been "girl living in France who makes French food." But now I was "woman back in Canada living in one of the most multicultural cities on earth where French food all the time just doesn't make sense." My new life and location needed a revamped repertoire, and it was hard to know where to begin.

So I can sympathize with anyone starting out—or, as was my case, starting afresh. We're so bombarded with recipes and food ideas from magazines, the Internet, and cookery shows, it sometimes feels like we'll fall hopelessly behind if we ever make the same thing twice. The foodie flood puts pressure on us in other ways too. We're expected to know our way around a baffling variety of products—curry leaves, fish sauce, lardo, agar agar, harissa—not to mention exotic dishes, half of which we can barely pronounce.

Initially I went on a bit of a rampage, chasing after every new recipe that crossed my path and eating my way through novel discoveries like a shredding machine, then discarding them to make way for the next. (It wasn't unlike one of those whirlwind holidays where you "do" Europe in five days, the result being that you see everything and absolutely nothing all at once.)

I'm all for ongoing learning in the kitchen, but at a certain point we have to put on the brakes and ask what the point is and whether the bombardment of images and expectations is really helping us be better cooks. Personally, I didn't find the scrambling sustainable. Instead it was stressful and frankly not particularly easy on the gut. There is such a thing as too much variety and unfamiliarity for one's poor gastric juices to handle politely.

Acknowledging that I'd always go through phases where I'd need to fling open the windows and let some fresh recipes blow in, I also knew that, more importantly, I needed to figure out what the solid fixtures of my repertoire in this new place would be. That way, I could get back to eating like a normal human being and start to feel present where I was. What collection of dishes would I become intimate with and grow to rely upon here? What recipes would stick with me through thick and thin in this new life? (I say "I," but, as you know, that suddenly became "we," so I was still in a pickle, but at least I wasn't in it alone.)

It turned out my impatience was unnecessary. What I quickly discovered is that as long as we're cooking often and in a way that's true to the place we're cooking in, a repertoire seems to emerge naturally. Repetition is key, and so is some coherence, which makes sense, because that's how cuisines work as well. In our minds, we associate Italy with dishes such as risotto, ragù Bolognese, tiramisu; America with corn on the cob, brownies, burgers; Mexico with enchiladas, guacamole; and so on. Cuisines are always porous, of course, but it's the recipes that rise to the surface and have staying power that ultimately define them. It's the same with a repertoire at home.

Within the first few months of living with Peter, I could already see our permanent collection taking shape: spaghetti with scallops, pot-roasted pork shoulder with garlic and wine, olive oil cake, fried chicken with coleslaw ... It was as invigorating as fresh mountain air. Building a new repertoire (not that I threw out the old one, but you adapt and evolve) not only revitalized my cooking and helped ground me to this spot, it's also incredibly bonding. Repertoire plays a huge role in keeping the people who share it together, defining them as a clan, and reminding them of who they are and where they belong. (It's why I never stop making things like fishcakes or squash pie: those and other recipes are emotional links to my beginnings.) A repertoire is also practical; having one lightens the load of everyday cooking because eventually almost every dish in it we can virtually produce on autopilot.

I have to wonder how many dishes my late grandmother Ethel would have had in her quiver. Buckwheat griddlecakes, beef stew with dumplings, baked beans, blueberry pie, ginger cookies ... Thirty? Forty? We never tired of her food. My mother is a similar style of cook, always working with the same basic, mostly local ingredients, preparing a handful of recipes over and over: lentil soup, potato scallop, lemon pudding ... When she announces she's making fish soup, I know exactly which soup she's referring to (the one and only "Mum's"). Our family has eaten her dishes (and my dad's) more times than anyone can count, and they're all excellent because they're so well practised. It's not to say nothing new is ever tried in my parents' house—it is, and when a recipe is worth keeping, it joins the throng—but their everyday eating, the core of their diet, comes from a basic household repertoire, one they've been honing for their entire marriage.

When I was a teenager, I collected all the family recipes, typed them up, and bound them to create *The Calder Cookbook*, a copy of which every family member got for Christmas. It was the book of "us," and it's still in active use, particularly in my parents' house. Later I produced three (published) cookbooks that collected the recipes from my France years, and a fourth from another brief era, which I should have called *Lost Soul Cookery*, but never mind . . . Now it was time to start a new cookbook. I went out and bought a hardcover notebook, and that's where I write down all the Peter-and-Laura keepers.

Five Ways to Build a Repertoire

⊣ Most people already have a repertoire, even if it's a small one, whether they realize it or not. If you're unsure, try this: list the top five to ten dishes you make regularly for yourself and never want to lose. (If you've never so much as boiled an egg, go boil an egg, eat it, and, if you like it, write down "boiled egg." There's dish number one.)

⊣ Keep a house cookbook. Write down or print out recipes you use regularly. Peter and I started doing this right away. So far, we have only about twenty-five absolute staples, but it's a start. Eventually it will grow into a precious collection of memories and of recipes we've known and loved and can hand down.

⊣ Make notes in the cookbooks you buy as you cook from them so that you know what worked, what didn't, and how you may have tweaked things. (I opened one the other day and, beside a baffling broccoli recipe, found I'd scrawled, "The single most disgusting dish

I've ever tasted." In another I discovered that, in 1996, I thought a particular potato tart recipe was "definitely not worth the frig," although the pork chops with capers and lemon a few pages later were apparently "great on a weeknight!") The point is that the recipes from cookbooks are all on trial until we've made them enough times that we adjust them to our own tastes, possibly reducing the sugar or adding a splash of vinegar or whatever the tweak may be. Once we get a recipe exactly where we want it, it can move into our handwritten house cookbook.

﹢ Help other people with their repertoires by sharing your recipes. Whenever we feed something to someone, we're shaping their experience in some way, adding to their story and to their store of memories as much as to our own. If someone has loved a dish you made so much that they ask for the recipe, be flattered and hand it over. (Hoarding is so ungenerous and unattractive.) Recipes are not about individuals and egos; recipes are about community. Every time we share one, we're helping to hold our people together.

﹢ If you have children, be sure to give them a handmade copy of your family cookbook when they leave home. They'll develop their own repertoires as they go through life, but this will start them off, and at least some of your recipes will be with them forever. Ties that bind . . .

The Goods

I remember from my single days one striking moment that made me realize how much I was craving a home. I was at my brother's house where his wife was making chocolate chip cookies for the kids. In the middle of mixing, she reached for the chocolate chips only to realize she'd run out. Then she opened another cupboard. "Oh, I haven't, actually. I've got another stash over here." My gut lurched with longing and with envy for my brother. Home is where you never run out of chocolate chips! Sob! Home is where the cupboards are always full of potential! Home is where there are people to make cookies for!

Keeping a pantry stocked is essential to keeping a kitchen lively and a home feeling like a safe haven. Whether you're the type of person who shops once a week or once a day, keeping up with what comes in and what gets gobbled up is all part of the home-cooking role. With it comes the hardest thing about home cooking; not the sizzling, simmering, and all that, but the shopping. Let's not whitewash this: it can be a soulless drag sometimes.

All those years in Europe spoiled me: the markets of France, Italy, and Spain, the bakeries of Germany, the staggering food halls of London department stores. The displays in such places are so artistic and sensuous, they make the eyes pop right out of your head: shimmering sardines, braids of smoked garlic, preserved lemons, bulbous artichokes, olives as bright as jade . . . If you weren't in the mood to cook before you went to the market, you'd be just raging to get back to the kitchen as soon as you were halfway down the first alley.

That's not the life I'm living at the present time. In my current

habitat, most vendors don't bother with excellent ingredients and artistic display to the same degree (although many butchers are fairly good). The norm here is leeks the size of baseball bats; fish massacred into willy-nilly pieces; potatoes and onions arranged with all the appetizing appeal of a pile of rocks in a quarry . . . I'd love to ask a genie to replace this utilitarian approach with one more respectful and understanding of quality and beauty—and of home cooks.

Think how many hours we spend every week chasing down our cheese, bread, lettuce, and all the rest. Surely I'm not the only one who's desperate for that time to be as pleasurable and invigorating as possible, rather than some slog I'm going to dread and resent because it's guaranteed to sap my energy and lower my spirits. Besides, having beautiful ingredients waved under our eyes in an enticing manner is a huge part of what inspires us to cook; grocery shopping and cooking go hand in hand that way.

For this reason, the average cathedral-sized grocery store of today's North America is not my cup of tea. For one thing, they're full of too many packages, which are about as motivating for a cook as so many shelves of power tools. Also, something about the overall aesthetic of these warehouses makes me feel disoriented, like I'm in a foreign airport having missed my flight and lost my luggage. I tend to avoid them and stick to smaller grocers, which, even though the displays may be no more artful, at least are more intimate and mercifully minimize the forced march to get to the milk and eggs (always in the farthest possible corner about half a mile from the door in the large places).

Luckily, we live not far from one very good grocery store where I go to restock the pantry with decent buckwheat flour, quality pasta, Italian tuna in jars, tiny pots of crème fraîche . . . It's manageable enough in size that I walk every aisle, something I refuse to do in the mega groceries, keeping my eye open for anything I absolutely don't need but desperately must have, like the exquisite bottle of pumpkin oil that's been in the fridge door for a year and that I've used only once. (I'm going to get to the bottom of it, I promise!)

We also live within walking distance of a funky urban market, which is really a collection of small food shops. What I like about shopping there is that it's social; on a Saturday morning you're bound to run into at least one person you know, and by frequenting the same shops regularly, we get to know the owners, which always leads to a chat and makes things fun. Our butcher, especially, understands true market spirit. The people behind the counter are jolly, knowledgeable, and keen to dole out cooking advice and suggest interesting cuts (tip: the lesser-known cuts are often the least expensive). Without them, I'd perhaps never have discovered capocollo, that piece of pork shoulder that collapses juicy and confit-like after a few hours in the oven. I have them to thank, too, for getting me hooked on lamb neck. I rarely used them before, but now wouldn't dream of making a spring navarin without them, because the broth from those bones is so much richer.

Another way that Peter and I have found to inject some zip into our grocery-shopping life is to make mini staycations out of excursions to exotic food shops north of the city. We've discovered a Persian market where we get sacks of fragrant rice, packages of dried orange rind, and sour barberries. (The displays in those shops are aesthetically different from those of the grocery stores downtown. I can't quite put my finger on why—it's not the ingredients, it's how they're laid out—but in them we feel like we're on another continent.) Near there, in a hideous strip mall, we found an Indian grocer selling divinely fresh green pistachios, for super cheap! The best fishmonger, and the biggest, is a destination, too, for when we want something out of the ordinary, such as a vast selection of oysters or a few bright-eyed bass.

So we do our best. Certainly by making as much of an adventure out of food shopping as we can and by getting to know as many of the people we buy from as we can, it's a more interesting experience. I still miss Europe, but when the weather warms up and tiny outdoor markets pop up around town selling ripe, fragrant tomatoes, stacks of sweet corn, and potatoes with real flavour, I get a bit of a fix. I go every week for the *joie de vivre* as much as for the fresh strawberries, the first crunchy peas in their pods, the sunflowers—and for a reminder of how marvellous shopping for food at least has the potential to be.

The Mega Grocery Store as Village

Having said all that, vast food emporia are now the norm, so there's no point pretending we're all out prancing about with our woven market baskets in flowery frocks every day, lifting melons to our noses to sniff out the ripest and looking every trout straight in the eye. It would be lovely if we were, but most of us are not. Even someone like me, who makes a point of supporting local producers, must still, if I intend to eat without making it a full-time job, jack through a turnstile like everyone else, grab a metal cart, and wheel myself under fluorescent lights through the maw—ahem, I meant mall.

The closest one to us now is, thankfully, not huge, but it's disheartening in other ways. I especially felt that when I first started going; regular beggars at the entrance, the same half-empty shelves of greens on a Monday, the same bloated breads that looked as though, with the help of a bit of helium, they might have been useful for floating inspired messages across the skies of downtown ... Yet strangely—amazingly—enough, after a while I started to notice things in there that I couldn't find in the majority of other places: decent endives, for example, fat and white, rather than premature and lime green; tiny radishes, rather than beet-sized bulbs; onions of a reasonable girth, rather than softball-sized.

Furthermore, the people working there were exceptionally nice. This too took a few visits for me to realize. It's fine and dandy to praise farmers' markets for their charming vendors, but grocery stores, however big, are also microcosms, and we mustn't forget. We may plow through them like robots after work, and it may seem as though the people working there are zombies, but if you actually stop and engage with them as they're stocking a shelf or scanning through your goodies, you'll suddenly realize that they're human too. They love a joke. They love to be noticed.

Not only that, but they notice things too, including us. One teller in my store in particular, a woman from Montreal named Rachel with blond curly hair, became so friendly after a few visits that I started queuing up at her checkout even when the line was long just so I could say hello. She was unfailingly curious about what I was buying. "What are you making tonight? That's a lot of vegetables," she'd comment; or "Who was that handsome guy with you last week? Your husband? Boy, good catch." Even the regular beggars at the entrance became part of the community. They'd yell out to me, "Nice coat! You look great today!" and, even if I couldn't spare change, "The smile's worth everything, miss."

A great deal of essential shopping these days is organized to be as sterile and anti-social as possible. (Even cashiers are increasingly being replaced by machines, which I refuse to use. What's next, grocery stores in the form of giant vending machines?) As someone who can spend whole days working at home alone, I sometimes rely on the human interaction I get while running errands to keep myself sane. This is another reason why smaller shops run by familiar faces seem healthier and happier to me, and why, even in a big store, I find it pays to make an effort to seek out what humanity is there, starting by lending the place some of our own.

The Inventory

I'm not this organized, but one job Anne Willan always used to get us to do at her house in Burgundy was to update "the inventory" regularly. She had typed lists on every fridge, freezer, and pantry door so you always knew what was inside, how many frozen chickens and bags of

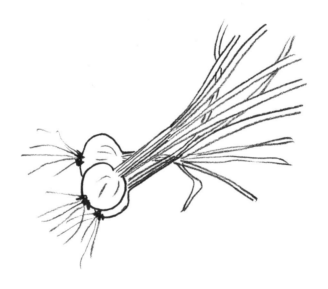

green beans, how many jars of tomatoes, how many sacks of flour and boxes of baking powder. It's an especially good system for anyone with a deep-freeze, because you know what it's like trying to dig down to the bottom in search of a pork chop or the quarter bag of frozen peas you were sure was in there. With the inventory, you could check without even opening the door. Whenever you took something out, you'd cross it off the list; whenever you put anything new in, you'd add it to the list.

I'd never have the patience to do this with a whole fridge, but I can see how it would be useful for things like condiments. Mirin, pickles, mayonnaise, jams—all that stuff has a dreadful way of wandering to the back of the fridge and hiding out until it grows moss. Ditto so many contents of a pantry. I keep forgetting that I have several prehistoric packages of cellophane noodles hiding in mine. Perhaps if they were on the inventory list, I'd get around to using them.

The Shopping List

With two writers in the house, we go through a lot of paper, which I recycle by quartering pages and stacking the squares in the kitchen for writing lists on the blank side. Some people have a blackboard instead (I used to, but now, for some reason, it's in a loo); but for the moment, I find the actual paper list more convenient anyway, because I can write it up gradually as I notice we run out of things and then it's ready to grab whenever I head out the door or need to pass it off to Peter.

For typical, everyday grocery shopping (as opposed to discovery-style market shopping), I am lost without a list. Not only do I forget things, but I dither and wander aimlessly, wasting time and growing agitated and cranky, which is no state to be in just before you start cooking or you might do yourself an injury. I don't remember when I got religious about lists, which I am, but they've certainly made me a better shopper. With list in hand, I am Wonder Woman and can whiz through my shopping in no time flat. Also, not that I have to be a slave to it, but a list does tend to keep me on track and prevent me from buying a zillion things we don't need that will just end up rotting in the crisper.

There's something fun about lists, too: they're so personal and tactile, which is always a pleasure in this digital era, and although I throw them out when I'm through with them, occasionally I'll find an old one in a pocket or in the bottom of a bag and think, "Hmm . . . pig's trotter, tonic water, thirty garlic bulbs, and crazy glue . . . I wonder what that day was all about?"

For the most efficient shopping lists, I find it helps to write products down by category so I can cross off whole sections in a single stop, like so:

BUTCHER
bacon
sliced salami (thin!)
8 chicken thighs

GREENGROCER
radishes (tiny only)
watercress
blood oranges

DAIRY
heavy cream (organic, if they have it)
butter

DRY GOODS
whole wheat flour
baking soda

HOUSEHOLD
floor cleaner
hand soap
loo paper

The Art of Unpacking Groceries

When everything you buy comes in a box or a tin, I suppose you just slide
it all onto a shelf. I don't know, because so much of what my mother
bought when we were growing up came spooned from bulk into bags that
it was mayhem. (One false move and the entire kitchen floor would be
paved with lentils and sunflower seeds.) The cupboards were loaded with
sacks of dates, brown sugar, dried figs, quinoa, brown rice—potentially
the messiest of all things. Our fridge, too, was always a war zone because
so much would end up in recycled yogurt containers to hide away until
it turned blue. It was enough to scar you for life.

It's not that I've turned into any genius organizer as a form of rebel-
lion to all that, but I am determined that there can be an art to putting

food away and that it can actually make us better cooks. I became suddenly focused on this one day when I was going off the deep end trying to unearth a bunch of dill that I knew I'd bought and that was supposed to be going (*right this minute before they get cold!*) onto my roasted carrots with goat cheese and black sesame seeds. I tore one wadded-up grocery bag after another from the fridge: parsley, no; yellowed lettuce, no (toss); rosemary and thyme, no. Finally I found the dill and gave it a rinse, which instantly makes it look like something that just flew out of the back of a lawnmower. What the heck? Chop, chop, chop . . . Oh, wet clumps. Great.

My herb storage, clearly, needed a makeover. The next day I went looking for a solution at a warehouse-sized bonanza store that claims to sell EVERYTHING! CHEAP! By and by, once I'd got past the plastic dolls and the discount fabrics, I found a piece of "Tupperware" (only a different brand) that was clearly designed to hold a large, rectangular cake. *Geronimo!* Back home, I lined it with paper towel, then I took all the various herbs from the fridge, washed them, spun them dry, and laid each herb in its own row, with more paper towel in between. (I was so pleased with myself, you'd think I'd just planted a herb garden out the back, complete with stone paths and a sundial.)

It sounds like the kind of thing you do once and then get lazy about, but in fact that box has become a permanent fixture in our fridge, a mobile drawer of sorts, which not only makes it a breeze to access ready-to-go herbs in the middle of cooking, but also inspires spontaneity. I might open the box for parsley and then, suddenly spying tarragon, use that instead.

Another habit I've developed is taking bacon out of its package as soon as I get it home from the butcher and laying the strips separately on a sheet of waxed paper. A second sheet goes on top, then I fold the whole thing over a few times and pop it into a bag and into the freezer. Bacon goes off fairly quickly and often we can't get through a package before it does, so this trick allows us to take out only as many rashers as we need at a time and thus save our bacon (forgive the pun). It can go straight into the frying pan frozen, and it's also easier to cut into *lardons* (tiny paperclip-sized slices) if I'm throwing some in a sauté or stew. I've also taken to freezing nuts because they go rancid quickly, dried mushrooms (to exterminate any bugs), baguette slices for ready-to-go tartines, and breadcrumbs for coating things and making gratins.

Not to turn the topic of food storage into *War and Peace*, but dry goods can also use some TLC. I find a lot of packaging makes for bad internal kitchen views, like having a row of abandoned, boarded-up townhouses awaiting demolition as the panorama beyond one's living-room curtains. (What can I say? I'm a sensitive soul.) Therefore, things like spices I put into my own spice tins; boxes of salt go into the salt jars; sugars, flours, grains, and dried fruits all go into jars or crocks too.

Basically anything in fussy or ugly packaging I repackage myself for ease of use and aesthetic appeal. Cooking, after that, is more efficient, and instead of staring at a bunch of barely identifiable sacks slumped in a cupboard, I get a jewel box of inspiration every time I open a door: red lentils, currants, oatmeal, cocoa power, couscous, candied ginger . . . How marvellous to live and cook in a self-made land of plenty!

Suggestions for Storing Food

- Keep a permanent bowl or bin for onions, garlic, and shallots in a cool, dark place within easy reach, such as in a drawer or under a counter.

- Keep fruit at room temperature, but keep berries in Mason jars in the fridge (bringing to room temperature before serving).

- Freeze nuts and dried mushrooms.

- Keep potatoes in a bin in a dark place (never in the fridge and always separate from onions).

- Keep fresh mushrooms refrigerated in a paper bag.

- Transfer flours, sugars, legumes, and grains to lidded jars, crocks, or bins. (Keep brown sugar in an airtight container. I've tried the terra cotta discs and the apple wedge tricks for keeping brown sugar soft. They don't work.)

- Store dried fruits in sealed jars.

- Have cooking salts and peppercorns in containers by the stovetop where you need them.

- Keep spices in well-labelled, size-appropriate tins (my cumin is in a large one, for example, whereas my turmeric is in a small one because I use less of it) and away from light and heat.

- As much as possible, group foods by category in the fridge so you can find them.

- Unwrap meats as soon as you bring them home, pat dry, and rewrap appropriately until using.

- Not before storing, but at least before eating, wash fruits and vegetables in water with a splash of vinegar to disinfect them.

Kitchen Kit

There is surely no category of equipment more likely to offer something completely useless to the unsuspecting consumer than gadgets and appliances for the kitchen. Oh, the vegetable peelers that couldn't take the skin off hot milk, the whisks with all the power of a ponytail, the hopeless chopping gadgets that massacre shallots and garlic and take longer to clean than a shotgun: beware them all.

In fact, before you let any equipment into your kitchen, you should almost interview it, as you would a sous chef. "OK, knife, where do you see yourself in five years?" "Are you always this rigid, Mr. Spatula? Because this job does require flexibility." "Dear Toaster, please explain the logic behind your need to beep like a moving van backing up every time a slice of toast pops." (I fantasize about raiding people's kitchens and weeding out all their junk.)

Of course, what equipment we have in our kitchens is a highly personal matter, depending on how it feels in our hands, the way we cook, our aesthetics, and our income. Objectively, most plastic cooking utensils, cheap serrated knives, and flimsy pans make it challenging for anyone to cook well, but once in the category of quality, whether we prefer copper to cast iron or European knives to Japanese is largely a matter of preference—mind you, it can take time and a certain amount of trial and error for us to discover what these preferences are.

Five Tips on Buying Gadgets and Appliances

⊣ Be wary of buying kitchen equipment in kits (pot sets, utensil sets, knife sets, etc.). I know these look like a deal and may be eye-appealing to those who like everything to match, but it's much smarter to buy only exactly what you need. For example, a fourteen-piece knife set for the average cook is at least ten pieces too large. You're never going to use the boning knife unless you know what you're doing with it, and you'll probably find the giant chef's knife unwieldy, so why not just buy a really good medium chef's knife, a bread knife, and a paring knife to begin with? It's less clutter and confusion, and you can always add on as needs arise. (Note: It's useful to keep one really cheap knife in the kitchen, possibly even serrated, for when people want to steal a piece of your kit to open mail or slice a cardboard box to turn it into a "car" for a two-year-old.)

- Think twice before investing in single-purpose equipment. If you're making room in your kitchen for a paella pan that serves twelve, be sure paella is one of your specialties and that it's going to be over a fire at least a few times a year. If you're going to have a flambé pan with its own tableside stand (as a friend of mine does), be sure you intend to become a pro at cherries jubilee and crêpes Suzette, otherwise it will end up in an unused room acting as a plant stand.

- Beware gadgets. Herb choppers, garlic-skin removers, plastic individual egg cookers, banana slicers, etc., etc. Run, don't walk.

- Buy quality the first time. Early on in my cooking life, I bought a very expensive pepper grinder, but before I even got it home I panicked, returned it, and bought a cheap one instead. The cheap one didn't work, so I threw it out and got a different cheap one. It didn't work either, so I threw it out and tried again. Four "cheap" pepper grinders into the game, I went back and bought the original good one (a Peugeot, as it happens) and it's still trucking after twenty years. Trust me: there's nothing more expensive in this world than cheap stuff.

⌐ Restrain yourself from buying too many appliances. If you have to have a rice cooker, sous vide contraption, microwave, popcorn maker, stand mixer, bread machine, and so on, you will eventually need a hangar at the airport to store them in. I do have a friend who owns a mill for grinding his own flour and rolling his own oats, but he's a bread geek and really uses it. I have another friend who has a vacuum-packing machine and she swears it prevents the premature deaths of untold quantities of cheese a year. Not all appliances are evil or destined to collect dust, but most are unnecessary, so buy only what you'll truly use and love.

A Wisely Selected Collection of Cookbooks

My cookbook collection was never huge to begin with, but I recently did a serious cull because it had started to feel like an obstruction, with too many books that never got used getting between me and the possibility of something to eat. I bit the bullet: any cookbook I suspected I'd never crack the spine of again, I set out on the street to let passersby peck away at until they were gone. Since then, it has amazed me how much I don't miss them. I can finally see the books I actually do use, which before were crowded into the wings by all the riff-raff.

I understand that cookbooks are often an impulse buy, like perfume or a scarf, because they're comforting and help lift our spirits when we're down in the dumps—superficially, anyway. There's nothing particularly wrong with being seduced by their Band-Aid effect, but in the long term it pays to be disciplined, because having too many, unless you're a serious collector, can be paralyzing. (I liken it to trying to shop for clothing in a discount warehouse; there's so much stuff in them, all in great heaps, that it's too overwhelming and I end up leaving without buying a thing.)

The older I get, the more I want to make space only for the cookbooks that are really going to get me into the kitchen cooking and up my game, so I have a few rules about buying them to keep me from going on a binge that I'll later regret.

My Personal Cookbook-Buying Rules

- Only buy a cookbook that has in it at least three recipes you know you'll make (or that is such an inspirational read, you know you'll go back to it again and again to feed your soul).

- Only buy cookbooks written by people with experience whom you know you can trust.

- Leave on the shop shelf any cookbooks that are hard to read, either because the print is too small or pale, the designs are eye-watering, or they're packaged like hardcover novels and are impossible to lay open. You won't use them.

- Beware any cookbook that's attempting to be overly comprehensive (e.g., five-hundred-plus recipes). The recipes too easily get lost. (It's that box-store effect again.)

Calling the Kitchen Muse

Glamorous though it's now meant to be, sometimes cooking is a pain. Even for people who love to cook, there's a lot of pressure when it comes to feeding people well and imaginatively, and it's a heck of a lot of work. Despite what social media would have us believe, it's not just about waltzing into the kitchen every now and again and whipping up a smoothie bowl strewn with flower petals and hemp seeds for an Instagram snap. Home cooking involves shopping, inventory, budgets, and organization, even before we tie on an apron. Then come preparation, cooking, serving, and, nobody's favourite, cleaning up.

This is a lot to throw on one person's shoulders day after day, especially when we all have a thousand other roles besides "cook" to play at the same time in life, many of equal value and that demand equally of our time and energy. A big question, then, becomes: How do we keep the romance alive?

Ignoring rules can help. They say one should never serve guests a dish not already tried before, but I often ignore that advice in an effort to ward off boredom. As long as I'm making something from a cookbook by someone I trust (and as long as I'm not attempting a totally new and foreign technique), it's rarely a problem. Indeed, sometimes it can take the pressure off, because if a dish goes off the rails, at least I can say "I thought I'd just test out this dish by so-and-so," rather than "Sorry, my own never-fail, signature specialty seems to have bombed."

Somewhat contradictorily, we're also told not to serve the same people the same dish twice, wisdom that I also ignore, not just because I'm interested in perfecting certain dishes, but also because people start to associate them with us, as they do dishes by their mothers. When they eat something for a second time at our house (not that I'd serve it to them twice in a row), it's a bit of a homecoming. "Ah, Laura's heart cookies!" "Hurray, Peter's steak with green sauce!"

One of the best sources of inspiration is season. When white asparagus hits the shelves, grab the nice fat ones and there's your first course. Ditto when blood oranges or heirloom tomatoes come to town; show them off, because they won't last. Cooking what's in season forces us to get creative, because for about a month we'll be continuously pummelled with the same ingredients. *Strawberries again! How can I make them feel new? Zucchini for the seventh time in two weeks! Well, maybe it's time to learn how to deep-fry after all . . .*

It's also savvy sometimes to buy an ingredient we have no idea what to do with and have to figure out only once we're home. I've tried quite a few things recently that I never had access to in France: napa cabbage, Japanese eggplant, collard greens . . . It's fun to make new friends.

Winter is the least inspiring season in terms of produce, but it's also the time of year when our appetites tend to crave proper cooking, which is motivating. In summer we stack a lot, and in winter we stew, which is where the real alchemy of cooking comes into play, where dishes become more than simply the sum of their parts. I like to go back to classics this time of year and get reacquainted with forgotten dishes like a proper beef daube, coulibiac, Wiener schnitzel, or trifle.

This may not be a popular suggestion, but leftovers are some of the best teachers in the kitchen. Anne Willan used to thrust things at us, like a quarter packet of old goat cheese and a wilted eggplant, and demand they be transformed into a first course. We, her obedient *stagières*, would roll our eyes and kvetch, but then, once we launched in, we'd actually find ourselves quite engaged in and excited by the challenge of how to turn those tired ingredients into a work of art. Still today, I have a habit of hanging on to leftovers, even if they're just a handful of squash purée or sliver of steak. They can be pleasantly provocative right around suppertime, especially for emergency hors d'oeuvres.

Never forget how kitchen ambiance can affect your desire to cook. It varies from season to season because of the light, but on average, by 6 p.m. every evening, I turn the house into evening mode (i.e., time out). I stop working, light all the twinkly lights, turn down the dimmer switches, turn on relaxing music, pour a glass of wine, and head over to the stove to see what I can rustle up. I don't rush cooking; I do everything at a civilized pace, taking a break for a glass of wine with Peter and whoever else is around, and we eat when we're ready. The last thing that will ever put someone like me in a cooking mood is turning the place into the set of *Iron Chef*—which some people do, especially when they're entertaining.

I'm of the kitchen-as-oasis school of thought: remove all tension from the scene and it's much easier to come home and want to chop. We put our mood in our food, as someone once said to me (it's so true!), so how we feel while we're cooking genuinely matters.

The Host I Strive to Be

We spend the first years of our lives being catered to, by Mummy or whomever, then we slum our way through student and single life until,

one fine day, we find ourselves shacked up or married, possibly with children, and guess what? It's our turn to host the house. Haaalp!

Sorry, kids, here's how it works: we all learn by doing. No matter how many times we may have seen someone else make vanilla custard, until we feel with our own hand a wooden spoon moving through the mixture and hear the sound the custard makes as it thickens, we can't know the precise moment to remove it from the stove before it curdles. (Take heart: it's by curdling custard that we learn how not to curdle custard.) How about knowing when a loaf of bread is done? My mother always told me, "When you tap the bottom of the loaf and it sounds hollow, it's done," which is a hopeless instruction until you discover for yourself what "hollow" sounds like (um . . . like a done loaf of bread being tapped?).

I had a friend in Paris, a single woman, who could make only two things for the first ten years I knew her: steamed individual pieces of salmon, and salad. I never thought she'd change. Then came a husband and children and, to my amazement, a sudden facility for salted caramel financiers and artichokes with hollandaise sauce.

It's not just beginners who have to find their feet. Another friend couldn't throw a dinner party for the first six years I knew her because her elderly husband wouldn't allow anyone into the house. When he moved into a home, she was dying to get back into the hosting game, but nervous about being rusty. One dinner party with close friends (a smashing success, incidentally) and she was right back at it. Finances, as I said earlier, can also be a factor, but I'd like to say at least this: whatever our circumstances, we must try not to compete, but rather to be generous according to our means. It's the spirit in which we do things that counts, not the money we've spent.

Years ago, on a trip through Sicily, some friends and I spent about an hour and a half driving up and up and up around a mountain to get to a desirable restaurant we'd read about. By the time we reached it, at the very top, we were ravenous (and dizzy), but the restaurant was dark. We got out of the car to stretch our legs, and as we were standing on the gravel trying to come up with a plan B, the front door of the place creaked open a crack. A tiny woman dressed all in black, probably in her sixties, asked us what we wanted. When we said we'd come to eat, she stated the obvious—"We are closed"—and shut the door. About half a second later, the door swung open again and a light flicked on. "Come in anyway," sighed the woman. "I'll feed you." Now that's the kind of host at home I aspire to be.

On That Note, Let Us Feast!

The best home cooks and hosts, I've always found, have a pleasure-seeking streak. They are connoisseurs of the good things in life and have a knack for knowing how to seize the day. They'll go the extra mile to ferret out a superior baguette or a prizewinning chicken from a secret address; they delight in shelling fresh peas, cutting corn fresh off the cobs, spotting wild strawberries in a field. If they see a fisherman's truck parked on the roadside with fresh clams for sale, they squeal to a halt.

Half the time, it's the spontaneous discoveries that lead these *bon vivants* to cook and invite in the first place; after all, it's no fun when we get our hands on something fabulous and have to eat it all by our lonesome selves. I was reminded of this when I returned from the east coast with a box of live lobsters for Peter and me. We opened the box to cook them, and for some reason felt half-hearted about it all. "This won't do," we realized, and immediately rang up some neighbours and announced, "Guess what we've got!" They cheetahed up the street and a much merrier lobster pasta in cream sauce ensued. (Lilly Pulitzer had the right attitude when she said, "That's what life is all about. Let's have a party. Let's have it tonight!")

So then there comes the question of what sort of party to have.

It's important to know what kind of host we really are and to stick, for the most part, to the kind of entertaining that will bring out our best and make us happiest. As I see it, hosts tend to fall into one of two categories: sit-downs or stand-ups. I am a sit-down type, by which I mean I lean toward dinner parties with conversation at their core and a meal to linger over. Others prefer big bashes with music, dancing, snippets of chit-chat, and a lot of tiny bites flying by on trays. One kind of party is not superior to the other, but they are completely different, achieving different goals and appealing more or less to different kinds of people.

The Dinner Party

Allow me to begin selfishly with one of the greatest passions of my life: the dinner party. I couldn't begin to count the number I've thrown over the years (or even in the last twelve months), not just in the places where I've lived myself, but wherever I've visited. It seems to be in my bones to want to gather people around a table for a meal every chance I get. Not only do I relish the creativity of it—who to invite, what to make, how to pull it off—but I find it the best way of getting to know people.

Sharing a home-cooked meal is entirely different from meeting up in a restaurant, incidentally, where the neutral turf limits intimacy. It's different, too, from a big party, whether in a home or a public venue, where people tend to remain superficial. At a dinner in a home, people are more likely to let down their guards and share a genuine side of themselves. (It's a certain willingness to be vulnerable—more on which later; a host makes herself vulnerable to judgement, and guests make themselves vulnerable to, well, I suppose to being poisoned or bored to death.) Also, the fact that the food has been prepared with our own hands means it will always be original, true to us, and inimitable. This is true luxury.

You may like your dinner parties formal, but in our house, for now at least, they are casual, because we like to be relaxed and because that's how our space is. (Mind you, even if I were to throw a gala in a palace, I'd make sure it was relaxed in its own way too, because who wants to stand around feeling like a steel rod in a tux?) Basically, I feed everybody who comes through the door like family; that's my cooking style, so what you get are things like ragù Bolognese, roast chicken with ratatouille, steak with chimichurri sauce, fish croquettes with tartar sauce—everyday dishes that seem to make everybody happy. (Unless, of course, all my friends are fantastic liars.)

I do step out of my comfort zone occasionally, say with a Japanese-style ginger-marinated chicken with smashed-up cucumber, or spiced quail with a Persian rice dish. Whatever it is, I serve it without any fuss or fanfare, and if I'm worried someone might be anticipating something fancier, I manage their expectations by telling them exactly what they'll be having at the time I invite them. "Would you like to come over and try my first attempt at Chinese dumplings on Wednesday?" I'll ask, or "I'm in the middle of making a couple of tourtières; any chance you guys are free tonight?" That sort of gambit works like a charm: people know they can just pop by after work as if they're going to their own mother's.

I've always been firmly against eating alone if it can be avoided. I don't believe human beings were designed to eat alone, and, in my experience, when we must do so over a prolonged period, for whatever reason, it takes a toll on our health, not only because we tend to eat less healthfully, but also because we lose the social and psychological nourishment that comes with eating as a group. (In fact, there are scientific studies that show eating alone to be a health hazard.)

If you had no other reason to host regular dinner parties, now you have one: it keeps friends and family from going off the deep end—and it keeps us from getting bored with our own routine. I love my quiet evenings alone with Peter, but if we didn't entertain regularly we'd feel cut off from the world. The conversation is good for our minds, the camaraderie is good for our hearts, and the cooking probably goes up a notch.

What most people tell me they worry about when it comes to cooking meals is getting the timing right on all the dishes. This is indeed tricky when you're starting out, but with practice it becomes instinctive. If you can swing it, try to do all your shopping the day before any serious feast, because that's a real time consumer and you'll be more relaxed preparing a meal if the shopping is already taken care of.

Anything you can prepare a day ahead takes pressure off considerably, but it's not always feasible. On the day itself, I always aim to get dessert out of the way first, usually in the morning, if I can, so I don't have to think about it. If I'm making a slowly cooked dish, I get that going early in the day (it can reheat later); otherwise, I get as much preparation out of the way as I can before anyone arrives, things like washing greens for salads, making any sauces, marinating meat, chopping vegetables. By the time people are coming through the door, I want to feel serene and in control, ready to sit down and visit for an hour with a drink in my hand. (This is especially easy in summer when so much can be served at room temperature.)

One last note: always make at least one serving more than you think you'll need for a dinner, because you never know when an extra body might get added to the guest list at the last minute (something I've learned it's best to be prepared for). In eighteenth-century France, hosts of a certain social class were apparently meant to be prepared at all times to welcome large numbers to dinner, whether expected or not.

I read a wonderful story about the night when one such host, Laurent Grimod de la Reynière, really got sideswiped. He reported, "It was ten o'clock; we were about to sit down to table, when ten or twelve carriages parading in the courtyard announced fifteen or twenty unexpected guests at a supper for three." I'll really know I've mastered the art of the dinner party when I can handle something that drastic without throwing myself onto a carving knife!

What Regularly Hosting Dinner Parties Will Do for Your Cooking

- You'll learn to plan better, so you're never scrambling at the last minute.

- Your menus will get smarter.

- You'll learn how to juggle food restrictions, such as allergies.

- You'll become more comfortable with your space and with moving around in it efficiently.

- If you're cooking regularly with someone else, a natural division of labour will emerge.

- You'll develop a unique hosting style that fits you like a glove.

- You'll start to realize that dinner parties are not that big a deal.

- Family dinners will suddenly seem that much easier.

Everyday Dinners

I am not terribly fond of the word "everyday," partly because it's wildly overused, but also because it feels dismissive and reductive. So let me be clear: by "everyday dinners," I am not talking about second-rate food nor about a second-rate dining experience. When Peter and I are having dinner at home alone, our attitude is that we're still hosting; we just happen to be hosting ourselves. The table gets set exactly as it would if we were having guests, and the food, although usually somewhat simpler, is prepared with as much care, even if it involves leftovers or is flung together using whatever we find in the cupboard.

In fact, we have a thing for what we call "accidentally delicious dinners." Those are the unplanned dishes that just somehow turn out to be miraculously good (like the spaghetti with scallops in rosé sauce we concocted one night). They're powerful, those accidental successes, because they can completely turn around an otherwise unpleasant day.

My favourite part about suppers to ourselves is that we get to knock around the kitchen à deux and cook without any pressure, one of our favourite ways to spend time together. It never feels like work; it's life in our happy zone, as is lingering over whatever the resulting meal turns out to be. The same can work for families. Even if the actual making of supper is the task of a single person, as long as the rest of the family, or a handful of friends, is gathered around, it should be satisfyingly social.

We are frequently given the message, through media and advertising, that we don't have time to cook. "Who has time for roasting peppers? Just buy them in a jar," we'll hear. "Who has time to make rice? Just dump water over instant." Well, I dunno, I have time. And I have time because I make time. (When you think about it, with the I-don't-have-time attitude, who has time for anything?) The fact is that we all have the same number of hours in a day and we all have the same full-time job: it's called life. How we carve it up depends largely on our own priorities and decisions. (If four hours on YouTube a day is a greater priority, fine, but it's no argument for not having time to look after ourselves.)

Do beware, because the "no time to cook" message is very much a sales pitch aimed at getting us to buy ready-made foods (as is the patronizing "cooking is too difficult" message). People have always led busy lives, been economically pinched, and had to learn to cook from that start line, yet until recently, regular home cooking was perfectly normal. It's ridiculous to believe that cooking is somehow a godlike talent that only so-called celebrity chefs can pull off. It's just human, as is hosting, and the activities circle back on each other: regular home cooking makes entertaining easier; regular entertaining makes everyday dinners easier, better, and all the more rewarding.

NICE RICE

Having grown up on a potato-based diet, I never really understood rice or how to make it properly. I suppose I used to steam it in a pot on the stove, according to package instructions, but it always led to rice that I found bland. It was when my older brother married a Korean woman that I became enlightened on the subject, because those two have a large rice cooker on their kitchen counter that is always on and always full (and always, weirdly, plays "Twinkle Twinkle Little Star" when the rice is ready). If you're hungry, you're never at a loss to find something to eat as long as there's hot rice in the house. I love this concept.

Then I became friends with a Persian woman, Parmiss, whose rice, the first time I tried it, made me moan with delight. It was light, fluffy, and delicious beyond any rice I'd ever tasted. This, I needed to know how to do. I went out and bought a giant sack of basmati and begged her for a lesson. It was one of the greatest aha moments I've ever had in the kitchen, and her rice method is now a staple feature of our weeknight life.

Lunch

If dinner feels too much like jumping in at the deep end, a great way to wade into entertaining at home is to invite people for lunch. The food can be simpler and lighter, there tends to be less of it, and there's no need to offer a full-blown dessert (which, even for a proper dinner, can always be replaced by a bit of fruit and cheese, a plate of cookies, or a smattering of chocolates, candied ginger, licorice and the like).

Noontime entertaining is ideal for guests with children, as well as for old people (ahem, like me) who don't want a late night out. It's also a useful time for getting together with one or two friends or colleagues for a private, clear-headed chat. (I know brunch is popular these days too, but I personally keep my distance because I find the food weird—one friend typifies brunch as "the pork chop waffle parfait"—and because eating at neither-here-nor-there hours of the day

Simple Persian Rice

— makes: 8 servings —

*The way to get saffron powder is simply to grind saffron
threads in a spice or coffee grinder with a pinch of sugar.
Store in a small jar in the refrigerator until using.*

2 cups rice

1 tablespoon salt

3 tablespoons butter

¼ teaspoon powdered saffron
dissolved in 1 tablespoon
boiling water

Rinse the rice in a colander several times, drain, transfer to a bowl, and cover with cold water. Let soak for an hour or so, stirring and changing the water occasionally, until the water goes from foggy to clear, which means it's ready to cook. Drain and set aside.

Bring a large pot of water to a boil (as for pasta), add the salt, then add the rice. Cook until it's shy of al dente (i.e., not quite done), about 5 minutes, although timing may vary depending on the type of rice.

Drain in a fine-mesh sieve over the sink, but do not rinse. Put the rice back in the pot, add the butter, poke a few holes in the rice with the handle of a wooden spoon, and drizzle over the saffron water. Lay a clean tea towel over the pot, then set the lid on top. Let sit off the heat for about 10 minutes (during this time, the towel will absorb any excess moisture in the rice, leaving it exceptionally fluffy). If you're not ready to eat quite yet, leave the pot covered for up to an hour before serving.

Fluff the rice with a fork before transferring to a serving dish. It will be beautifully light, with threads of saffron yellow running through it.

throws my body out of whack. *Chez nous*, therefore, midday eating means lunch proper.)

Lunch can be exactly the same as what we'd serve in the evening, albeit in smaller portions, but I think unless it's meant to be the main meal of the day, it's nice if it has its own flair and unique stamp. The soup-and-sandwich combination is classic and may sound a bit slapdash, but can be quite stellar. I love corn chowder with lobster sandwiches; tomato soup with grilled cheese; gazpacho with sardine or chèvre tartines; asparagus or watercress soup with chicken salad sandwiches... The options are endless. I lay the sandwiches out on a platter, cut them into churchy-sized pieces so people can help themselves, and then ladle up the soup. Easy.

Another fine option for lunch that's quick and relatively light (and inexpensive) is an egg dish such as a Spanish tortilla, cheese soufflé, or quiche with a green salad. Even salad alone is fine, as long as it has a bit of substance or you serve some cheese, charcuterie, and a baguette on the side. Generally salads are treated as afterthoughts and aren't very interesting, but an intelligent salad is a thing of beauty and really hits the spot (see "On Salads," page 202).

HOW TO MAKE A SANDWICH

Most sandwiches are dreadful. Perhaps because they're so easy, people tend not to give them proper thought, so you end up with results such as overly thick, inadequately buttered bread holding together a flimsy piece of unseasoned meat and a wilted leaf of lettuce. Airports and roadside stops excel at revolting sandwiches, but you see plenty in lunch spots around town and in homes too. We must turn this neglected opportunity around, because a proper sandwich makes a fine midday meal indeed. Think of the perfect brie and butter on baguette; ham and mustard on rye; egg and mayonnaise with crisp lettuce on slim white bread (crustless); bacon, lettuce, and ripe tomato on light toast; grilled cheddar—the salivating list goes on!

Whatever your combination, the way to a good sandwich is thoughtfulness, so consider the following:

- Is the bread fresh and delicious in its own right, and of the right thickness and texture for the fillings to come? If toasted, is the bread toasted enough? Too much?

- Is the butter, mustard, mayonnaise, or whatever spread right out to the very edges of the bread so every bite includes some?

- Do toppings have taste and good texture (i.e., ripe tomatoes, crisp lettuce, roast beef sliced thinly enough)? If there is more than one topping, do they belong together? Is anything gilding the lily?

- Are the toppings evenly distributed rather than clumped in the middle, like a cat hiding under a rug?

- When appropriate, is the sandwich seasoned with salt and pepper?

- Is the sandwich wrapped or plated to look enticing?

ON SALADS

Again, what a missed opportunity salads can be! Too many are bland, or overdressed, or underdressed, or full of conflicting combinations of ingredients. Even the classics, which have been well thought out and, when done right, can be grand, are far too often massacred by a sloppy approach. We can't do much about what we order in restaurants, but at home we have the power to make our salads remarkable. We just have to come at them with care.

I often serve a simple green salad after a main course, but I try never to let it be dull. I buy at least a couple of different lettuces in case I want to combine them, and I also like to have a variety of herbs on hand in case a handful tossed in makes sense. I prepare the greens ahead of time by washing, spinning, and wrapping in tea towels in a plastic bag in the fridge so they're nice and crisp when I'm ready to mix them.

I also give dressings my full attention. There are too many kinds to describe them all, but I can give a few pointers on basic vinaigrette. If you've ever heard the mantra "three parts oil to one part vinegar," forget it, because it's not true. You'll end up with way too acidic a dressing. What I usually do is start with a spoonful of Dijon mustard, a pinch of salt, and perhaps half a clove of grated garlic, then I add just a teaspoon or two of vinegar before mixing in the oils (I often like to combine different kinds of oils). Next I taste it, and if I think the dressing needs more acid, I add, carefully, either vinegar or lemon juice to finish it off. You might like a squirt of soy or a handful of Parmesan cheese, or maybe a pinch of stock powder, to lightly coat the greens (but still remain a mystery ingredient). The options are many, but with all of them what's key is adding things slowly and tasting as you go along to get a perfect balance of acid, salt, and oil.

First-course salads, especially, deserve to be interesting. They're meant to be appetizers, after all, so they must be appetizing. It's worth making to the letter a few recipes devised by chefs just to get a sense of what really works. I make a Raymond Blanc endive and radicchio salad with walnuts, apple, and blue cheese that's very good. I'm fond of my own butter lettuce with flower petals, pine nuts, and lemon, and of another recipe from a friend that includes fennel, orange, and a fascinating anchovy dressing. Root around in books and you'll find plenty. Test them out, see what surprises you, and soon you can acquire a fine leafy repertoire.

As for main-course salads, which often come into play at lunchtime, I recommend learning a few classics before branching out into experiments. Salade niçoise is one of the best known and looks smashing on a big platter when arranged with a good eye. That and a baguette, and there's lunch. Cobb salad, chicken salad, seafood salad: there are many variations on each, so practise a few by professionals before trying to invent something new.

My final advice on salads is to ditch the tall bowls for serving and use either a large shallow bowl or even a platter (the latter for composed salads for sure). The trouble with high-sided bowls is that all the good bits fall to the bottom and you're left with a pile of lonely leaves on top. It makes for difficult serving. (Indeed, thoughtful presentation, no matter what the dish, is vital to its success at the table.)

The Sunday Roast

There is one so-called lunch that is not so easy—the infamous Sunday roast—but it's definitely worth mastering because it's basically smaller-scale practice for all the grand-scale family celebrations that come dotted throughout the year to terrify us all. I was inspired to resurrect the tradition in our house after I'd spent a small fortune on a big white linen tablecloth. (Where more appropriate to use it than at Sunday roast?) The stroke of genius with our Sunday lunches is that we roped a particular group of friends into the game and turned ourselves into somewhat of a club. Sunday roast happens roughly once a month (summer months excluded) and we rotate houses, which lightens the workload for everyone and spreads expenses out evenly (meat isn't—and shouldn't be—cheap).

A Sunday roast is essentially the dreary old meat/starch/two veg formula of dining, only at its most glorious. Christmas dinner is a Sunday roast, with a few special fixings; Easter lunch is a Sunday roast; Thanksgiving is a Sunday roast. Because these feasts are so substantial, no first course is required; the main spread just goes on platters on a buffet or straight on the table where chaos ensues as people pass dishes around and around and around in circles like so many minds gone mad. This is how such family-style celebrations should be: total chaos, with shouting children, barking dogs, wine glasses knocked flying in the heat of a good tale... There is no reason not to stray from the traditional menus (I do it all the time), but it's also worth being familiar with the tried and true, because they're comforting and familiar, always appropriate, and never go out of style.

Host's First Roast

— Makes: 6 servings —

*If you're new to Sunday roast, take the easy route and serve cold roast beef
with an array of enticing sauces: grainy Dijon mustard and horseradish cream,
both of which you can buy, along with walnut mayonnaise and green sauce,
both of which you can make in a wink.*

1 3-pound sirloin roast
Salt and pepper
Olive oil

Heat the oven to 425°F. Season the roast and rub it lightly with oil all over. On the stovetop, heat an oven-friendly skillet that will accommodate the roast and brown the meat on all sides until you get a nice dark crust, about three minutes per side. Transfer to the oven and roast until a meat thermometer reaches 120°F, about 40 minutes. (If the meat is not quite to temperature, return it to the oven, but check every few minutes because things can go overboard very fast from this point on.)

When it's ready, remove the roast from the oven and set aside to rest for at least 15 minutes. If you're making the roast early in the day, wrap and refrigerate once cool, then remove from the fridge an hour before slicing ultra-thinly and arranging on a platter. Serve with the four sauces, each in its own bowl.

Walnut Mayonnaise

— Makes: about a cup —

Depending on the strength of your walnut oil,
you may want to use half walnut and half grapeseed oil.

1 egg yolk

1 teaspoon Dijon mustard

1 teaspoon sherry vinegar

½ teaspoon salt

1 cup walnut oil

Lemon juice to taste

———————————

Whisk together the yolk, mustard, vinegar and salt. Whisk in the oil, adding it only drop by drop so the mixture emulsifies. Taste and add lemon juice and more salt, if needed, to taste. Refrigerate until serving.

Green Sauce

1 cup parsley leaves

½ cup mint leaves

½ cup basil leaves

2 anchovies, rinsed (optional)

1 heaping teaspoon capers

1 heaping teaspoon Dijon mustard

1 garlic clove, grated

⅓ cup olive oil, more if needed

Salt and pepper

Lemon juice

Put the herbs, anchovies, capers, mustard, and garlic in a food processor and pulse fine. With the motor running, add the oil in a stream to sauce consistency, thinning with more oil if necessary. Taste, and season to your liking with the salt, pepper, and lemon juice. Transfer to a bowl and refrigerate until serving.

SAMPLE CLASSIC SUNDAY
ROAST MENUS

Roast Beef and Gravy
Horseradish Sauce
Classic Roast Potatoes
Green Beans
Yorkshire Pudding
———
Trifle

Roast Leg of Lamb with Jus
Mint Sauce (if doing English style)
Petits Pois à la Française
Buttered Baby Potatoes
with Herbs
———
Lemon Tart or Mousse

Pot-Roasted Pork with Jus
Applesauce
Roasted Carrots and Parsnips
———
Green Salad
———
Pecan Pie

Roasted Venison with Red Wine Sauce
Buttered Egg Noodles
Sautéed Mushrooms

———

Green Salad

———

Baked Pears

Roast Turkey with Stuffing
Gravy
Cranberry Sauce
Mashed Potatoes
Brussels Sprouts or Sautéed Spinach

———

Squash Pie

Glazed Ham
Gratin Dauphinois
Asparagus

———

Chocolate Cake

Roasted Salmon
Lemon Cream Sauce
Spring Vegetable Medley

———

Blueberry Crumble

Vichyssoise

Roast Chicken

Ratatouille

Ice Cream with Berries and Vanilla Cake

Planning a Menu

This is where every party involving a meal must start, and even if you're not ready to get into entertaining just yet, by plotting dinners on paper you can already learn a lot. I always begin, almost subconsciously, by taking certain general factors into account: who, if any, the guests are; weather; season; my energy level; whether there's an occasion; our appetites; whether there's food in the fridge, including leftovers; whether people have food restrictions . . . All of these details come into play and help determine what food will be appropriate.

If this sounds overwhelming, don't worry, because in fact it takes our brain only about a minute to compute all this. For example: close friends are coming, it's hot out, tomatoes are in season, I'm feeling lazy, one person is allergic to nuts. Once we have a clear scenario, the vast possibility of things to eat suddenly gets narrowed down and dinner feels more manageable. Then the real creative stuff can begin.

Assembling specific dishes for a menu is a bit of a juggling act, because variety is important. In my overzealous youth (I think I was about twelve), I once created a fatal menu: five courses, all of which contained cheese. Don't do that. Any of us can get wildly enthusiastic about making certain individual dishes and then forget to consider whether or not they actually belong in the same meal, so before you start cooking, scan your plan. If you've plotted chicken-liver mousse followed by poached halibut in cream sauce followed by crème caramel, rethink. It's just too much cream and squoosh, so at least one course should be swapped out for something with crunch and perhaps some colour. (Try imagining yourself eating each dish in sequence to see how you feel about it.)

To achieve balance, it helps to isolate one course of a menu first as a starting point, and it should almost always be the main—the most important, the one we can't lose (whereas the others, if we get overwhelmed, can be dropped). So decide on roasted halibut, steaks, stuffed peppers, whatever it is, and then structure side dishes and other courses around that, keeping in mind contrasting ingredients, textures, colours, and so on. If we're serving asparagus as a first course, we're not going to want green beans with the main. If we're serving macaroni and cheese, we should avoid rice pudding for dessert. If we're having a hearty stew, we might want to consider a green salad afterwards rather than a hefty pâté to start.

Many hosts go overboard, and I've done it myself. What I've learned is that it pays to be honest with ourselves: if we don't relish the prospect of a seven-course menu on a weeknight in someone's house, then why would we ever impose such a thing on our own guests? That's suffering, not supper. So if we find ourselves about to launch into the creation of five different hors d'oeuvres, we might want to step back, shut our eyes, take a deep breath, and repeat the Goldilocks formula: not too big and not too small, but juuuuuust right.

Another common error when menu planning is coming up with a

handful of dishes that, we discover at the last second, all need the oven at the same time. Whoops. The standard set-up in kitchens today is a single oven with a four-burner stovetop (lucky you if you have more). If this is your situation, you cannot hope to achieve a seven-hour leg of lamb, a chocolate cake, roasted parsnips, and warm dinner plates all on the same night. Most roasts can rest, covered in foil, for a good hour, so that will free up the oven, but otherwise you have to limit oven-cooked dishes to one or two and do everything else on the stovetop. (I wonder if this explains the traditional British predilection for boiled veg alongside roasts.)

You might also choose a first course that involves no cooking at all and a dessert that can be made well in advance. "You've got to use your head, see?" as my late grandfather used to say, and writing things down on paper certainly helps. (By the way, if you're about to renovate your kitchen, do consider a warming drawer for plates. Such things exist now, and I'm desperate for one.)

Questions to Ask *Before* Planning a Menu

+ Who is coming? Close friends with their children is different from colleagues.

+ Why are they coming? Celebrating an engagement is different from just getting together to watch football.

+ What season is it? Wild boar stew in July, fresh strawberries in February = no-nos.

→ Is it lovely out (something fresh and light) or is the weather dreadful (comfort food)?

→ Does anyone coming have food restrictions? No seafood in the house at all? Make a buffet so there's choice?

→ How much time do I have to cook? All day? An hour? None, so I should cook everything in advance?

→ How much time do we have to eat? An hour? Five hours?

Questions to Ask *While* Planning a Menu

→ Are food groups balanced: starch vs. meat vs. vegetables vs. dairy, etc.? Goat cheese salad followed by chicken in cream and vanilla ice cream is dairy overkill.

→ Do I have colour contrast? White asparagus followed by sea bass followed by banana pavlova is a visual yawn.

→ Do I have textural contrasts? Foie gras needs thin toast; cheese soufflé should not be followed by mousse for dessert.

→ Is everything at the right temperature? Fruit is best at room temperature; green salads are generally best cold; stew should be piping hot.

→ Do I have the right amount of food? Don't be mean, but don't overdo it either.

ⴕ Does the menu suit the people eating it and the occasion? I doubt the Queen wants a burger for her birthday; your hockey buddies probably don't want caviar, consommé, coulibiac, and flambéed cherries after a game (or *do* they?).

ⴕ Do I have the right equipment and appliances available at the right times to make all the dishes and serve them? If not, what dish can be changed? If a ham needs to be in the oven for hours, perhaps a refrigerator dessert makes sense.

Minimalist Daytime Hosting
. . . because not all entertaining has to involve a meal

It is such a rarity for anyone to visit without warning these days that when the doorbell rings unexpectedly, we immediately assume it's a salesman or a fundraising type. Although it's tempting to dive into the flour bin and wait for them to go away, we usually drag our feet to the door, working out a good line on the way ("Sorry, I can't vote in this country"; "Sorry, I don't actually live here, I'm just cat sitting"), only to discover it's Mollie on the doorstep delivering a pot of geraniums, or Robert, en route to the post office, returning a cake plate. *Yippee! A proper excuse to take a break!*

I realize there are people who don't like these sorts of surprises (some even consider it rude), and I know they're not always convenient. Still, I adore callers. It flatters me to think that my house is considered the sort of place where the door is always open, or that I might be thought the kind of person who can always find a quarter of an hour to spare even when I don't have it. Besides, it's not that these spontaneous drop-in types are expecting to stay the weekend. The very definition of a caller is someone passing by for a *brief* visit, just enough time for an exchange of light gossip and a little refreshment. It does wonders for everyone's morale and it's as undemanding as entertaining can get. I say embrace it.

Little visits like these don't necessarily have to be unannounced or unexpected—and indeed often won't be, because, as I've said, calling on people is not really done anymore. If we want these precious stolen moments to happen, we have to encourage them. Rather than thinking that we have to orchestrate a state dinner every time we want to see people, we can just invite them over for a beer (perhaps even a shandy: half a beer topped up with an equal amount of lemonade or ginger beer, which the French call a *panaché*).

This sort of effortless hospitality is particularly ideal for anyone unaccustomed to hosting or without adequate space for full-scale entertaining. If you think you're out of the hosting game, master the art of these *hors*-mealtime moments and you'll be a champion, in an admirably original way.

READY IN THE FRIDGE

The least we can offer the unannounced passerby is a glass of water, especially if they're on foot and not intending to linger. Even this can be done with class. Be the host who offers a choice of ice or no ice, sparkling or still, and do use a nice glass, never plastic. If it's high summer and you're one of those enviably organized sorts, you might have a carafe of water already in the fridge, infusing with cucumber slices, lemon slices, or mint sprigs.

Something I love is cold herbal tea. I brew it in the morning, let it sit on the counter, and sip away at it at room temperature all day (I much prefer it to hot).

Iced tea or coffee are other fine hot-weather weapons, and don't forget lemonade. The homemade drink really delights people, like running into a long-lost friend.

And it's simple to make. Combine 1¼ cups sugar and 1 cup water in a saucepan and bring to a boil for a few minutes to dissolve the sugar. Cool, then stir in 1 cup freshly squeezed and strained lemon juice. This makes your base, which travels well and stores easily. To serve, pour it into a large jug, top up with 7 cups still or sparkling water, and give it a stir.

(P.S. This is also very good when infused with mint. Just add a few sprigs to the pot when you boil the sugar and water, leave it in the liquid while it cools, and remove.)

TEA

I can't offer advice about coffee because I rarely touch the stuff (I don't like the taste, although it always smells good); I do, however, practically underwrite the Sri Lankan economy with my orange pekoe consumption.

To my mind, inviting people over for tea seems a bit old-fashioned now (unless you're a Duchess, which statistically speaking you probably aren't), and to turn it into a Jane Austenesque affair feels downright pretentious unless it's done with tongue welded firmly to cheek. I never extend an invitation for tea, but, being a tea drinker myself, I do know how to make it and, naturally, think any self-respecting host should (says the self-respecting host who's hopeless at coffee, but then that's what my co-host is for). What torture it is to be offered tea at someone's house and then, upon acceptance, to be served a mug of weak swill made from decade-old bags pinched out of a long-unopened canister that looks like it was salvaged from the *Titanic*.

To be clear, I'm talking about classic black tea here (basically, a British cuppa). The main rule is to use enough bags (one for every 2 cups of water) or leaves to give the pot of tea strength (too many will make it bitter, but too few, which is the more common mistake, and you get dishwater). Pour boiling water over the bag(s) (do not, *shudder*, hand someone a mug of hot water with a teabag passed separately for futile dipping, as nearly all restaurants do). After a quick stir, let the tea steep a good three minutes, by which time it should be ready to pour. If in doubt, pour a splash into your guest's cup and ask if it's strong enough for their liking before filling the cup. Let them add milk (cold) themselves if they want it.

LONDON FOG

This is a nice twist on tea that an opera-singing friend once served me. It's wonderful on drizzly, off-season days, especially mid to late morning

Brown Butter and
Sea Salt Shortbreads

— Makes: 75 cookies —

I generally serve these as they are, but you can also sandwich the cookies
together with red currant jelly or raspberry jam if you like.

1 cup salted butter

¾ cup sugar

2 teaspoons vanilla

2 cups flour

1 teaspoon soda

$\frac{1}{16}$ teaspoon salt

Fill the sink with about 2 inches of very cold water. Put the butter in a saucepan and melt, stirring with a wooden spoon, until it reaches a dark caramel colour. Set the pot into the cold water and stir the butter until it becomes opaque, about 5 minutes. Add the sugar and vanilla, followed by the sifted dry ingredients, mixing well. Set aside at room temperature to sit for 2 hours.

To bake, heat the oven to 325°F. Cut the dough into small spoonful-sized pieces and roll into balls, then cut each ball in half. Lay cut side down on a parchment-lined baking sheet and bake until done, about 15 minutes. Let cool slightly before trying to move them from the sheet, and store in an airtight container.

when people are already caffeinated to the brim. It's somewhat of an Earl Grey cappuccino: brewed Earl Grey tea topped with warm, frothy milk. For those who like it, a spoonful of maple syrup added is nice, or a drop of vanilla, although for me that's gilding the lily.

THE COOKIE JAR

This is embarrassing to admit, but I don't own a cookie jar. In my parents' house, there were (are!) always cookies, and it's a very reassuring thing because it means you always have something to offer people if they pop by during the day, and you always have something to offer yourself if perchance nobody does. If you have children or grandchildren, it's absolutely *de rigueur* to have a cookie jar forever full with one of your signature household cookies. My father used to make up his own names for his cookies, such as "anti-apartheid cookies" for his chocolate and vanilla balls, or "camel turds" for some healthy mounds involving chocolate chips and coconut.

I don't make cookies often enough, but when I do, one of the favourites, given to us by Peter's aunt Lee, are these brown butter cookies, which look rather plain but taste sensational (see p. 219).

THE CANDY JAR

I'm not much of a candy eater, but I do remember with fond nostalgia how the old houses around where I grew up all had candy jars, which was bliss to me as a child. Miss Newcomb, up the road, had hers full of striped hard candy hidden behind her television set (we found that in no time). Vida Bostwick kept several little bowls scattered around her coffee tables, at least one of which contained "chicken bones" (those perky pink sticks with chocolate for marrow). Uncle Freeman displayed giant jars of pink-and-white peppermints on a pine sideboard in his living room. When you're little (or even just young at heart), this is the stuff of magic—forbidden fruit, but because you're visiting, Mummy will nod and let you have one, maybe two.

This all sounds terribly old-fashioned, I'm sure. In those days, there wasn't the sugar problem we have today (neither were allergies epidemic), and children ate much less candy, so it was always a treat. Perhaps it means less to people now, but I still find a candy jar devilishly inviting. It's easy to find a cheap but groovy vessel at a flea market—or something more upmarket in an antique or modern design shop—and fill it with a candy that can become your signature variety (candied ginger and black licorice seem to be mine). Always have the jar sitting somewhere that makes clear to people they're welcome to help themselves, say on a side table in the living room or on a console by the front door. It's also nice to set out a few after a dinner for those who fancy a fix.

"For Drinks"

The cocktail hour is special: that mysterious turning point between day and night, the mellowing space between active life and repose, a period during which time passes, with or without alcohol, almost liquidly, transforming us from our public personas to our private selves. In short, it's a transitional interlude that has "host" written all over it. I'm not talking about a full-on cocktail party, by the way, which is an ordeal. I just mean popping a cork or mixing a few negronis and kicking up our heels for an hour or so with one or two friends or acquaintances, then parting ways. All very chill.

North Americans tend not to invite people to their houses solely for drinks; they'd rather meet out for their after-work tippling. Nothing wrong with that, obviously, but one should keep in mind that the drinks-at-home scheme is a wonderful way to entertain without committing to a lot of time or going to great effort or expense. I reckon it's possible to offer drinks and a nibble for four to six people at the same cost as paying for one's own two cocktails and a cone of frites in a noisy bar.

IN THE APERITIF CUPBOARD
FOR IMPROMPTU GUESTS

Jars of high-quality jalepeño-, lemon-, almond-,
or anchovy-stuffed olives

Gourmet potato chips

Pretzels

Popcorn (for making on the spot and serving hot)

Pistachios

Roasted almonds or cashews

> And in the fridge: Dried sausage
> (to slice very thinly before serving)

The cupboard stuff is really for emergencies. If we've actually asked people to drinks, then I think it's only correct to stretch ourselves beyond pulling the lid off a tin of roasted peanuts (certainly if we're not promising a meal afterward). For one, people are hungry at that time of day and we don't know where they're going afterwards (possibly nowhere). Furthermore, if we like the people we've asked (one can only assume), then it's nice to show them we've actually anticipated their visit and put some thought and effort into it.

You're being preached at here, don't forget, by someone who is pretty hopeless at canapé cookery and can't stand doing it because it feels friggy. I am not, for any money, about to start skewering melon balls and mozzarella on toothpicks or start deep-frying threads of ginger to top daikon cubes with miso mayo.

My advice, if you're anything like me, is to get friendly with the notion of toast. I'm talking about slices of baguette or boule drizzled with olive oil and lightly toasted in the oven (400°F for 10 minutes usually does it), upon which you can pile just about anything: goat cheese and soft ribbons of red pepper, a slice of cold butter topped with fish roe or a curl of ham, conserved mackerel with lemon ... A popular one in summer is tomato bread, which I learned to prepare long ago in Spain by rubbing tomato directly on toasted bread, but which Peter has taken over making by the method shown on page 226.

Popcorn

— Makes: about 10 cups —

Fun for the whole family, folks, and cheap!

2 tablespoons grapeseed oil

½ cup popcorn

3 tablespoons melted butter

Salt to taste

Put the oil and two to three kernels of popcorn in a large, lidded pot and set over medium-high heat until the kernels pop. Pull off the heat, add the remaining popcorn in a single layer, and let sit, covered, until you hear the next pop, about 30 seconds. Return the pot to the heat and shake gently while the rest of the kernels pop. Toss with the melted butter and salt and serve.

For Hosts Who Hate to Cook
(or Sometimes Can't)

At least three good friends of mine absolutely loathe cooking. Fortunately for them, they're rich, so they can order all the takeout, caterers, personal chefs, and ready-made goodies they like. With the exception of the private-chef approach, I admit I tire of that sort of food rather quickly, no matter how high-end. Too often, dishes prepared for vast numbers taste like exactly that. There can be a non-ness about them.

However, sometimes catered food can be incredibly useful and very good indeed; when it is, it's a godsend to the kitchen-phobic like these particular friends of mine (or to anyone who actually likes to cook most of the time but on certain occasions can't, or hasn't planned to and suddenly has guests, which could be any of us). We don't actually need to be capable of cooking a thing to be a great host; we do, however, want to be known for serving lovely food in a lovely way.

TAKEOUT AND OTHER
READY-MADE FOOD

One friend of mine entertains often, in a variety of ways: sometimes she cooks, sometimes a catering company is called in, and sometimes she just goes out and gets stacks and stacks of takeout boxes from, say, the small Vietnamese restaurant down on the corner. However she does it, she never fusses. What she cares about is bringing people together in a jolly atmosphere, and for this she has a real knack, partly thanks to her flexible attitude when it comes to food.

Pan Con Tomate

— Makes: 6 servings —

6 slices rustic white bread
(such as boule)

Olive oil for drizzling

2 large ripe tomatoes

1 clove garlic, halved

Fleur de sel to taste

Anchovy fillets (optional)

Heat the oven to 400°F. Cut 6 not-too-thick slices of the bread, halve them on a baking sheet. Drizzle with olive oil, and toast lightly in the oven, about 10 minutes.

Meanwhile, cut the tomatoes in half and rub each half on the large side of a box grater until you're holding nothing but skin. Discard the skin.

When the bread comes out of the oven, rub very lightly with the cut side of a garlic clove half (too much will be acrid), then spoon on a small amount of the tomato, spreading it evenly to the edges. (You do not want a thick layer of tomato; it should be thin to the point of transparency.) Drizzle with olive oil and sprinkle with fleur de sel. If you're an anchovy fan, you might lay on one or two fillets per slice, well rinsed and patted dry, in which case go easy on the salt.

What's key, whether we have guests or not, is never to eat ready-made food out of the cardboard and plastic containers it comes in (that's for seagulls). It takes no time whatsoever to transfer food to proper serving dishes and it will make all the difference to everyone's morale. Spill that tabbouleh salad from its Styrofoam carton into a colourful pottery bowl and watch it transform. Marvel at the difference between meatballs in their flimsy tin tray and those same meatballs hot and steaming on an earthenware platter. Such simple actions can dramatically transform the eating experience: in the blink of an eye, something that looks completely third-rate is made glamorous. (We might even get away with pretending we made it!)

Three Golden Rules for Eating Food Brought In

- Buy good-quality prepared food to begin with, to the extent you can. (And remember, you can always add your own garnishes for a personal touch.)

- Transfer all food to proper serving platters; the less sterile and the more personal, the better.

- Set the table nicely with well-loved household dishes and proper cutlery.

THE INTIMATE BUSINESS
OF HIRING A COOK

I am my own cook and have rarely hired anyone else to take my place; however, I do know people who have full-time kitchen help; I also know people who *have been* the full-time kitchen help. It's probably too personal a business to make sweeping generalizations about, but everyone should bear in mind a few things if hiring a home cook or personal chef is in the cards.

YOUR COOK'S FOOD STYLE
SHOULD MATCH YOUR LIFESTYLE

If you're at a cottage for the summer, you probably want a cook with a light touch, someone who likes to barbeque and finds making things like simple salads creative and satisfying. (The cooks with a heavy hand for sauces may not be for you, at least not in that context.) On the other hand, if you've just been appointed ambassador to France, you'll probably want to find someone who takes pride in the occasional display of opulence and has the serious skills to pull it off.

Peter tells the story of a chef his father once had in London, where he served as Quebec's delegate general. A group of businessmen from the aviation industry were coming to his house for dinner, and the aim was to impress them and seal a deal. The cook went quietly about his usual affairs all day, or so it seemed, but when the doors to the dining room swung open at the appointed hour, guests found themselves filtering in to a table decked out with a magnificent airplane centrepiece sculpted out of sugar. Very smooth.

SET OUT CLEAR HEALTH GUIDELINES

This seems obvious, but professional chefs aren't necessarily trained in or instinctively interested in nutrition. There are those who can be shockingly liberal in the fat and salt department, which you may or may not appreciate. There are also those who will be bored cross-eyed if all you ever let them make are green smoothies. Make sure your cook's idea of healthy food (and of interesting food) mirrors yours.

CONFIRM YOU CAN SHARE A ROOM

Unless you plan never to set foot in the kitchen, be sure you're hiring someone who shares your standards of tidiness, cleanliness, and organization. I know more than one chef who cooks like a dream, but also like a complete slob, capable of turning the entire kitchen upside down just to fry an egg. On the flip side, make sure your presence in the kitchen—and the kitchen itself—agrees with the cook. Is the kitchen you're providing workable, well equipped, and as cheerful as it can be? Are your schedules for using the kitchen compatible, so you're not going to be under each other's feet all the time?

WASTE NOT, WANT NOT

Whether it's food or actual money, be sure you and your cook share the same values about spending and waste. Money matters can cause the demise of any relationship, especially one like this, where you're essentially entrusting your wallet to another hand. That said, don't be cheap either. You can't expect your cook to make you a feast if you equip him or her with nothing but a rind of cheese, a few rusks, and a bag of bones.

CHOOSE YOUR CATERER CAREFULLY

Just because a caterer is professionally trained doesn't mean they're actually any good or that they'll be your style. (This is true of any profession, of course. Think of dentists, seamstresses, carpenters . . . Trained or not, some have skill and some don't; some share your taste and some don't.) Research is important, and not just on the Internet. Before hiring a caterer, it's important to consult with friends in the know, read the menus on offer, and ask for samples of the food. You need the right fit or you'll be disappointed. Once you've found someone you can trust, you'll be able to build a relationship that can last a long time. (The better the caterer gets to know you and your house, the smoother every party will run.)

Whomever you hire, it's essential to be clear about what you want and to make sure you've been understood. I once did a dinner with a friend for something like thirty people, and we hired a caterer. It was a bit unusual, because the idea was to throw an intimate dinner around my home cooking but to have the caterer actually cook it because it was a big crowd, and in any case I was meant to be a guest. I drew up the menu, provided recipes, signed my name to the deal, and did no more worrying until the night itself (which, surely, is the main point of hiring a caterer in the first place).

It turned out to be slightly embarrassing. Everyone had come expecting my cooking, but the caterer, whose brand was flawless, fancy food, had decided otherwise: they'd come with their own recipes, which they presented with three-star flourish, completely ignoring my requests. It's not that the food was bad (indeed, it was excellent), but it was impersonal, which made hearts sink a little and affected the tenor of the evening.

I suppose that's a general risk when it comes to caterers: it's difficult to put our own personality into what's basically someone else's show. Maybe the use of a caterer with a homier style for that particular evening would have made the difference, but the lesson I took away was that when you hire someone else to cook, it's best to stand back, disassociate, be grateful, and let them do their thing.

More Catering Tips
(Because catering isn't just about the food.)

→ Have the team arrive early to set up. You want your house looking host-ready when everyone arrives, not like the erection of a movie set in progress.

- Make sure waiters are identifiable, so it's clear who is working. You don't want people approaching their fellow guest the Marchioness of Manners and asking her where the loo is, so perhaps specify a uniform of, say, traditional black trousers and white shirts (also, no scruffy beards, etc.).

- Request that staff not carry mobile phones (even in their pockets, because they often forget to turn them off).

- Ensure there's sufficient staff to take and return coats.

- Show staff where the washrooms are before people arrive so they can direct guests, if asked.

- If you want to save money, buy your own service ware, making sure it's suitable to the food being served and that you have enough. (Particularly for a cocktail party, make sure serving plates and trays are light, but sturdy, and easy to carry.) Renting dishes is convenient because they'll all be taken away at the end and you won't have to think about them; that said, it's also an expensive charge (and a bit boring, because they're virtually always blah).

- Instruct staff to clean as they go, not only so the kitchen appears organized and the party zones remain welcoming, but so that you don't experience problems such as running out of glasses or other dishes. (People moving about at a party often lose a glass and reach for a new one, sometimes more than once.)

꙳ Ensure the caterers are contracted to clean up everything afterward so you're not left with a mess. This includes taking out all garbage, so be sure to have plenty of garbage bags at the ready.

Nibbles for Dinner

A cocktail party is definitely the time to consider hiring a caterer. I've thrown them where I've done all the food myself, and it's a lot of work (best done teamed up with a cooking buddy). If you have nobody to serve for you, set out a buffet of nibbles and then keep an eye on it so you can make sure supplies aren't dwindling or, if they are, transfer bites to smaller dishes so they still look abundant and beautiful.

Most people I know hire out the whole job, which is fine, but don't be fooled: hiring help doesn't mean we get to throw our hands up and not participate. We're expected to give guidance (although a good caterer will guide us too). What's crucial to remember is that party food often replaces dinner altogether. If a cocktail party is organized for 5 to 7 p.m., people will expect just a few bites, but if it's a party proper that will last into the night (and not involve sitting down to a meal), then we really have to give the food serious thought because what we serve will be the only food people see for many hours.

Successful cocktail food is:

꙳ eye-catching and imaginative

꙳ seriously tasty

⇥ varied (and mindful of allergies and other food restrictions)

⇥ copious and, in some cases, substantial

⇥ easy to eat in no more than two bites using one hand

I remember attending a Fashion Week party years ago in Paris and hovering with friends near the kitchen door, positively writhing with hunger. Suddenly, like a spider popping up out of a drainpipe, a single waiter would tentatively emerge carrying a plate of something like spice-coated cubes of beet, and the multitudes would pounce and clean him out before he'd taken so much as two steps. He would then retreat again, leaving those who hadn't managed to snatch so much as a cumin seed to twist in agony until he reappeared.

Nobody can have fun when they're distracted by hunger. If the food is bad or insufficient, people can't be blamed for leaving. Where there is plenty of drink, there must be plenty of food, and it's not much of a party unless the food is good.

What If the Night Goes On and On and On?

I'm not really saying this for me, because I don't "do" late nights, but perhaps you do, so here's the message: if you have a cocktail party that goes overtime, the food's all gone, and people still aren't going home, it's wise to be prepared to rustle up some proper fodder so that your guests don't crash their bicycles and limos into poles when they finally do make an exit. I was at a cocktail party not long ago at which the host (perhaps knowing her audience well) had pasta hot and ready for anyone who was simply having too much fun to want to leave. Brilliant.

A very easy all-season pasta to have on hand is spaghetti tossed with garlic and chili pepper–infused oil and a handful of finely chopped parsley. It's called Spaghetti Aglio, Olio, e Peperoncino (you can look it up). It's even good at room temperature.

In the winter, we love bucatini or spaghetti tossed with the famous Marcella Hazan tomato sauce, which is prepared thus: Put a large tin of San Marzano tomatoes into a sauté pan with their juice. Cut the tomatoes up a bit with scissors lowered into the mix. Add 5 tablespoons of butter and half a medium onion, peeled. Season with salt and simmer (i.e., on low, murmuring heat) uncovered for 45 minutes, stirring occasionally and squishing any oversized chunks of tomato with the back of a spoon. When the time is up, discard the onion and check the seasonings. If you're in the mood, add some high-quality canned tuna, drained and broken up. Toss with bucatini (or spaghetti) and serve with freshly grated Parmesan cheese.

In the summer, we serve Ina Garten's Summer Garden Pasta (angel hair with cherry tomatoes, basil, and garlic). Essentially, you combine halved cherry tomatoes, olive oil, shredded basil, minced garlic, red pepper flakes, salt, and pepper and marinate this at room temperature for a few hours. When you sense your crowd growing restless, boil up some angel hair pasta and toss with the tomato mixture and a few handfuls of finely grated Parmesan cheese. Always a hit.

And Just in Case Anyone Stays Over . . .

Breakfast is the most personal meal of the day, the most ritualistic and repetitive and generally the least social. I'm one of those tiresome people who rarely eats it; I start off the day with tea, go to yoga on an empty stomach, and the next thing I know it's lunchtime. However, I did grow up in a household where not eating breakfast was considered unthinkable; not only that, but the first meal of the day was always hot. The point is that we each have our own breakfast preferences, so it's nice to be sensitive when feeding overnight guests.

Coffee and tea are basically givens. At breakfast, we almost have to think of them in the same way as the requisite cocktail before dinner: nobody wants even to think about food until they have the appropriate mug of hot drink thrust into their hands. Only then does one ask, "What do you eat for breakfast?"—a question that has built right into it an acknowledgement that breakfast is a meal of habit and that a guest will probably want something along the lines of their usual.

My first rule is never to force breakfast on anyone, because I resent it whenever it's forced on me. There are some strange, heavy American egg dishes out there, usually in casserole form and full of all sorts of mystifying chopped-up bits, which are dreadful, indeed torture, to eat if you generally can't stomach breakfast anyway.

Continental breakfast, which implies something like hot, milky coffee with a croissant or an apricot tartine, is a completely opposite approach and not to everyone's taste either, but at least it's simple and fairly inoffensive (except to the sort of people who are croaking for yogurt and fruit, or oatmeal). The nice thing about continental breakfast is that you can basically set it all up and walk away, which is good if you have, say, a crowd of people staying for the weekend and no idea when everybody's going to get out of bed.

All you do is set out a pot of coffee, hot milk, sugar, a basket of croissants wrapped in a napkin and another of bread with a toaster nearby, butter, and jams. Coffee cups, plates, and knives should be at the ready so people don't have to ransack the kitchen searching for them. Then, as guests trickle down at various times over the course of the morning, they can take what they like and go read the paper while they sip and nibble away, leaving you in peace.

Pancakes, particularly buckwheat, are traditional where I come from and are what my parents generally serve to guests at the table. I'm not talking about fluffy, thick white pancakes, but rather a thinner, earthier kind—not crêpe thin, but somewhere between that and blini height. They're cooked on a special cast-iron griddle, which is a bit of a conversation piece (actually, Peter and I have one too, so when guests come, we carry on the pancake tradition). We serve the pancakes on a warm platter and set out butter and maple syrup so people can help themselves.

My Dad's Pancakes

— Makes: 8 to 10 pancakes —

Earthy, healthy, and easy.

2 tablespoons melted butter or oil,
plus more oil for frying

½ cup water

1 egg

½ cup spelt or buckwheat flour

½ cup whole wheat flour

2 teaspoons baking powder

½ teaspoon salt

Whisk together the wet ingredients, then sift in and whisk the dry until smooth. Achieve a thin batter by adding more water as needed.

Heat a griddle to medium-high and brush with oil. Set a plate in a low-temperature oven (no higher than 225°F) to keep pancakes warm as you fry them, plus plates for as many people as will be eating so they're warm too.

Pour batter onto the griddle to make roughly a 5-inch pancake. Bubbles will appear all over the surface; let them disappear until the pancake is almost completely cooked through, about a minute and a half, before flipping to finish on the other side, about 30 seconds.

Transfer to the plate in the oven to keep warm while you cook the rest. Serve with butter and, if you like, maple syrup or molasses.

Granola Crackers

These crackers are granola-to-go, perfect for anyone who wants to strike out across the moors in the early hours with something savoury in their pocket.

2 cups rolled oats
¾ cup flour
¼ cup sesame seeds
½ cup sunflower seeds
2 tablespoons sugar
1½ teaspoons salt

1½ teaspoons dried oregano
1½ teaspoons dried thyme
1 teaspoon garlic powder
3 eggs, lightly beaten
¾ cup grapeseed oil

Heat the oven to 375°F. Mix all the ingredients thoroughly and spread evenly over a parchment-lined 11½- × 17-inch baking sheet, going right out to the edges. Bake for 20 minutes. Remove from the oven and cut into squares immediately. Allow to cool on the sheet before removing with a metal spatula. Store in an airtight container.

The Not-Quite-Full
English Breakfast

— Serves 4 —

I like the idea of English breakfast much more than I enjoy eating it,
but many people adore the feast, and any self-respecting host should probably
know how to prepare one, just in case. It's a production, be warned, not because
any element of a "full English" is difficult, but because there are a lot of moving
parts. Being organized and having the timing down is crucial. A really full English
breakfast might include—in addition to the essential eggs and bacon—baked
beans, blood pudding, sausages, fried mushrooms, fried potatoes, and fried bread.
Adding even a couple of these extras is for me complete overkill (but do check with
your guests in case anyone wants them), which is why this is a pared-down version,
the bonus of which is that the whole performance is easier on the cook.

(P.S. If you're too scared to invite people for Sunday roast, you can
always get your feet wet by starting with this breakfast.)

4 plum tomatoes,
halved lengthwise

Salt and pepper to taste

Olive oil for drizzling

Butter

12 slices bacon

4 slices white bread,
preferably a day or two old

4 to 8 eggs, depending
on appetites

First, cook the tomatoes. Put the oven rack to the top of the oven and turn on the broiler. Season the tomatoes with salt and pepper, then lay skin side down on a baking tray. Drizzle lightly with oil, and dot with butter. Broil until fully cooked through and golden on top, about 5 minutes. Remove from the oven.

Turn the oven down to low (from now on it's just to keep things warm) and put the rack back down to the middle of the oven. Set in four dining plates (woe betide anyone who tries to serve English breakfast on cold plates). Keep the tomatoes warm in the oven while you cook the rest of the breakfast on the stovetop.

Next, fry the bacon. Start it off in a cold pan over medium heat so that a good pool of fat melts off before it gets crisp. Set the cooked bacon onto paper towel to drain, but leave the fat in the pan. Keep the bacon warm in the oven.

Fry the bread for 2 to 3 minutes per side in the bacon fat, adding butter if needed. You want the fat not so hot that it burns, but hot enough to make the bread evenly golden all over. Keep the bread warm in the oven too.

At last, the eggs. Melt a good amount of butter in the pan until bubbling but without browning. Crack in the eggs and let them set for half a minute. Season with salt and pepper and cook to your liking, covering with a lid after about a minute. As the eggs are cooking, either divide the other breakfast components among the four plates or arrange them on a platter. When the eggs are ready, slip them alongside and hasten to the table.

The Weary Traveller

Once I arrived at my parents' house after a fourteen-hour road trip to possibly the most bewildering reception I ever had. I'd been travelling with my friend Mollie and we'd really motored, eating junk along the way in anticipation of proper restoration of the civilized sort on the receiving end. When we landed, to my astonishment, there was pizza. (It was homemade by my dad, but still ... We'd been driving for the equivalent of two full workdays, subjected to gas-station gastronomy, and now this? From *my* parents, of all people?)

It turned out that Mollie and I were not the only guests, which would later explain the situation. The others, who had been staying already for a few days, were fast-food devotees, and my parents, being of the homemade-everything camp, were trying to find a compromise to please everyone—hence the pizza. Around the table we all sat, the junk-food visitors navigating the homemade pesto et al. whilst dreaming of the next day when they could finally hit the road and find a McDonald's; meanwhile, Mollie and I munched away in a baffled state like two teenagers who'd accidentally wandered into the wrong movie at the Cineplex. (Poor Mummy and Daddy.)

You have to know your guests, I suppose, and perhaps I'm no benchmark. But if I'm the arriving visitor, the last thing my body wants to find on a plate is any food even remotely resembling that of the trains-planes-and-automobiles variety. No heavy starches, no deep-fried anything, etc. So what does the weary traveller crave?

On my last visit home, my mother made an enormous pot of hot soup. It was 100 per cent vegetables, but, as she explained, that's what makes it

Traveller's Soup

— Makes: 8 servings —

*A healthy restorative that says "Welcome home!" Feel free to vary the vegetables
and to add protein, such as cooked white beans, ground beef, or chicken.
In the case of the last, I tend to omit the tomatoes. If you have a rind of Parmesan
in the house, throw it in the soup early on to release extra flavour, then remove
before serving. If your stock is very lean, a spoonful of butter added to the
soup toward the end will enhance the taste.*

4 carrots, quartered
lengthwise and sliced

½ rutabaga, sliced the size
of the carrots

3 stalks celery, sliced

2 onions, finely diced

2 garlic cloves, minced

1 tablespoon summer savory
or herbes de Provence

1 or 2 bay leaves

4 cups chicken or
vegetable stock or water

2 parsnips, quartered
lengthwise and sliced

2 to 3 waxy potatoes,
quartered lengthwise and sliced

2 cups tomato purée

Salt and pepper

Put the carrots, rutabaga, celery, onions, and garlic in a large pot. Sprinkle over the savory and add the bay leaves. Cover with stock (or water), bring to a simmer, and cook about 10 minutes. Add the parsnips and potatoes and continue cooking until the vegetables are tender, about 15 minutes. Stir in the tomato purée, if using, and season to taste with salt and pepper.

such a versatile recipe: you could add cooked, seasoned hamburger meat or sliced cooked sausage, perhaps cooked white beans or lentils, or stir in some cooked pasta, barley, or rice. In our case, we just topped our bowls with grated cheddar and ate it with bread and butter. It's a convenient dish for hosts because it suits virtually any diet and can be made well ahead and reheated at whatever hour the coach pulls up to your door.

Can Do

One of the smartest things I ever did was to buy a bushel of Roma tomatoes and can them. It was a September weekend a few years ago when Peter and I were in Montreal trolling the Jean-Talon Market, which is strongly Italian in character. The displays of vegetables were spectacular—eggplants, artichokes, garlic, zucchini flowers—and it was killing me that I couldn't buy everything, take it home, and start cooking immediately. Alas, we don't live in Montreal (yet!) and were leaving town that day, and I didn't think porcini mushrooms and little radishes would make practical travelling companions.

Then, just as we were exiting the market, passing through a seemingly endless corridor of tomatoes, I buckled. "Let's get a bushel of those," I pleaded. "Let's get three!" I got called a "crazy old bat," but in the end, Peter let me buy one.

Back home the next day, bursting with domesticity, I set out in search of canning supplies. I'd never canned a thing in my life, but I'd seen it done often enough. My parents, great gardeners, preserved loads of fruits and vegetables every year, so I knew I needed Mason jars (my mother insists on buying lids with no BPA) and a very large but light-weight enamel-coated steel canning pot that came with a metal basket inside, which makes it easy to lift jars out of the simmering water. Between Honest Ed's and the hardware store, I found everything I needed for a song, and by the time Peter got home from work, I was running my hands over a row of glorious jars of canned tomatoes like a model on *The Price Is Right*.

The satisfaction of making any kind of preserve is off the charts, like seeing the speck of dust you planted in June produce green beans

Canned Tomatoes

Be not afraid. This may be time consuming, but it hardly rates as difficult,
and the effort pays off in spades.

Roma or San Marzano
tomatoes

Lemon juice
Salt

BLANCH AND PEEL THE TOMATOES

Bring a large pot of water to a boil. Make an X in the bottom of each tomato with a sharp knife. Fill a sink with ice-cold water. Working in batches, blanch the tomatoes until the skins split, about 30 seconds, then remove them with a small sieve or a spider and immediately plunge into the cold water. Remove from the water and slip off and discard the skins. Set aside. Continue until all the tomatoes are done.

STERILIZE THE JARS AND LIDS

The easiest way to sterilize jars and lids is to run them through a dishwasher cycle, then leave them in there in the steam until just before you're ready to pack them. (Note: Buy lids with no BPA.) You can also put them on a baking sheet in a 225°F oven for 20 minutes.

PACK THE JARS

Working a few two-pint jars at a time, put a tablespoon of lemon juice and a teaspoon of salt into each (for single pints, halve that). Pack with tomatoes, pressing them down well and leaving a ½-inch head at the top. Stick in the handle of a wooden spoon to remove any air bubbles. Wipe clean around the top of each jar before putting the lid on.

CAN IN HOT WATER

Fill a canning pot with a fitted metal basket with water and get it hot. Set the jars down into the basket, allowing the water to come at least an inch over the top. Bring to a simmer, cover, and let bubble gently for 45 minutes. Remove from the water and set on the counter to cool. As they cool, you will hear the lids pop, which means the jars have success-fully sealed. You can confirm this by checking the centre of each lid, which will have become indented. Squeal with delight, and enjoy the coming-on of winter.

in August. It's magical and extremely confidence boosting: having a pantry full of summer-flavoured, nutrient-packed food for winter makes you feel as safe and secure as a cashmere blanket. Those tomatoes changed our lives. We popped a jar every time we needed a quick week-night supper, and when at last we ran out and had to resort to our first sauce from tinned tomatoes, we realized we were ruined because, until that moment, we never knew how much tinned tomatoes taste like tin. Blech. The next year, I got away with buying as many bushels of Roma and San Marzano tomatoes as I wanted (225 pounds!).

And so was born to our house a new tradition of preserving. Now we do a lot more than just tomatoes, mostly pickles, but I plan to branch out and do more vegetables too. I had a friend in Paris years ago who came from a farm in the southwest, and she would throw impressive weekend lunches on the turn of a dime with no stress whatsoever. I could not imagine how she did it, until one day I opened a cupboard in her kitchen and inside discovered an entire wall of jars containing everything from green beans to ceps to foie gras to jam, all sent up by her mother from the farm. Aha!

And Bear in Mind— It's Not About the Food

Hosts can tend to concentrate too high a percentage of their entertaining efforts on what appears on people's plates. This is a mistake. We may be the most genius chef on the planet, but if our guests somehow feel unwelcome, uncomfortable, or intimidated, the meal is guaranteed to be a failure.

Some of us are brilliant with piping bags, others have noses for spices, some have the knife skills of a Samurai, yet others have the money to buy the best caviar and Wagyu beef in the world. None of it really matters if we forget that our guests' needs go deeper than their appetites. No matter what we've got planned for their bellies, it's more important to learn how to feed their hearts and souls.

FOUR

Host

In his book *Great Hostesses* (1982), Brian Masters suggested that we no longer live in hosting times. "The grand hostess cannot flourish in the modern world," he wrote, which made me want to cry. I assume by this he meant that too few of us have enough money to ride up to our mansion's poolside dining tables on the backs of elephants and have eunuchs serve us caviar in ivory dishes for breakfast every morning. Presumably every era has those who can and those who can't afford such indulgences (not to mention those who'd want to and those whose eyes would backflip into their sockets at the very thought), but that is beside the point.

We can have money by the truckload and still make horrible hosts. What we can never buy, and therefore never offer to others, are imagination, a generous spirit, a genuine interest in other people, a willingness to be vulnerable, and an ability to put people at ease. These qualities are the non-negotiable prerequisites of great hosting, making it more of an even playing field than it might at first appear. Standout entertaining doesn't begin with a butler and three-star canapés, but with a state of mind, something that more or less anyone with the will to do so can adopt.

The great host, in a way, is an ideal figure, an almost platonic form. My own mental image of a perfect host is someone with a strong personality and a giant heart whose aura draws people like moths to a glowing light. It would be someone with original style; a relaxed informal manner and easy laughter; a person who sprinkles good vibes and wit around like fairy dust, with an invisible hand, and brings out the best and most fascinating side in everyone they meet. It would also be someone with a knack for uncovering delight even in the most unlikely corners, a real *carpe diem* type. Whatever the exact combination of qualities, a fine host is someone who everybody wants to be around (ditto a fine guest). No wonder: they're people living as the best possible version of themselves.

The English language, playful and rich as it is, lacks pitifully in vocabulary for describing the pleasures of joining people together to enjoy food and one another's company. (This surely explains why we're so often borrowing words from the French.) "Entertaining," for example, is a misleading term. It denotes performance, which, while any social situation will involve some degree of that, is miles from the main point most of the time. Even without the tap-dance and top-hat nuance, "entertaining" is a word that puts a great many people on edge, largely because it too often either drags our minds back to formal, self-conscious dinner parties of bygone eras or it conjures up images of today's socialites hosting low-cal ladies' lunches on private islands with the help of caterers and florists, the sort of dreamy and largely unattainable images featured in glossy magazines.

I rather love that stuff—"aspirational" inspiration has its place—but it can also be intimidating, causing too many to feel that they can't get people together unless they're that person with that palazzo and that shoe closet, which simply is not the case. With a little verve and originality—and the desire to offer the best of ourselves to others—enjoying people's company can happen pretty much anywhere and be a success. Most people show up flattered to have been invited at all, curious about who else will appear, and excited about what they'll discover. (And if they don't, are they the sort of person whose company we want to keep anyway?)

That hosting makes us all a little nervous is really a positive sign, because it suggests we instinctively know we're dealing with something in life that matters and we care about getting it right. We might as well get used to it, too, because most of us, however reluctant we may be, are going to need to host at various times throughout our lives. Think of a child at her sixth birthday party, a boss hosting a team-building barbeque, a grandmother laying out the family Thanksgiving feast, a young man trying to impress the object of his desire with a first attempt at quiche . . .

Occasions demanding some form of milestone-ing, usually involving food, crop up constantly, and all of us, now and again, will be expected to take charge, apply a bit of flair, and, with any luck, transform these moments into happy memories. Hosting, in other words, is an indispensable life skill. Whether we want to host or not, at some point we're going to have to take on the role, so we might as well learn to do it with panache.

Bear in mind that while society hostesses are great fun to read about, they are not the only ones keeping the world spinning. It can be dangerous to gaze too much upon what the *gratin* are doing (or did—i.e., the grand hostesses from days of yore), because it can make us feel powerless in the present.

Celebrity culture, which is the one we happen to be living in right now, can be a royal pain in the *derrière* in this regard, as I'm sure spectator culture has been at every other time in history. Here's the rationale behind it: some people get to *live* (or pretend to, like Greek gods or Napoleonic courtesans) and the rest of us are supposed to sit around *watching* them live. Rubbish! Take inspiration, sure, but otherwise, stop gawking and start hosting, I say. We have our own lives to live and our own worlds to make as inviting as we can.

Why We Host

The word "entertaining" covers a lot of ground. Sometimes we engage in the activity just because we want to amuse ourselves, to break up the ho-hum and/or stress that everyday life can be and bring some pleasure into it for relief. But often it's far more complex than that. We entertain to celebrate people's achievements, sometimes to help people mourn, to thank them, or to reciprocate their own hospitality. We invite so that we can get to know people and bond with them, build our communities, and hold them together. We also host for the purpose of refining our knowledge and taste, cultivating ourselves. Some people make it a game of social climbing; for others it can be about power tripping. For many of us, it's simply about love.

There is a lot of meaning buried behind the words "host," "guest," and "hospitality." In Italian, the word "*ospite*" is used to describe both host and guest, which highlights how, in a way, they're one and the same. If you go back far enough linguistically, the word refers to "other"—and "other" may be either friend or foe. (I suppose entertaining is one way to find out.)

Above and beyond every other reason for offering hospitality is that it is essentially the opposite of hostility. Being a host is about keeping the peace, which in my lifetime I've never seen a greater need for. I don't know about you, but if I'm going to be a peacekeeper, I'd much rather do it in a dress while holding a coupe of Champagne than in fatigues while holding an automatic weapon.

Inviting People Over

I can be shameless about inviting people over, especially for a meal. If someone interests me, I don't even care whether I know them well or not, I'll track them down and ask them to come dine. (Once we even had a "Twitter dinner" and invited some people we'd never met in the flesh. Another time we let a friend of Peter's show up for dinner with ten of his friends whom we'd never met before either.) It can be a bit like running an eighteenth-century Parisian salon sometimes, but there's nothing

I'd rather do. As Carolyn Coggins wrote in her 1952 book *Successful Entertaining at Home*, "Liking to have company is like being one of those characters who bet on the races. You simply can't help yourself."

I'm lucky to live with someone who doesn't mind this addiction of mine. If three days happen to go by with nobody coming over, Peter will notice a sudden antsiness on my part. "Uh-oh, you're reaching your limit," he'll say, and he's right: I can't relax until I've rung up a few friends and plotted the next menu. (You'd think I should be running a restaurant, what with this compulsion, but I'd never consider it. If money were to become involved, the whole business would immediately lose its allure.)

People seem to love being asked out, so assembling a party isn't difficult. For anything that's not a milestone occasion (which means most of the time), I usually send out an email. Where this particular method can be a problem is with the slow responders (who have clearly been raised in a dark forest by rabid wolves, but are thankfully rare). I have been known to send an email on a Sunday night asking people for Thursday, then been forced to send another out on Tuesday when I still haven't heard back, only to be left in limbo until the day itself, whereupon I send a final, really nasty email blasting them for their bad form ("Dear you utter savages . . . ," etc.). All it takes is one ghastly-guest stunt like that and they get the "invite by telephone only" stamp on their foreheads (plus they lose a point, moving them closer to being dropped from the invitee list altogether).

Too harsh? Not if you ask me. Hosts do a lot of work organizing and preparing for their guests' benefit (we also spend a lot of money). If a guest is in limbo about coming, it's not fair for them to hold us hostage, making it impossible for us to know if we should invite someone else instead, or whether we need to buy food at all, or whether we're free that night to accept another invitation ourselves. (Guests, pay heed.)

For special occasions requiring proper invitations, evites are fairly standard these days (at least they are in North America), and although I've yet to send one myself, I recognize their convenience. They're delivered in a click and they're secretarially smart about keeping track of RSVP lists. Obviously they're cheaper, too, than cardstock and stamps, and they're useful for guests who appreciate a Google map of the party location to click through to. While I do bow to these advantages, paper invitations are still far nicer and pretty much irreplaceable for seriously special events. I love how loaded with anticipation a paper invitation is as it sits there promisingly on the mantel. Also, paper invitations make touching souvenirs of fine soirées, well worth collecting to pore over in old age with a lace-edged handkerchief close at hand. Sniff!

Whether zapped electronically or sent via the post, all written invitations should cover the following (though not necessarily in this order): who, what, where (with directions, if appropriate), when, why, and how. In other words: host's name, date, place, occasion, RSVP contact information, plus dress code if it's not obvious.

So, for example:

To celebrate our elopement

SMITHS

Wednesday, April 10, 2020

Cocktails: 6 to 9

121 Happy Street

RSVP to smiths@emailaddress

If that's too plain and bureaucratic-looking for your tastes (as it sort of is for mine), then obviously add design, or perhaps handwrite the invitation and print copies, or knock yourself out and make them all by hand with coloured pencils, doodles, stickers, Photoshop, or whatever your inner six-year-old desires. Personal invitations like that are always fantastic fun, and a cool invitation suggests that the event will be equally cool—and is therefore all the more irresistible. For example, wouldn't you love to get an invitation like this?

SMITHS
Annual Hair-of-the-Dog New Year's Breakfast
11 a.m. to 3 p.m., January 1, 2020
121 Happy Street
Dress: Pyjamas
RSVP by December 15 to smiths@emailaddress

In any case, an invitation sets the tone of the event, so we want to make sure the style of invitation and the style of the party are in sync. Here are some general guidelines on invitation etiquette:

Impromptu Dinner or Drinks with Family or Close Friends

HOST   Last-minute invitation by phone or text

GUEST   Immediately reply to the invitation. Then, following the event, send a thank you by phone, text, or email. (Please don't send a thank-you text from the taxi on your way home. It looks lazy.)

Casual Dinner with Friends or Acquaintances

HOST   Email or phone invitation with three days' to a few weeks' notice

GUEST   Thank you a day or two after the event via email or telephone

Moderate to Highly Formal Occasion
with Friends and Acquaintances

HOST   Designed electronic invitation or paper invitation by post. Send three to six weeks in advance, or more if someone's coming from far away. If for a party further out in time, send a "save the date" notification prior to the invitation (well in advance if considerable travel is required or if it's a seriously special occasion). If you really need to nail people down, you might send a post-invitation *pour memoire* too. It feels a bit like nagging on, but it *is* astounding what people can forget.

GUEST   Thank you sent by post within three days following the event, possibly with flowers or a gift, if appropriate.

Formal Invitation for Public Event,
Such as Product Launch, Art Opening, Ball, Etc.

HOST   Designed electronic invitation or luxurious paper invitation by mail, depending on the event.

GUESTS   No thank you required, unless you personally know the host, in which case thank on paper.

Thank You

Thank yous can almost be an art form. My friend Jill once gave me a fabulous set of formal thank-you cards that had printed on them "Laura Calder regrets her behaviour at...," which was a useful (and *très drôle*) starting point. I wish I'd kept every thank you that my friend Pamela has ever written me over the years, because they're always personal, specific, imaginative, and hilarious (she signs off every one "Kissage, Lady Pamela"). I've decided that's how all thank-you notes should be: not proper and generic, but exciting, memorable, and bursting with personality (which that set Jill gave me always guaranteed). In other words, we should never write anything as banal as:

Dear Host,
Thank you for dinner. We enjoyed ourselves and found the company interesting. Thanks again for your hospitality.
Kind regards,
Mr. and Mrs. Yawn

What we want to give people is a note worth ripping an envelope open for, and I think what's key is to be specific about what we genuinely loved. Like so:

Anne,

What a swell soirée that was! How DO you always manage to get your hands on such brilliant humans? The Cohens were delightful and I was especially thrilled that Ralph knocked the red wine all over my white trousers, because I've been dying for a proper excuse to burn them for months. Besides, I looked eons better in the kaftan you lent me to change into. (Do you want it back? I hope not.) Coq au vin positively superb, and if you don't give me the recipe for that chocolate pudding I'll have to have you kidnapped.

Eternal thanks for yet another sensational evening.

Love and smooches,

Ella (*et* Tom *aussi*)

Obviously we're not going to write something quite that theatrical for someone we barely know, but we can still be original—and, again, specific—rather than cookie cutter. For example:

Dear Trevor and Jonathan,

What a delightful evening—and such a delicious cast of characters! We felt utterly spoiled by all that lobster and were downright in awe over your ability to get a roomful of strangers to break into *Auld Lang Syne* over digestifs. *Merci* so very much for including us; it was splendid.

Laura and Peter

P.S. That pug of yours is too cute for words. A true party animal.

Hostess Gifts

We have friends who bring us such amazing gifts whenever they come over that it's almost embarrassing: fur slippers, whimsical lights, designer tea towels... It's sort of their signature thing to do, and it's a treat because every time they bring us something, it's so personal we know it was bought specifically with us in mind. *Quel honneur!*

I'm not in their league in the hostess-gift department. More often than not, I show up with wine like most other Joe Schmoes (although not, I hope, like the Joe Schmucks who show up with plonk). This isn't merely a lack of imagination on my part; it's also because I know that with many friends, it's expected. Wine is expensive, and for many, what makes entertaining possible is knowing that everybody will pitch in on the booze front. I certainly appreciate it.

This said, there is no point bringing wine to the home of well-off friends with giant cellars. A better gift for someone with a *cave* of their own fine wine would be, say, a grappa brought back from travels, a special olive oil, some designer-label chocolates, or a beautiful candle. To avoid having to run out every time you need something like this, it's convenient to keep a gift drawer loaded with last-minute presents such as special soap, candles, sea salt, hand cream, candies, oils, preserves, vases, designer gadgets... these sorts of things make presents suitable for anyone.

Some people also have a drawer for unwanted items they plan to re-gift. Fair enough, but it's wise to label them so they don't end up being given back to the original giver. And if it's something we hate (the Darth Vader mug, the cinnamon barbeque sauce), we shouldn't hand it on. The gifts we give say something about who we are and about how we see the recipient. It's usually painfully obvious when we're giving something without any genuine thought.

Some of us bring flowers for our host, which can be controversial. I've heard people say that it just gives the host another thing to deal with as guests are arriving. But, personally, I love having a bouquet thrust into my bosom—any old time! It's no trouble: if I can't deal with it in the moment, I just pop it into a vase of water and it can wait until I have time to arrange it properly. Sometimes people send flowers the day after, which is chic, but not cheap, and depending on your social circle perhaps a bit over-the-top. A potted plant or flowers already in a vase are another way around this conundrum.

My own preferred way of offering cut flowers is to make it seem as though I just picked them from the garden I don't have (yet!). What I do is bring flowers home from the shop, trim the bases, strip excess leaves, tie string or a ribbon around the bouquet, and deliver them just like that, with no tissue paper or plastic or other fuss around them. That way, the host just has to plunk them straight into water and they're done.

IT'S A WRAP

My friend Johanna always brags that when she was growing up, her family had a wrapping room in their house. Her mother, a former archaeologist, was a bit of a pack rat, so the room was towering with bubble wrap and ribbons, rolls of Christmas paper, tags, and string. It's rather a thrilling and extravagant concept, especially for a paper fanatic like me, not to mention a wrapping addict.

When I lived at Le Feÿ in France, every Christmas my boss used to set me up at the long dining-room table with sparkly paper and bows to

wrap all the outgoing presents to my heart's content. It was a job she couldn't stand, but I adored this break from my normal routine to play crafts, even though it took at least a day. There's magic in wrapping, I feel. The "thought that counts" is almost more apparent in the wrapping job than in the contents of the package.

The need to wrap presents can happen at any time of year, of course, so it's good to be prepared. Variety is important, especially if we have a lot to wrap: one box covered in silver tissue paper and tied with a yellow ribbon is delightful; six of the same gets to be a yawn for the wrapper. Knowing this, I'm always sure to have plenty of different papers and ribbons on hand, sometimes buying paper by the single sheet. I save scraps, too, for smaller presents or for making tags or collage-like decorations on top of other paper. Peter's mum is so organized that she keeps tape and scissors right with her wrapping supplies in a giant box under a bed so she never has to do any searching. Her wrapping box is so well stocked, it's practically as good as a whole wrapping room—a model I intend to follow.

THE WRAPPING ZONE

Whether it's a room, a shelf, or merely a box, having supplies ready for wrapping in a set place where you can always lay a hand on them is an organized way to be. Here are some essentials you'll want to find there:

Saved paper, ribbons, boxes, etc.
from gifts past that can be reused

New wrapping paper
in various styles and sizes
(including brown paper for parcels)

Bubble wrap

Tissue paper

Ribbons, twine, and bows

Tags

Scissors (Merchant & Mills makes
a great pair with extra-long blades)

A hole punch

Tape (including double-sided tape)

A ruler

A black felt-tipped pen

Silver and gold pens

How To Mastermind a Guest List

I once had a friend who had no sense whatsoever of how to put together a guest list. He would often invite me and a couple of my friends, then flesh out the table with his boyfriend's extended family. *Oof.* Everyone came from such different worlds that it was downright hard labour trying to find things to talk about, feign interest in one another, and pretend to get one another's jokes. It's not that everybody wasn't basically decent, but the mix was impossibly incongruent, and therefore those evenings, for everyone, had what another friend of mine would call "a certain *je ne peux pas.*"

In theory, the guest list for a big party should be easier to compile than for a more intimate one. With plenty of people, surely everyone will find someone to talk to, and anyone who'd rather keep to themselves will be absorbed by the crowd to the point of invisibility.

Well—not so fast. You can't just open the floodgates to everyone you've ever met. I know someone who very nearly does this when she entertains on a large scale; her whole unemulsifiable life shows up, everybody from the banker to the bongo drummer from the market, and I find it gives a room such a lack of cohesion that it's next to impossible to read the scene and feel you can let down your guard.

It may sound cruel, but the magic of a large party depends almost as much on who's *not* invited as who is. (Weddings and funerals are notoriously impossible to control in this regard, so we just have to go with the flow, but don't worry, everyone has the same trouble with these.)

In any case, the bottom line is that, to be a success, any party, large or small, must have a sense of harmony, of recognizable rhyme and reason. The guest list is what creates this, and it's why a truly fine one takes the skill, thoughtfulness, and instinct of any great collector or curator. Fashion designer Rebecca Moses likened it to creating a fine dish; she wrote, "Each guest is like a flavour . . . a spice . . . a texture, the mix is EVERYTHING."

I've always had a great range of friends from a lot of different backgrounds and from across a wide social spectrum. I love everybody equally, but I don't necessarily mix everyone together, and when I do I try to be thoughtful. We live in fairly democratic times, but it can't be denied that humans are great categorizers by nature and tend to be most comfortable amongst their own kind. So it's a juggling act sometimes; while it's wonderful to give people the opportunity to shift slightly out of their usual comfort zones (otherwise social life grows stale), there's no point forcing anyone into company they'll feel completely awkward around (perhaps even hostile toward).

Mixing too many people from the same profession or pursuit (unless it's an industry- or hobby-related event to begin with) is also risky business. The tendency in those situations is for everybody to talk shop, which is dull for them and absolutely lethal for any outsider who might have been invited. (Woe to the person who couldn't plant a kiss finding herself surrounded by members of the garden club who are all prattling on about azaleas.) Remember, people get together not simply to divert themselves, but to refine themselves, to learn, broaden their minds, expand . . . This can't happen if everyone in a room is already a carbon copy of one another, and it can't happen if people come from worlds too disparate. A balanced mix, on the other hand, means that everybody can intermingle naturally and rub off a bit on everybody else.

I reckon it takes a lifetime of entertaining to become a real expert in guest lists, to be able intuitively to fine-tune the mix of brains, personalities, manners, tastes, and so on. Sometimes I've got it wrong. I've invited people who, on paper, looked a perfect match, but who, once face to face, turned out to be oil and water. It's rare, but it can happen, and when it does, that's where I expect guests to be grown-ups. As much as it's the host's job to make guests comfortable, it's also the job of guests to put their host and their fellow guests at ease.

"John, Jane. Jane, John."

Don't you hate it when you're with someone in the street and they run into a friend you don't know and suddenly launch into a conversation, leaving you on the sidelines to inspect your fingernails and twirl your hair? A quick introduction, even if you don't join their conversation, per se, puts you at ease and is inclusive. (If I'm not introduced, I size up the situation and sometimes just barge in and introduce myself. You never know, it could be that the person we're with has forgotten a name and needs rescuing. It certainly happens to me!)

It's no different at parties: everybody must be introduced. If you have two hundred people, it's impossible to present every single person to every single other person, but as host, you should at least greet each guest and make sure that anyone who doesn't already know someone is hooked up with someone else of potential interest. (P.S. If you're a guest and the host is not at the door, you should track them down to greet them.) When making these introductions, it's helpful to give the guests involved a start to conversation, as in "Linda, Bob you absolutely have to meet because, fancy the coincidence, you're both water-polo fanatics," or "David, Paul, are you aware that you have both lived in yurts?" Once we get people mixing and mingling, they can more or less take over and introduce themselves, although it's wise to keep an eye out in case we spot anyone later on who seems to have turned into wallpaper.

Standard etiquette books, which frankly seem less written for the nobs they appear to be aimed at than aspirational fantasy fiction for everybody else, give the general rule always to introduce a junior, younger, or "less important" person to the senior person or VIP first (e.g., "Lucy, I'd like to introduce you to the Dowager Duchess." Or "Billy, meet my grandfather."), but most of the time it's safe just to say "John, Jane. Jane, John." If you find yourself moving in circles where a strict etiquette of introductions matters and you don't know your way around, then obviously get yourself a reliable etiquette book and follow protocol so you don't make a faux pas with the Crown Princess of Newfoundland or the Archbishop of Avalon. Otherwise, let's face it, outside royal and international political spheres, introductions aren't exactly strategic diplomacy.

The great horror, of course, of introductions is the business of forgetting names. We all forget names all the time, so I'm not quite sure why it's such a source of mortification, although I suppose it does slightly imply that the person didn't quite make enough of an impression on us the first time.

One tactic for remembering is to repeat a name as soon as you hear it. If someone says "Laura, this is Ursula," then I say "Hello, Ursula," and then try to get that slippery little name into another sentence or two immediately afterwards to etch it on my feeble brain. Like so: "Isn't this gorgeous weather, Ursula? . . . I detect an accent, Ursula, where do you come from? . . . Vienna, Ursula! Why, Ursula, that is one of my favourite cities!" (There, that oughta do it.) Of course, I usually forget to do any of this and then I want to kick myself when I suddenly have to introduce what's-her-name to somebody else. (Ute? Erica? Oonaugh?)

Our friend Phil taught me a tactic for handling those mortifying moments. (It may have come originally from Ronald Reagan, now that I think about it.) Here's his method:

Phil to person whose name he has forgotten: "What's your name again?"

Person of forgotten name: "Ursula."

Phil to Ursula: "Ach. I *know* you're Ursula, for heaven's sake; I meant what's your surname?"

Ursula: "Ohhhh, of course! Shufflebottom. Ursula Shufflebottom."

Phil: "Ah, that's right. Ursula Shufflebottom, meet Walter Winterbottom."

Et voilà. Saved by the skin of your teeth.

Tone

I've said vulnerability is a key factor in hosting. That's not a word anyone is terribly comfortable with, but it is one we have to warm up to if we're ever going to allow people into our lives. If your hair looks funny, your cooking ability stops at crackers and cheese, or you live in a wooden shoe, don't worry about it. "All that matters is ambiance and you," as that wise

French friend of mine said. What she did not say, but which has also become clear to me since, is that ambiance, in fact, largely *is* you.

The first of our roles as host is to set the tone, which starts with managing how we feel about ourselves and the aura we project. If we desire a tone of conviviality, we shouldn't exude a chilling properness; neither can we expect a tone of seriousness if we're prancing about like a buffoon. No, we have to *be* the tone, embody it. This is not always easy, because moods and feelings aren't easy to control; the negative ones in particular have a nasty way of sneaking up on us like bad weather. (Most of us can relate to that sad line from Hamlet: "When sorrows come, they come not single spies, but in battalions.")

All kinds of things can get between us and our ability to present our best selves to the world—bounced cheques, overcooked duck, flat tires, lost loves, bad hair, hormones—but the experienced host must learn to wipe all evidence of unhappiness from his face and be gay no matter what, or at least appear to be. If it's any consolation, this is not something that comes easily to me. I'm exceptionally sensitive (so much so that I have to avoid reading the news) and I wear my heart on my sleeve and (very embarrassingly) my thoughts on my face, so if something gets me down when I'm supposed to be a vision of levity, I have to think of the Queen in her most trying moments and do my best to follow her steady example—throwing in, perhaps, a bit of a Princess Margaret live-it-up twist. "Be the party you want to throw," I tell myself, taking a deep breath. (I love that the Queen reminded us in a Christmas Day address that "to breathe in" in French is *inspirer*, inspire.)

This reminds me of something a yoga teacher of mine once said. We carry energy with us wherever we go, so before we enter a shop or a meeting or any space—before we open our front door!—we should check what kind of energy it is we are carrying and, if necessary, change it. This is not about being fake. It's not as though we have to shuffle through a whole array of masks to wear for every occasion we show up to. ("Oh, ballet gala, better put on my I-have-a-right-to-be-here face." "Ah, backyard barbeque, that calls for the down-to-earth, I-loves-me-a-burger look.") No. If we're hosting, the most effective way to make people feel welcome and put them at ease is to take our own mask off first and give people authentic us (without, as per above, any hint of internal crisis if that's what's going on). Being kind, open, warm, and real, in my experience, is generally the best way to be when we hope to draw the same out of other people.

We are a fear-addled, untrusting species, highly self-conscious, suspicious, and socially on pins and needles. It's a fascinating pain in the ass, but there you go. A great host wants to cut through all this crap as much as possible and make people feel safe and free to be themselves. That can only start with the host being the first one to drop any stuffiness, snobbery, stiffness, or insecurity and to infect everyone with the party spirit. As my late grandmother, Alma, used to say, "No fools, no fun!"

Presence

Is this too obvious for words? You would think so, but it's not. How many times have I attended parties in public venues for things like product launches or magazine fêtes, supposedly "hosted by so-and-so" (usually someone marginally famous), whom you never even end up laying eyes on let alone being greeted by or talking to. I find this the height of bad taste. It implies—nay, is proof positive—that the host believes he or she is too good to associate with his own guests.

If we have put our name on an invitation as host, we must be there, I say, and we should be positioned to greet people as they arrive, or at least be circulating widely. (What's the use of a host who just swans in halfway to get her picture taken for the social pages and then ducks out again?) Ditto at home: we can't just say hello and then disappear into a secret back room with a handful of our favourite peeps, leaving everyone else to their own devices and the contents of our fridge.

At a small party at home, the absent host is usually one who has planned badly and is off in the kitchen trying to pull off a three-star feast beyond their ability rather than serving a roast chicken liberally garnished with their own lovely, relaxed, and engaging company. It's the host people come for, along with the company of the fellow guests, so it's our duty to indulge them and save that first attempt at spun sugar for another night.

Weaving the Night

Where hosting becomes a magician's art is in striking the perfect balance between being visible and invisible, between knowing how to control without appearing to hold strings. No party we throw is ultimately about us, after all; it's a gift we offer other people (and, in a way, every guest is a gift we offer to other guests). So, yes, we host to connect ourselves to others, but also to connect other people to each other. In doing so, we become the hub of a wheel of our own making, and it's up to us to keep it spinning. (Mind you, it's also true that every guest has to do an element of hosting too.)

We must be on alert so that no guest is ever left feeling anonymous, insignificant, or forgotten—though we mustn't, of course, keep hovering over everybody. I like Emily Post's take on this: "In popular houses where visitors like to go again and again, there is always a happy combination of some attention on the part of the hostess and the perfect freedom of the guests to occupy their time as they like."

Something else a host must do is save guests from any potential embarrassment. A friend once told me a story of being at a snazzy dinner, toward the end of which a rather drunk countess slipped under the table. Apparently, the hostess (clearly a brilliant one) got under the table with her and said, "I always prefer to have pudding under here too." That brings to mind that astute line from Horace: "A host is like a general; it takes a real mishap to reveal his genius."

I feel, at least at big parties, that a host should also bring a room (or table) all together at least once, either with an announcement, a toast, or a short speech—something that anchors the evening. If you invite, say, fifty people to a cocktail party and just let them mill around for hours and then go home, the evening is left dangling. On the other hand, if you cling-cling your glass with a spoon at some point fairly early on in the proceedings, thank people for coming, and tell the room that after fifteen years you're finally leaving the convent to be a roadie for the Rolling Stones, then it creates a shared emotional moment that helps bring people together (and gets conversation going).

Obviously, there's not always something quite that dramatic going on in one's life, and of course nobody wants a smoothly running soirée to get hijacked by someone on a podium; nevertheless, a few words can work wonders, even if they're just "Friends, Romans, thank you for coming! I've been dying all my life to roast a pig on a spit and here you all are to witness this crackling moment! Let us all then raise our glasses in honour of my dream come true: To the pig!"

A great wordsmith I know often writes a poem about the guest of honour to read aloud after dinner. These are always a scream. We know a few musicians who occasionally give us a merry tune. I've been known to make everybody at the table go around, one at a time, and give a wish to the person on their left. *"I wish you a lifetime of good health!" "I wish you luck getting that job!" "I wish you would quit checking your blasted Apple watch! . . . Oh, all right: I hope you find true love before the year's out. Sigh."*

There's something very warming about bringing people together by taking a step beyond just letting them through the front door. For one, it's kind of like a benediction upon each guest, which helps everyone in the room feel that they belong and share something in common with everybody else. It also grounds the evening, imbues it with meaning, and makes the party not just a party, but also a memory that can live on.

Bores

I once heard of an optimist who felt it was important always to invite a few dull people to parties, because then he himself would look all the more fascinating. I don't buy it. You have to be careful, for a start, not to confuse dull with shy, because they are quite different qualities. In fact, really boring people, in my experience, are rarely the wallflowers, but rather more commonly the types who can't get enough of themselves and won't stop drowning everybody else out with their great bellowing voices and attention-seeking gestures.

Reading *On Green Dolphin Street* by Sebastian Faulks, I discovered a passage on the "boring" topic. The late American journalist Joe Alsop had something he called his "amendment," which, as Faulks spelled it out, "stated that with eight people at dinner there could be no bores present; with ten there could be half a bore; with twelve a whole bore could be absorbed; with fourteen, a bore and a half, and so on. Half-bores, in Alsop's definition, were dull but very powerful men or vacuous but very beautiful women."

Another splendid definition of a bore comes from the nineteenth-century French dramatist and writer Louis-Sébastien Mercier, who of a certain group dismissively said, "Such men are like empty chairs in a circle that encumber the room."

Now this is all rather harsh, and once again I'd warn not to judge too quickly, because sometimes people just take a bit of time to be coaxed out of their shells. I remember finding myself seated beside a painfully shy young banker once, for example. I thought, "Oh no. Tedious night ahead. I can't talk banking, so now what?" With a bit of digging to root out where his mind might be otherwise, I managed to discover that this fine-boned, soft-spoken creature had grown up in Cape Breton (it's hard to be boring and from Cape Breton) and was dying to tell me all about his brother, of whom he was clearly very proud, who had just run off to become a musician. (No doubt his brother was in a jazz club downtown at exactly the same time telling some gobsmacked bassist that his brother was a banker. ("No!" "Yup." "Not possible! "Cub's honour.")

So there you go: if you're stuck in a corner with someone who seems about as sociable as a sarcophagus, follow Dorothy Draper's fine advice from her 1941 book, *Entertaining Is Fun!*, and make it your mission to "find that smouldering spark of interest that nine times out of ten can be fanned into flames." (Forgive the onslaught of quotations, but so many people have been brilliant on this topic, I can't help myself.)

If your arm is about to fall off from fanning madly to no avail, then you probably have found yourself a true bore, a real thoroughbred. Take note (should you ever find "bore" on a treasure-hunt list, right after four-leaf clover, at least you'll know where to find one), and better luck next time. Meanwhile, a greater concern for all of us is perhaps to take care we're not being bores ourselves, blathering on about ourselves, telling stories about people who mean nothing to anyone, never giving anyone else the floor. I got an excellent piece of advice from Russell Lynes's book *Guests*, wherein he shares a lesson pounded into his brain over a lifetime by his mother: "If you are interrupted in the course of telling a story, never try to finish it unless you are asked to."

Key to not being boring is to be curious about others and never to bang on for too long about any of the following:

- Your health

- Your children and grandchildren or friends that nobody present knows

- Your technical devices

- Your trip to _____

- Your wedding plans

- Your line of work

And here's a useful tip: Lady Elizabeth Anson, cousin of and event organizer for the Queen, claims her best tip for dealing with bores at a sit-down event is to seat them all together. "They don't realize they're bores and they're happy," she told the *New York Times* in an interview.

Dress

My father's parents were real dresser-uppers, guest-ready at all times. So engrained was their habit of being well turned out, I remember my dad's exasperation one time when he had to screech over to their house to take my grandfather to the emergency ward after a heart-attack scare:

he found his father bent over trying to polish his shoes. Weeks later, when my grandfather was still in hospital and very weak, he'd still drag himself out of bed every morning and put on a suit (with tie and the works). That's how he believed people should present themselves in public—with dignity—so he dressed to the nines, on principle, even though he was a lone wolf in a pale blue sea of hospital gowns.

It makes me all the more ashamed to admit that I've always been rather shy when it comes to clothes, and as a result have never risen to my style potential. Quite young, I remember going through a phase where I'd get home from school, shut myself away in my closet, and spend hours putting various pieces of clothing together to see what might make nice outfits. Whenever I thought I had a good combination, I'd stand back, hand on chin, and study my creation to figure out "Does this work?" and "Is this me?" (Perhaps it's a game I should learn to play again.)

One of the impediments to my developing a proper wardrobe has always been my endless moving, because a person can lug around only so much stuff at a time. (Alas, that's not an excuse I can trot out anymore.) Another trouble is that I don't like shopping for clothes. Sorry, but I find the "trying on" just deadly. And then there's the fact that I used to have a habit of literally giving the shirt off my back whenever somebody complimented me. "What a great jacket, Laura!" "It will look even better on you!" I'd exclaim, and button it up right on them. Despite my aversion to clothes shopping, I've bought a fair number of pieces in my time, now that I think of it. But it was never long before they were turning up at my house on other people's bodies.

So this is a confession that I am not particularly good at something that, in fact, I believe is an important skill. I'm not talking about fashion, which doesn't overly interest me, but rather about knowing how to dress in a way that brings out the best in us and is a true expression of who we are (even when we're home alone). The wrong clothing choices can be disastrous for morale and, by extension, for behaviour, so getting it right matters for legitimate reasons, something for hosts and guests alike to keep in mind.

Another perspective on appearances took me a few years to absorb properly, but essentially it's this and it's French in attitude: you are not just you; you are someone else's view. I'd never thought of that before. I'd always assumed people dressed to please themselves or without thinking at all (because to give too much attention to the act would obviously be shallow and frivolous).

How we dress says a lot about how we feel about ourselves and how we feel about the people who will be looking at us. It's a sign of respect to dress well for others, and it makes life more fun. If a host has gone to the trouble to dress up the house—and himself—for a party and then we show up in a ripped T-shirt, what are we saying?

A number of years ago in Montreal, I found myself staying in a hotel where a big Fashion Week party was being thrown. Management had tried to avoid complaints about the noise by inviting all hotel guests to come. Not normally my scene, but my friend and I decided to go. Well, step aside Paris (where I attended a certain number of fashion parties back in the day): this was the single most gorgeous and surprising display of fabulousness I'd ever seen in my life! No two people looked alike. Everyone paraded around like a page out of *Vogue*. It was a spectacle, and it's the moment I understood the value of spectacle, which leads me to another example, albeit a dismal one.

I got invited to watch the Rogers Cup a couple of years ago. Not a tennis aficionado myself (Peter is), I just assumed the crowd would be dressed *à la* Wimbledon—in other words, that they'd be as much fun to watch as the players. Nope. As far as the stands went, it was about as exciting for a fashion watcher as shopping at Walmart. Every bleacher and every box just screamed "missed opportunity!" If you can handle another example, I attended a funeral once and to my horror found the cathedral packed with mourners wearing ball caps and jeans. You could have counted the dark suits on one hand. Appalling (because the message is a lack of respect).

So there's my case for thoughtful dressing, from host and guests, both at home and out in the world. It's pretty rich coming from me: I've hardly been a poster girl for style, but maybe I'll try harder now that I'm aware of a few more important reasons why it matters.

P.S. If you're at a loss for what to wear to dress-specified occasions, see debretts.com to be safe.

The Host as Bartender

(Ahem. After all that, I'm sure we could use a drink.)

One of the first things a host does when guests land is offer them a drink, so a bar is important, whether it's an actual bar, a tempting trolley, or just some twinkling glasses and a bottle on a tray. Ah, such a charming vision: a promise of woes about to be soothed at the denouement of day! (I even once knew a host who, if a crowd dropped in at 10 a.m., would belt out, "Now, would anyone like a brandy?" Nice touch, in a way, although it was usually only the host himself who ever wanted one.)

People start to get nervous at parties, you may have noticed, if they're standing around for too long without being offered something to sip on. Pretty much as soon as guests are through the door and have had their coats and bags tucked away, we should be prepared to play Jeeves, unless of course we've hired a Jeeves, in which case we can just swan about being adorable in the secure knowledge that pouring is happening. (We might also take the Kingsley Amis approach. Christopher Hitchens recalled Amis telling guests: "I'll pour you the first one and after that, if you don't have one, it's your own f****** fault. You know where it is.")

My favourite "cocktail" is a glass of Champagne, so I'm quite useless when it comes to the bar situation. We do, however, have among our friends a master: Ian, who has the most impressive home bar we've ever seen. His is an entire room with bottles floor to ceiling, 80 per cent of which I've never heard of, and row upon row of glasses in every shape and size. Plus he owns infusers, ice picks, fermenting gizmos, oak casks... (Poor lamb. He really missed his calling as a hipster by being born in the seventies.)

Anyway, our bar (Peter's, really; I keep my distance) is, in fact, the top of a console, so it's not exactly Raffles. Still, it serves its purpose for now. Since cocktail culture is such a boon these days, we may have to flesh ours out eventually, and when we do I shall consult Ian's recommendations for respectable home bar kit and caboodle.

THE BAR KIT

Two shakers (one large and one small)

A mixing glass (you can use a pint glass or a beaker, but if you want classy, get the real thing)

A Hawthorne strainer and a julep strainer

A bar spoon

A Y-peeler for garnishes

Two jiggers: a ½-ounce/¾-ounce one and a 1-ounce/
2-ounce one (some people like an angled plastic jigger
or an all-in-one multi-level jigger instead)

A citrus press

A corkscrew

A muddler (the barman's equivalent to a pestle)

Ice bucket and tongs

Straws: metal or paper, not plastic
(metal spoon straws are cool)

THE CABOODLE (I.E., BOOZE BASICS)

London dry gin

Blanco rum

Dark rum

Blanco tequila

Vodka

Campari

Vermouth: one sweet, one dry, and make sure you
refrigerate them between uses; they're essentially wine
and won't last forever once open

Orange liqueur

American whiskey

Scotch whisky

French brandy

Anise: Pernod, Ricard

Maraschino liqueur

Tonic, soda

Bitters: Angostura, Peychaud's, orange

Simple syrup (whip up a batch before a party by
whizzing together equal parts—weighed—of water
and sugar in the blender, and store in the fridge)

Olives

Citrus fruits

For big parties, by the way, even Ian hires a bartender. (Teenagers are very useful for this job, so if you have a few of those, you can put them to work.) He sets his good man up at an easily accessible station (far from the kitchen so he's not in the way of the food) and plants a sign beside him listing three or four drinks for people to choose from. It's smart to offer only a limited number of cocktails for a party rather than the entire contents of *The Compleat Mixologist*, or whatever the latest drinks bible is. Remember you are a home, not a cocktailery. And if it actually is you mixing the drinks, then more importantly, remember that you're primarily the host and not Colin Peter Field. (For more on drinks, see "The Co-Host's Drinks Job," p. xx.)

The Host as Sommelier

Most hosts have no choice but to be guided by price in selecting wine. Where I live now, there is a strict government monopoly on what wine gets sold to the public, which further limits options. I prefer wines with character (just as I like my guests), but it's difficult to find such wines in this market (to the point that one wonders sometimes if everything with personality isn't downright banned). So let me put it this way: I'm not in a place at the moment where it's easy to be a connoisseur or even a snob. We get the selection we get, which, if I'm looking for an upside, I suppose keeps us humble. ("It's the kind of wine that improves enormously when everything else has run out" is one of Peter's favourite "Laura lines," uttered once when he discovered I was having a glass of wine from a bottle I'd rejected outright the previous day.)

If you live in the middle of world-class wine country, you'll probably find that your neighbours like what you like. Elsewhere, different strokes for different folks must be accepted. I have some friends with otherwise excellent taste who for some reason like the sort of generic wines that are identical year after year after year (and that have about as much in common with Mother Nature as Coca-Cola). I know others (some with excellent cellars) who wouldn't know the difference between Château Margaux and cranberry juice. I also know a few so passionate and knowledgeable about wine, they taste everything like forensic scientists. I've learned to go with the flow.

In an ideal world, my preference is for wines to be chosen to go with a meal and shared by the whole table in order. I don't do this all that often these days, but when I do, I find it can be useful to ask a salesperson with sommelier-status knowledge to advise on pairings with my menu. Most of the time, I just buy several of the same red and white and let people have what they want, because many prefer to stick to one or the other throughout an entire meal. Often guests bring wine to dinner too, and although we can decide not to serve those bottles, the eventuality that they'll get drunk must be factored in, especially since having to buy all the wines for a dinner would make entertaining impossible for many hosts.

I don't mean to make any of this sound complicated; wine is, after all, just a drink. I do have some extremely fussy wine friends (don't worry, most live on the other side of the ocean), but I find that most people are just grateful to be offered a decent glass. In any case, this continent is relatively new to the world of wines, so there's no point pretending we've been barrel aging cabernet since the twelfth century. Let's just pop those corks, then, and let the merriment begin.

A Few Tips for Tippling Democratically

- Always buy a couple more bottles than you calculate you'll need in case any are flawed.

- Help ward off morning-after headaches by trying out my friend Horia's rule, which is to offer a single decent red and white at parties rather than a selection.

- If you can accommodate a wine fridge, they're very useful for avoiding kitchen collisions with the cook.

- When offering wine, say "Would you like a glass of wine?" or "How's your glass?" as opposed to "Would you like another glass of wine?" The latter sounds a bit like a judgement, as in "What?! More?!" (Peter has a similar trick with cocktails. Instead of asking if someone would like a second, he always asks, "Would you like the other half of that sazerac/martini/white lady . . . ?"

- Unless you're tasting with a roomful of winemakers or critics, refrain from discussing "nose" and "legs" or using other technical wine terms.

- When serving wines, generally move from lightest to heaviest so that guests' palates aren't dulled too early on. The French have a little rhyme that takes another reason into account, which I've always found amusing. It goes: *"Blanc sur rouge, rien de bouge; rouge sur blanc, tout fout le camp."* The spirit of the message might be translated thus: White before red, you'll sleep well in bed; red before white, you'll be up all night. (You catch my drift.)

A CURE FOR HICCUPS

I'm sure you will never need this advice yourself, but you might one day come across someone having a hiccup fit who needs your help. Here's the remedy: suck a lemon. (Seriously. Get a wedge, sink your teeth into it, and hold until the juice is gone. Not yummy, but effective.)

Setting the Table

I love setting a table and I love everything tabletop. It's my dream, in fact, to have a giant walk-in closet sort of arrangement just for dishes, glasses, cutlery, and linens. Even if nobody was coming over, I could play all day long at setting the table in various ways, trying out mixes of colour and pattern, experimenting with arrangements from formal to *très rustique* and everything in between.

When you think about it, with few exceptions what sets formal dining apart from informal dining is more the table setting than the actual food (and, I suppose, service and the way people are dressed, but those are other matters). Obviously a taco doesn't belong on a black-tie menu and red wine sauce doesn't belong at a picnic on the beach, but a salad, an apple tart, roast beef: these and most other dishes are as happy at a gala as they are at the cottage, albeit with the presentation tailored to suit the rest of the scene.

Funnily enough, for someone who loves setting tables, my least favourite Google search is "table settings." I take that back; my least favourite is "tablescapes." Try googling either, go into "images," and you are guaranteed a voyage over the very roughest seas of bad taste: boldly patterned napkins folded like fans and jester's hats; floral centrepieces so enormous and tacky that you can picture them in plastic on top of tombstones; clown-like colour schemes bounding back and forth across the table from water glass to seat cushion to vase ... It's a wonder guests ever find their food beneath such vibrant rubble or manage to focus their attention spans long enough to notice they have dining companions to talk to.

If that sounds biased, let it be known that I'm equally stuck-up when it comes to self-conscious minimalism, which, it seems to me, is almost more prevalent today. When simplicity—fine in itself—comes accompanied by any whiff of preciousness or self-righteousness, it can be just as off-putting and stiffening as ostentation. (I recall someone who had a most annoying way of arranging magazines on his coffee table. The apparent goal was to make them look as though they'd just been casually tossed down, but they were always at such a precise angle that it felt as though he'd used a geometry set to get them into position. An exercise in tension if ever there was one.) Good taste, high or low, glamorous or next-doorsy, must always feel comfortable, appropriate, and effortless. Contrived nonchalance is *not* a thing.

Alas, there is no magic formula for pulling this off any more than there is to decorating a room or getting dressed. It requires we be true to ourselves and learn through trial and error. I used to have a couple of scrapbooks full of two decades' worth of magazine clippings of tabletop items, dining rooms, and set tables I admired. The books were borrowed and lost by someone whom I still dream of strangling. I don't think I've grieved so much over a lost possession in all my life.

In my mind's eye, I still try to pull up some of the lost images from those books: the stone room in a French château with a large table in front of a marble fireplace, covered simply with a rumpled, heavy, taupe linen cloth; another French table in a Paris apartment whimsically strewn with white poppies and etched glass over a dramatic cloth of fat, royal-coloured florals; the worn wooden table in a courtyard with cherry-red café chairs; the fetching collection of thin-lipped Champagne flutes in every shade from violet to chartreuse . . . Gone. But I do hope, having spent so much time poring over those pictures of glorious design, that perhaps my beauty-starved brain absorbed some sense of what constitutes flair and that, when I do acquire that walk-in closet of tabletop toys from my dreams, I'll be able to set my table differently every night with the whimsy and imagination of a world-class set designer.

Tabletop Pet Peeves

(Listen, my scrapbooks were lost; I'm allowed to be grouchy for another minute.)

- Cutlery set in weird positions on the table, such as all to one side of a plate (very widespread these days), like chopsticks, or in an X across the plate, as though dinner were forbidden. I always rearrange it as soon as I sit down so that it's where I need it when it's time to pick it up. Sure, change is good to help us see things in a new light, but things have to make sense.

- Cutlery rolled up in a napkin. This perhaps makes sense at a casual buffet, but set on a table, it just makes work, it's awkward, and it rumples the napkin—especially off-putting when the napkin is paper.

- Oversized wine glasses. (What are we about to drink, goldfish?) They take up too much space and are far too easy to knock over.

- Clunky, oversized, awkwardly shaped dishes (square are the worst culprits) that hog the whole table and cause congestion.

- Plastic and paper anything (best left on the crafts table at kindergarten)

- Clumsy or cutesy centrepieces, such as full-on hedgerows planted down the middle of a table or painted porcelain Easter bunnies carrying baskets of jellybeans, etc.

- Excessive colour coordination

- Salt and pepper in shakers that make it impossible to see how much is coming out

The Placement

I bother with place cards if I'm doing dinner for eight people or more, because it avoids confusion when people go to sit down. Because of where our table is positioned, I always nab the seat on the end that allows for the quickest getaways to the kitchen, since I'm the one trotting food and dishes back and forth (although I have got stuck in the back once or twice and had to yell orders to people at my usual end). Apart from that, I basically try to keep couples separate, for a bit of fresh air, and men and women staggered. And when I've got a group of people who don't know one another, I take extra care not to put a lion alongside a mouse, no two studs across from each other, no flighty butterfly anywhere near a Siamese cat, and so on. (See p. xx regarding how to seat bores.)

If, for you, place cards feel even remotely like you're overdoing things, bring them down to earth by making your own, a bit tongue in cheek, perhaps with a doodle on them. If there are children around, it's fun to let them make the place cards; having something made by happy little hands is always amusing and can help break the ice even at the most buttoned-up of tables.

Serving Dinner

I feel like a voice in the wilderness sometimes, but I really think that casual dinners at home should be either family style, with platters of food set on the table, or buffet style so people can serve themselves. The reasons are that (a) it's convenient, (b) it gives people the freedom to take only as much as they want to eat at a time (rather than forcing quantities upon them that they don't want), and (c) it encourages interaction. These are all bonuses that we miss out on when individually plated food is set before us, as though we were in a restaurant. (The exception might be for a first course such as soup or a slice of terrine, but even when desserts are individual—say, in ramekins—I tend to lay them out in the middle of the table so that anyone who isn't in the mood for something sweet doesn't feel obliged.)

A buffet system is useful for a large table where passing platters would turn into a roundabout at rush hour. When I do that, I set the table as I normally would, but put the plates at the end of a side table where I've laid out the main dishes. When it's time to eat, I get everyone to trail along and help themselves to whatever they like and sit down. Once I notice their plates getting low, I just invite them to go help themselves to more without waiting for everyone else. This way the table doesn't all of a sudden get evacuated like a sinking ship.

Buffet 101

- Stack plates at the front of the buffet to be picked up first.

- Organize dishes of food in logical order for going onto plates and within easy reach. Also, make sure each dish has appropriate serving spoons.

- Make sure food on the platters is ready to pick up. You don't want people having to slice and carve with one hand (which is not only awkward, but also holds up the line).

- Set cutlery (a few more pieces than you need, to be safe) and napkins at the end of the buffet so people aren't stuck holding them the whole way through the line.

- Gradually reduce the size of serving dishes so that when people go back to the buffet, they don't find three forlorn chicken breasts left behind on a platter the size of a toboggan. As quantities go down, the size of serving dishes must as well so that the food continues to look appetizing.

→ If drinks are also being served buffet style, set them up in a separate location so that you don't create a traffic jam.

Table Manners

As a child, and I cannot tell you where I got it (in the womb, I suspect), I was very finicky about how everyone behaved at the table. My older brother, Gordon, used to drive me to distraction, because no matter how perfectly I'd set the table (I volunteered for the job regularly), he liked to switch his fork out for one that didn't match the rest. He also had a habit of tipping back on his chair. I'd spiral into fits, night after night, trying to get him to conform to my standards, but to no avail.

Compared to some people, though, Gordon was a prince. Something that used to drive me even more out of my tree was seeing other children eat food on the school bus. I had to avert my gaze, so strong was the disgust, and I still do when confronted with a similar sight on public transport or in the street.

Many would quickly dismiss my squeamishness as snobbery, but that's not it; this reaction of mine is straight from the gut, which makes me believe it must be primal. In fact, I have a theory about why table manners exist in the first place: eating is gross to look at. And so is some food. There is a reason people apologize if they have to eat in the company of another person who is not eating at the same time, and that's because it's highly unappetizing to watch somebody else's mouth negotiate a piece of steak or a soft-serve ice cream unless we ourselves are doing the same thing at the same time. Why? I don't know why, but when we are also eating at the same time, we don't seem to notice the other person gnawing away at their chicken wing—unless, of course, their table manners are so repulsive that our attention, despite ourselves, becomes riveted to the distressing scene. (I suppose another reason is that it's anti-social not to share.)

We were at a dinner party not long ago where one of the guests was a senior-level investor type. I have no idea how he got to be a senior-level anything, because he ate like a low-level grunt, licking his knife and holding his fork practically from the tines; it amazed me that he managed to get any food from the plate to his mouth at all, so inept were his skills.

If I were a bank, I would never hire someone who didn't bother to fix this defect in himself, for two reasons: he would be an embarrassment around high-profile clients, and anyone who can spend a lifetime eating socially and *still*, at the age of fifty, use the shovel approach with one arm while wrapping the other around his plate like he's about to toss a Frisbee strikes me as a person worryingly lacking in social intelligence and unobservant of the world around him (i.e., not someone I'd want handling my money).

I also notice people's eating methods in restaurants all the time, unfortunately, and wonder how on earth some survive in this world, handling forks and knives as awkwardly as they do. "Do you drive a car?" I want to ask. "I hope not!" Or "Do you use a curling iron? Well, not on me, thanks." From an observer's point of view, it's painful, and largely because it looks so painful for the eater too. It's a wonder they don't perish.

My unsolicited opinion is that everyone should consider it part of their basic education to learn good table manners and to use them. It's called being civilized. When we sit around a table with people to share food, we're not there to watch one another masticate and swallow, because, as I've said, it's quite ugly. (Note that most royals refuse to be photographed eating for the very reason that it's about as unflattering as, well, a lot of other basic physical human needs.) Instead, we're there to commune, to nourish our minds and souls along with our bodies. Bad or highly unusual table manners distract from this and make people uncomfortable. Conforming to standards is not about being fancy, then; it's about not offending, not grossing other people out, essentially not drawing attention to our animal side, but instead covering it up.

It's not for me to order people to follow standard dining etiquette, but I would feel irresponsible if I didn't mention to anyone unawares that, rightly or wrongly, not to do so will have social consequences. If you think table manners don't matter at all, at least trust me on this: they only don't matter to you. Other people are watching how we eat, and they are judging the rest of our personas based on what they see. There's nothing empowering about ignorance: learn the rules so you can feel confident and socially at ease.

The Most Basic of Dining Rules
(with apologies to anyone for whom this is like being told the sun sets
in the west)

- When you hear the words "à table," they mean "come to the table,"
  not "make a last-minute dash to the loo." Get that business out of
  the way well beforehand so you don't hold things up. (This is a good
  rule beyond the table, of course.) I love the story about the Duke of
  Windsor told by the late American socialite Fleur Cowles. She once
  asked him at a dinner party what had been the best advice his father,
  George V, had ever given him. The reply was "My son, pee first."

- Don't start digging into food until everyone is sitting at the table,
  including the hostess, and you've been given the go-ahead. (Tip:
  The hostess picking up her fork is a sign.)

- Do put your napkin in your lap when you sit down. It's not décor;
  you're meant to use it.

- If you're serving yourself from communal platters, take a reasonable
  amount the first round so that the guy at the far end of the table
  isn't left with just one green bean and a shrimp. (P.S. Avoid that
  two-serving-spoons-in-one hand trick, unless you're the waiter.)

- Do not talk with your mouth full, the way every American actor
  seems to think they must do on TV (smack, smack, talk, slurp—ugh).

- Do talk between bites. In other words, don't just put your head down
  and put food away like a starved wolf, ignoring the conversation
  around you.

- Use cutlery like a grown-up human and not like an octopus. (If you don't know how, finding out is all over the Internet and costs nothing to watch. Debrett's is a good source for this sort of thing.)

- Don't reach across people to get things (or to shake hands) like you're diving into side-angle pose at the yoga studio. Ask to have the gravy, etc. passed to you.

- Pass the salt and pepper together, even if someone asks only for the salt. Set them down on the table so the person can reach them, rather than thrusting them into their hands.

- Once the hostess has initiated the clearing process, do not immediately leap up and start helping unless you're given the go-ahead. When too many people jump up to be helpful, the party is broken up and those left behind at the table feel guilty and awkward. (P.S. Clear the same way your hostess does. If she carries off two plates, don't start scraping and stacking, which is generally frowned upon because it's ugly and the noise isn't nice. Also, send everything up that's asked for. Don't leave knives and forks straggling.)

A SERVER-FREE TABLE-CLEARING METHOD

I got this system from a chatelaine who hosts large weekend parties with virtually no help. At the end of each course, she asks for plates and cutlery to be handed down the table in sequence (i.e., not stacked along the way). As they reach her, one by one, she stacks and then silently carries off the whole pile. Neat and discreet, as long as you can get your guests to obey and not stack along the way.

Family Affairs

The main thing to remember about the major celebrations of the year, no matter what one's background, is that they're usually bedlam. When gatherings are large with all age groups flung together, we really can't expect anything else. The upside of this sort of feast is that they're seldom precious, which means that the food, while it should be copious and often includes traditional dishes, is generally family style and quite relaxed, which isn't to say it's necessarily easy to orchestrate.

The sheer volume can be intimidating, especially for people who don't cook regularly the rest of the year. The good news is that several people usually pitch in to help for the big, family affairs, which means the pressure isn't on one cook alone (ditto when it comes time to clean up). Another relief is that the foods usually stay the same from one year to the next. It's not as though you have to keep coming up with new ideas for Hanukkah; you know the doughnuts and the latkes are going to be there.

In my case, Christmas is basically Christmas, and the menu at my parents' never changes: roast turkey, stuffing, cranberry sauce, various vegetables, and a plum pudding or trifle. By the time I'm seventy-five, I expect to be a master. Right now, I'm still fumbling somewhat, and that's the other reality of major feasts: responsibility for them gets handed down. We can go for years only marginally helping out—peeling the odd potato, filling the water glasses—and then one day, kerplunk, the main load for the whole feast is on our shoulders. Well, there's nothing to be done; embrace the madness and dive in. It's the only way to learn, and family, surely, is the most forgiving audience anyone could hope for.

One thing about taking over as host for a long-standing family holiday tradition is that we've often by then joined forces with another family, so the traditions may change slightly. One of my brothers married a Dane, which is how a whole new Christmas cookie entered our holiday repertoire. Peter and I, meanwhile, have started making a giant foie gras terrine every year at our house, which erodes gradually over the holidays as various visitors come and go. In other words, because we've seen things done a certain way all our lives doesn't mean we can't change them once we take over. My own approach is to hang on to tradition while adding at least one personal twist. I like to think that before long, any new tradition I add will take on memory and meaning of its own, to the point that the next generation won't be able to imagine a holiday without it.

Whatever the holiday menu, remember that the house is bound to be full of people, so it's essential to prepare as much of the food as possible in advance. Nobody wants to be deep-frying orange-flower beignets while herds of toddlers race underfoot. The other thing that makes life easier is having the table set before anyone arrives. In my family, we're about sixteen now for a sit-down extended-family feast, so it's not easy to pass things around the table.

My preferred solution is, once again, the buffet route (see page 297) so people can serve themselves and find their places, then get up and help themselves to more at any point during the proceedings. Another idea is to put food on the table, but in double, with the same dishes at either end. I also like to set up a *Katzentisch* arrangement for any children; to keep the chaos to a minimum (see "*Der Katzentisch*," on the next page), although, as I've said, that's a fairly futile goal and perhaps not even a desirable one. The best memories always come from the craziest goings on, and if disaster strikes, well, at least we've got a good opening gambit for dinner conversation next year.

DER KATZENTISCH

Germany has a whole word for what I suppose we'd call the children's table, the table apart from the grown-ups that helps keep major family celebrations from turning into the running of the bulls. When children are really little, they often like to be at the big table (and need to be because they can't feed themselves), but from about age three to four comes a phase when the young and old are best kept apart for the sake of everyone's sanity, especially if there are quite a few children. Children can't sit for as long, so if they leave, the table becomes full of holes. Also, conversation during dinner can be nearly impossible above the din and flying food.

What we want is for children to feel not that they are being got out of the way, but rather that they're privileged and special. Enter *Der Katzentisch*—the cat's table. I recently pulled this off at my parents' house by setting up two children's tables in the living room to seat five—one on a piano bench with lower benches on either side, and the other on a table with big soft chairs—so the whole room looked rather club-like, only in miniature. Each table was decked with a pretty cloth and a bouquet of wildflowers, appropriately sized cutlery, and small crystal water goblets that my mother immediately whisked out of sight and replaced with plastic mugs. (Oh well, I tried.) All the nephews and nieces had a jolly good time in there, while the grown-ups got to eat in peace within view and earshot.

The Drinks Party at Home

If there was ever a sentiment I can relate to, it's this one from the American etiquette maven Letitia Baldrige: "You have accomplished your mission of going there tonight—you were 'seen' and you furnished your host and hostess with the sincerest proof of your great love and friendship for them—you have endured their cocktail party."

Tell me about it! If you wonder why I never throw drinks parties, there's your answer. Despite the smile plastered on my face all night, I'm very often suffering through them. Loud music, scores of total strangers, dice-sized bites of stuffed puff pastry flying past on trays like drones, soggy handshakes: all that stuff turns me into a person I can't even recognize.

Now let me quote Jean-Jacques Rousseau, because I often feel the same way he did: "I would enjoy society as much as the next man, if I were not certain to show myself there not only to my own disadvantage, but as quite different from what I am." I can never quite be myself at cocktail parties, although I'm working on it, because knowing how to mix and mingle and make small talk is part of life.

There are, of course, people who just *love* going to parties of this kind (these are the same sort of people who keep nightclubs and stadiums in business). I was talking to a friend the other night (at a dinner party, naturally) about the phenomenon of crowd entertainment, and her take on it was that people crave shared emotional experiences because, in groups, our energy levels get heightened somehow by feeling, hearing, yelling, and seeing all together. It gives us a high. (Ahem, and by "us," I mean "them.")

Big parties, by their nature, are more superficial in tone than a dinner, which is why I tend not to favour them—and why they're what make a great many people feel safest. (F. Scott Fitzgerald complained that small parties offered no privacy. He must have been the kind of man who also appreciated the anonymity of big cities. That, or perhaps he just liked to hide his epic drinking in plain sight.) My friend Stephan, who's nothing like F. Scott, adores a cocktail party, and once (again at a dinner party) gave me a great long list of reasons why:

- If you're single, you don't run into the couples problem.

- You know you have something in common with everybody in the room (i.e., the host), so you're free to march up to anyone and introduce yourself.

- You can see a lot of people in one night rather than in over, say, forty separate nights.

- If you're the host, you can pay back a lot of people all in one go.

- People are usually "happy" at cocktail parties (i.e., they've had a few), so you can be quite ballsy about asking for their contact information and then getting in touch the next day with the people who interest you.

- You have no risk of getting stuck for hours beside two people you can't stand.

- You're not forced to eat anything, including the rest of something you've already taken a bite out of.

- You have the flexibility to arrive a little late and leave a little early.

I have to say, the guy was almost convincing. He then offered four tips for what to do if you're an anxious cocktail-party attendee, like me:

- If you're shy about meeting people, but want to, plant yourself in one of the top strategic schmoozing spots: (a) next to where the food comes out, (b) in a narrow hallway, or (c) by the loo.

- Don't eat squishy things; they go all over the place. Also, never mix sweet stuff and booze. Guaranteed headache.

- Know where your coat is, at all times, for a discreet escape.

- Never sit on a sofa. It's a trap.

And then he gave me three tips for what to do if I ever throw one:

- Get help. At a cocktail party, your hosting skills need to be 100 watts. Never mind trying to mix drinks and serve. You can't do it all. You're there to greet, introduce, mix and mingle, and make the mood. Just wear that one hat and let someone else sweat the rest.

- Choose music carefully and always keep it in the background. Too often, people allow the music to get intrusive, which is a conversation killer. Music should be an atmosphere enhancer, not the enemy of interaction, which is the whole point of a cocktail party.

- Keep booze simple. A cocktail bar may *sound* nice, but if you have great, long lineups of people waiting for drinks that each take five minutes to mix, it's a disaster. Offer wine, water, and maybe one cocktail or a couple of mixed drinks, but unless you have an army of mixologists at your disposal, that's it.

Introverts

Despite appearances, I'm afraid I fall into this camp. Introverts are people who, amongst other things, find being at parties rattling and draining, yet most of us don't want to be considered social outcasts, so we show up. The smart thing, if you can manage it as host, is to make sure your party space has a few quiet nooks—a few chairs in a corner, perhaps a small side room opened up—for people who need to get away from the crowd and the noise to compose themselves. The extroverts, who are most people, will be happy to stay on the dance floor, but the silence-seeking minority will be grateful for your thoughtful provision of places to retreat to, and perhaps able to stay longer as a result.

Modern-Day Dilemmas That Every Host Must Face

FOOD RESTRICTIONS

Miraculously, all my friends seem to be like me: bon vivants who love to eat, drink, and be merry. I can't imagine life any other way. Pity the hosts who set cakes on their tables thinking "Num num num!" only to have some killjoy make a comment about calories. And how must they feel having spent all day making homemade ravioli only to have some guest waltz in and announce they're suddenly off carbs?

I have great sympathy for anyone with a serious food allergy. It must be just dreadful to see other people enjoying things the afflicted would die to sink their teeth into but can't because that is in fact what would happen. I also understand religious food restrictions. One friend of ours, whenever he's asked to dinner, always sends me a reminder note to say "No piggy!" This is considerate, because, with so many food limitations out there, I just can't keep track of who won't eat what unless I've fed someone several times before.

Some food restrictions are serious and real while others are fashionable and faux, but whatever their status, all together they have turned modern-day communal dining into a minefield. A can't eat fish, B can't eat nuts, C can't eat wheat, D can't eat shellfish, E is vegan, F won't have sugar, G goes dairy-free, H is off carbs, and I . . . I, and everybody else trying to host a dinner party, practically have to draw up a spreadsheet just to plan a single menu. There is no mercy. Yet if we want a social life, we must deal.

Whenever we invite people to eat, I find out what they can't or won't eat right away by enquiring, say, "If I ever want to kill you, is there a particular ingredient that would make swift work of it?" (If a host fails to ask, it's the guest's responsibility to give warning, well in advance.) One person with an allergy is no problem; three people with their respective restrictions cancelling each other out (no meat, no fish, no dairy, etc.), and I immediately lose my will to cook. It happens rarely, but when it does, I pull myself together and plot a buffet arrangement, laying out a variety of options so people can pick and choose. (If anyone has a lethal allergy, I keep the deadly ingredient out of the kitchen altogether.)

SMOKERS

An antiques-dealer friend of ours stands firm on the conviction that all living rooms need ashtrays. He believes this even as a staunch non-smoker. In his mind, a gracious home is all about possibility, and ashtrays, for him, are a symbol of that, whether you allow people to smoke in a house or not. I agree with him, but I'm not sure why, perhaps because ashtrays seem to hearken back to a more civilized hosting era. Anyway, this is why we have them.

Although ours is not a cigarette-smoking house, I don't get too fussed if we have guests who smoke (which in any case is almost never) because I don't think one night is going to ruin the place. Besides, if I've invited someone to dinner who smokes, it's because I want their company, so I hate to see them constantly disappearing outside and leaving the rest of us stragglers behind. This said, many people mind tobacco smoke, so for the sake of those people at the table, it means it's best to have smokers doing their puffing somewhere else. I make sure they know where to go and that there are ashtrays available there (and no guilt required). Certainly for drinks parties, a smoking section outside is imperative; even the non-smokers end up out there half the time (it's that introvert thing again).

MOBILE PHONES

When I go to someone's house for dinner or any other party, my phone stays turned off and in my bag until I need it for calling a taxi at the end of the night. To take out a phone during dinner or a party is unacceptable, unless we're with close friends and desperate to look up the capital of East Timor or whatever. (Once we've found the trivia, we should put the phone away—and certainly never start checking emails and social media).

The other thing I never do is take pictures at private parties, unless it's encouraged by the host (like at the Great Gatsby party we attended once). Otherwise, if I do take pictures, it's for me alone, not to share on social media. Little in life is sacred these days, and I think it's only respectful to hosts (not to mention to friendships) not to splash their parties, homes, menus, friends, faces—in short, their private worlds—all over everywhere, at least not without permission. A number of our friends wondered why, when we got married, no photos of our wedding, or of any parties celebrating it, showed up on Instagram. In the moment, it never occurred to me to post photos because I was too busy being present where I was; when questioned later, the very thought of doing such a thing actually made me shudder.

For the Co-Host

Back in my single days, I used to be shameless about hijacking other people's husbands to carve the roasts and pour the wines for me. (How's that for playing damsel in distress?) If it weren't for Peter, I'd still be recruiting them. Entertaining is a zillion times easier and more fun when we're not doing it by ourselves. I say this not to honk the horn for married life (although having a constant co-host with whom you can really work in sync is pretty great), but to remind single people that even if they're hosting solo, they mustn't feel they're expected to do everything alone.

As the principal host in our house—and I claim the role because usually I'm the one dreaming up the dinner parties—I am the one who holds the master plan. I know how many people are coming, what food I need to buy, what the cooking schedule will be, what wines we need ... If it's a weeknight, and often that's the case, then I've got everything under control up to the point when guests arrive, by which time Peter will have come home, mixed us a "psychological," and steadied himself to play Mr. Front of the House.

THE CO-HOST'S DRINKS JOB

Once coats are out of the way, the co-host's first on-stage performance of the night is drinks. The easiest route is to open and pour from one communal bottle of bubbly rather than going all pharmaceutical with a zillion different elixirs, potions, and the rest.

That said, it can also be nice, if you have it in you, to offer a few cocktail options (emphasis on "few") for pizzazz.

The chief thing to remember when it comes to offering cocktails is that you're a home, not a bar. There is no need to apologize for not turning yourself into a full-fledged bartender, complete with suspenders and meticulously trimmed beard. Unless you have an academic interest in mixology, I recommend bothering only about perfecting the few drinks you habitually make for yourself at home. Unless, of course, you feel like doing a feature cocktail for a party—perhaps Pimm's cups for a royal wedding or Americanos for the Fourth of July—in which case you could try anything as a one-off, following a recipe from a book, and let anyone too timid to try it have wine or beer instead.

Among the tried and true in our house, available at all times, is the martini: strong, sophisticated, shrouded in snobbery, and a wonderful way to transform oneself into Auntie Mame at the end of a gruelling week. Everybody has an opinion about the correct way to make a martini, but, after all, it is your house. For example, many insist that the taste of vermouth in a martini should only be as noticeable as if you'd done no more than whisper the word over the shaker. That's what you'd call, nose aloft, an extra-dry martini.

Well, pfft, we like it wet. In our house, we appreciate the taste of good vermouth (high quality and kept refrigerated so it doesn't go off). Peter mixes ½ ounce of vermouth for every 2 ounces gin or vodka, and sometimes even throws caution to the wind by adding two drops of grapefruit bitters. This gets poured over quantities of ice in a metal shaker, at which point one must decide whether to shake or to stir. I suggest you let season dictate the choice. In summer, it's rather nice to bring the bracing, crystal frostiness of a shaken martini to one's lips. Some argue it's more diluted than when stirred (maybe, maybe not), but it's marvellously nippy. In winter, the smooth, thickly silken intensity of a stirred martini may be preferred. There: a peaceful solution.

For a shaken martini, put the ingredients in the shaker with ice, slap on the lid, and shake like mad. For stirred, never mind the lid; just lower in a long, metal spoon and stir sixty to ninety times. Whatever you've chosen to do, the next step is to strain into glasses and finish with a strip of lemon peel, twisted over the glass to release the oils, then tossed in. A word of caution: when it comes to martini glass size, small is *de rigueur*, ideally not larger than 4 ounces, otherwise you'll end up with a cocktail that, within minutes, holds all the appeal of a room-temperature oyster.

Chill is crucial when it comes to a good martini. (Although my editor Tim says: "I find a large glass, consumed very quickly, is the ideal solution to this problem.")

Now, if you only ever learn to mix one drink in your life, it should probably be a gin and tonic. Why? Because, for one, if the Queen ever pops by and discovers you don't know your way around a bottle of gin, you'll be a disgrace. This particular rendition of the G & T may be a bit racy for Her Majesty's tastes (she's said to prefer a gin and Dubonnet anyway), but not for ours: we adore a pink G & T. This is not pink as in pink gin—i.e., gin with a drop of Angostura bitters—but something even more delicious.

First of all, use an old-fashioned glass (i.e., low ball, not high ball, to avoid the fatal error of overdoing the tonic). In the glass, put an eighth of a lime, cut as a wedge, skin side up. Pour over 1½ ounces of your favourite gin and mash with a muddler to extract the juice from the lime (a tip from my younger brother, Stephen). Add plenty of ice, stir in a drizzle of Campari for tint and a touch of bitterness (2 teaspoons is about right), then top up with a scant ½ cup of tonic, not more.

It goes without saying that, splendid though they are, G & Ts are not for winter, which is very unfortunate because it happens to feel like winter most of the time where we live. No, when the snow falls, one tends to turn away from all that's bright and zingy and move toward things more mellow, such as the old-fashioned, that masculine, spicy-sweet concoction beloved of *Mad Men*.

Again, start with a low-ball glass, only this time with a sugar cube dropped into it, preferably brown, although white is fine too. Choose season-appropriate bitters and fill up a dropper, which you then release over the sugar cube and let soak in. The sugar will immediately start its dramatic breakdown and you can then add a splash of water and stir, stir, stir until the whole business is reduced to a grainy veil. Drop a large square or round ice cube into the glass (the gargantuan kind that can't melt too quickly), then pour over 2 ounces rye or bourbon. A strip of orange zest is optional before you putter over to a cozy spot in front of the fireplace.

For a non-drinker, soda or sparkling water with a liberal lashing of bitters is simple enough to produce. Apart from that, a small repertoire of drinks such as this (your personal arsenal may be different) is enough to make you a respectable co-host. Should you find yourself with guests who are connoisseurs or who crave something flashy that you've never heard of, you can save face simply by pointing toward the bar (slightly off the mark of it, actually) and declaring, "I still haven't quite recovered from my laser surgery. You might be wise to fix your own drink."

THE FIRES

It's rare these days to encounter a real wood fire in a home, and whenever I do I get so drawn in by the mesmerizing qualities I can barely tear myself away to talk to anyone. I love the crackle, the smoky scent, the warmth, the leaping flames, the smouldering coals . . . It's a feast for the senses. For the moment, Peter and I are stuck with one of those electric fireplaces that you turn on with a switch. It gives off heat and light, but it does about as much for ambiance as a plastic waterfall. I yearn to live with the real thing (preferably tall enough for a grown man to stand up in), and when the day comes, as I trust it will, I'm going to count on Peter, my beloved co-host, to keep it roaring.

You can't have a fire without wood, obviously, so it's important to be organized. My parents have their firewood delivered in spring. It sits out all summer to dry in the sunny air, then it gets stacked indoors in early fall to get them through winter. Incidentally, having been brought up in the country, I'm well acquainted with the pride people take in their woodpiles. You can tell a lot about a person by the quality of their stacking job; it's a real art. But back to the hearth itself:

To make a fire, inside or out, start with crumpled-up paper as the base, preferably laid on a thin layer of ashes from the previous fire. Next, lay kindling on top of the paper, crisscrossing the sticks so that air can pass through. Finally, lay on two logs, in parallel fashion, topped with two more going in the opposite direction, if there's room (or upright, for certain fireplace models). If you're dealing with a stove or a fireplace, open the draft before lighting the newspaper, which will catch quickly and, in turn, light the kindling, which, in time, will light the larger logs. Set a fireguard in front of an open fireplace and move it away whenever you need to add more logs, a job that may require the help of a poker to shift around pieces of burning bits. Remember to shut the draft once the fire's in full swing to slow the burn.

Thanks to candles, the calming and comforting powers of fire can be had even without a fireplace. My co-host is very good about keeping them in stock, and if I haven't got around to lighting the ones on the table, he's onto a box of matches like a cat on an open tin of sardines—a minor job, but a big help. (P.S. When lighting candles on the table, it's a good time to check if the water has been set out yet or not. If it hasn't, that's a co-host job too.)

SERVING WINES AND OTHER
DRINKS AT THE TABLE

Some people are quite controlling about their wine service. They fill glasses and remove the wine from the table completely, bringing it back to refill as they see fit. This does tend to pace people, which is good, and I like to be served this way; I just don't like having to do that service myself, because it requires too much staying on the ball. For that reason, and because it makes no sense to use waiters in our place, what we tend to do instead is plunk bottles right onto the table. Peter keeps an eye out for empty glasses and fills as the evening progresses, but we also encourage people to help themselves. (All very gauche, I know, but what do you want me to do?)

Where Peter does take the reins on drinks at table is when it comes to digestifs after dinner. I don't even know what half his fancy bottles contain, but they're fun to look at, as are the charming silver thimbles, pink-stemmed liqueur glasses, cut-crystal whisky glasses, and so on. When he brings those out, I grab the chocolate-covered coffee beans and the candied ginger, etc., to do my part. For some reason, Peter takes all coffee orders and I make the herbal tea. That's how it is when you co-host with the same person repeatedly: you fall instinctively into your own special routines.

CARVING

I joke that I'm not going to be able to cook meat ever again because, at least when it comes to anything grilled or fried, Peter has taken over as chief cook. It makes me feel slightly from another era whenever I'm fussing around with a salad while he sears a giant steak, but the truth is that I kind of like this division of labour and, at the risk of sounding completely sexist, I like it when my man carves.

Carving seems to be where caveman meets knight in shining armour, at once primal and genteel. It really separates the men from the boys, too, because anybody can stick a roast in the oven, but not everyone can slice it expertly once it's out and present it with honour. I think of it as a traditional skill that's best handed down from one generation to the next, but perhaps that's a bit romantic in this century of chicken nuggets. Oh well, if you didn't learn from Daddy, there are plenty of books to guide you, not to mention the mentoring available from Uncle YouTube.

To kit yourself out for being an expert carver, you'll want a high-quality carving fork and knife along with perhaps a boning knife for any tricky dismantling. You'll also want a carving board, which is a cutting board with an indentation furrowed all around the edges for catching any juices. From there, the basics are to rest meat at least twenty minutes under foil before carving and to cut against the grain when you slice. With roasts, I am adamant that thin slices are the only way to go. Whether it's roast beef, turkey, lamb, or ham, thin slices are nicer for mopping up gravy or other sauces and essential if your aim is to make sandwiches from the leftovers the next day. (P.S. Serving whole fish, while technically not carving, should be added to the co-host's list of skills to master.)

A NOTE ABOUT KNIVES

In case that little sermon just gave you the brilliant idea of giving someone you love a carving set, hold back for a moment. I am not generally superstitious, but I give some credence to the old wives' tale that presenting a knife as a gift will sever the friendship, unless the person on the receiving end reciprocates with a gift of metal coins, which apparently turns the gift knife into a sort of purchase and breaks the spell. I once made the error of giving a very dear friend a pair of beautiful bone-handled picnic knives as a wedding gift. Even though he gave me coins in return, the cherished friendship, which dated back to my youth, was sadly over before the year was out. Call me crazy, but I've never offered a knife to anyone as a present since.

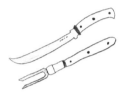

A Hosting State of Mind

Nobody can be a great host if their spirits are in the mud. Even for people who love company, there are times when the door must simply be slammed shut and when our first order of business must be to take care of numero uno. This may sound selfish, but it's not: if we don't look after our own well-being and happiness, it's impossible for us to be of use to anyone else. ("Put your own oxygen mask on first," as they say on airplanes.)

I know about this from personal experience. I'm more capable than most of going into overdrive. I have a tendency to want to look after everyone, which is no doubt a big part of why I'm such a chronic inviter, but I can end up a bit threadbare from trying to be all things to all people. Hosting is fun, but it's also work—a fact of which I sometimes need reminding.

December, take heed, is wipeout month. We're all hosting and guesting like socialites on steroids, and by January 2, half of us are ready to check ourselves into the nearest monastery. But any time of year, we can find ourselves doing too much socializing too fast, or working too hard, or squeezing in too many meetings, conferences, or presentations (September is another doozy). Sometimes we have too many people to look after all at once and we feel drained. Eventually, the very *thought* of being "on" for anyone apart from ourselves makes us queasy.

Retreat, restore, revive: this is what has to happen to attend to the physical and emotional glitches that arise in life for all of us so we can keep on keeping on. As a culture, we'd do well to stop making ourselves feel guilty about taking time out when we need to shut off and go inward. It doesn't mean we're crazy or lazy; it just means it's time for a different kind of party, one at which we look after the most important guest in our lives: ourself.

Useful Phrases for Anyone Suddenly Craving the Womb

→ Sorry, I'm on deadline.

→ Sorry, I'm out of the country.

→ Sorry, I seem to have developed the strangest, very itchy, probably contagious rash.

- Sorry, my in-laws are in town.

- No.

Pre-Party Mood Boosters for the Frenzied Host

- Meditate for twenty minutes. Sit in a quiet spot and shut your eyes. Don't open them until the kitchen timer goes off; just breathe and listen to sounds.

- Do five sun salutations (no mat or change of clothes required).

- Go for a twenty-minute walk outside, without mobile devices. (I find labyrinths to be especially therapeutic, but they're rather tricky to come by.)

- Wet your head. Sticking your head under a not-too-hot shower or under the tap is an instant way to clear out the cobwebs.

- Soak your feet in water as hot as you can stand it for about fifteen minutes. (This bit of unsolicited advice was given to me once by an Indian taxi driver, who, when I climbed into the back of his car, informed me that I looked only about 60 per cent happy. According to him, soaking my feet would wash my negative thoughts away.)

- Change your clothes. Put on something that makes you feel attractive, confident, and charming.

- Sit down with pen and paper and write down everything you can think of to be happy about in the moment. Be specific. In other words, don't say "I'm glad I'm not dead." Instead, go micro with statements like "I'm thrilled my amaryllis came out today" or "I'm so grateful I was able to borrow that croquet set for this afternoon."

⇥ Do as I was advised once by a woman who was both an ex-ballerina and, to make the understatement of the century, a bit of a peacock (if peacocks were female). She used to yell at me, whenever I'd let myself slump into a question mark, "Don't walk like that! Shoulders back! Get tall, like you're being pulled by a string coming out of the top of your head! There!" And then she'd add, demonstrating all the way, "You never walk into a room. Neeever. You *arrive!*" She'd step over an imaginary threshold, pause grandly, and then stride in like a queen, looking left and right as if acknowledging a roomful of admirers. Tip: Use the "arrive" method when the doorbell rings.

⇥ Smile! Even if it's at a wall. Just walk around smiling for five minutes. If it doesn't cheer you up, at least it's bound to amuse anyone else who catches sight of you.

⇥ If all else fails, mix yourself a "psychological." My favourite among these remedies is something called the Corpse Reviver #2. Google it.

The Door

I admire the French enormously for their dedication to hellos and goodbyes. From the earliest age, children are taught to *faire la bise* (i.e., air kiss every greeting and farewell). When I did *stages* in French restaurants, way back when, I remember being astonished by the cooks who shook the hand of every other cook in the kitchen when they showed up, and again after lunch break. Such a commitment to peace!

We all yearn for acknowledgement in life (one reason it's important at least to nod to beggars in the street, thank bus drivers, make a friendly joke with the mailman, etc.), and it's a host's job to make sure guests feel our pleasure in their having taken the trouble to come, both when they arrive and when they leave. I love that line (author unknown but wise whoever she was): "To be a successful hostess, when guests arrive, say 'At last!' and when they leave, say 'So soon!'" (A little originality is always good too. I remember once leaving a party at my friend Genni's with a few friends. As Genni walked us to the car, she yelled over her shoulder to her husband, "I'll be back! I'm just going to go frisk these girls for silver.")

A Digestif

It's a given that when we host a party, or attend one, we're expected to put our best face forward: we're at ease, we look good, we're smiling and welcoming, we're showing genuine interest in other people's comfort, and we're being generous and helpful. It's not realistic to maintain these levels of grace and charm around the clock, day in and day out, but it isn't a bad notion to have that ideal in our minds as a guide and at least to strive for that, not just at a black-tie event or a community barbeque, but everywhere—at the office, on public transport, in an overcrowded shopping mall. For one thing, it's a good way to snap ourselves out of being grouch almighty or from acting like a sulky opera heroine whenever we find ourselves in situations that push our buttons, say in a traffic jam or dealing with a customer-service rep over the telephone.

I suppose every era has the same complaint (at least somewhere on the planet), but I have to say that in my lifetime, the world has never felt more uncivil or full of hatred, violence, and fear. The Middle East is a disaster; much of Africa is in strife; Europe is straining at the seams; the states of America feel about as united as pieces of a jigsaw puzzle spilled out of their box onto the floor; the World Wide Web is a perpetual warzone of differing opinions and standards of behaviour. Not that anyone ever said life was all roses, the world one giant, fragrant garden of justice and kindness. Evil is always with us, jerks always among us, and every era has its reasons for getting up in arms.

Thomas Hobbes famously wrote, "No arts; no letters; no society; and which is worst of all, continual fear, and danger of violent death: and the life of man, solitary, poor, nasty, brutish and short." If you want to get depressed, it doesn't take much. It's overwhelming, too, because when the world is in so much trouble all at once, those of us who care can feel powerless and wonder how we can begin to try to fix it.

I'm hoping that the answer is "little by little." Our tiny, so-called insignificant daily acts—helping someone across the street, watering a flower, making a good soup—are cracks in the gloom that let in light. The more rays we allow through, perhaps the sooner the skies may clear. "That best portion of a man's life, his little nameless, unremembered acts of kindness and love," as Wordsworth phrased it, is, at the end of the day, what's at the heart of hosting and making home.

These are the thoughts and actions that can flip the coin from hostility to hospitality side up. These oft-dismissed activities in fact can be important leadership roles, major civilizing forces vital to the health of society and an essential place to start taking back power and changing the world.

Ten Ways to Make Life More Inviting Right Now

- Get in touch with someone you haven't seen in a while and find out how they are (especially if it's to heal an old wound).

- Cook something delicious and invite someone over to eat it, even if it's just a baked potato.

- Clean something dirty, even if it's just a doorknob.

- Fix something broken, even if it's just a fingernail.

- Make something ugly or banal into something beautiful, even if it's just your thoughts.

- Say something nice, even if it's just a whisper to yourself.

- Do something kind, even if it's just to smile at a stranger.

- Give a thoughtful gift, even if it's just a wildflower.

- Lend a hand, even if it's just holding open a door.

- Write down ten more ways to make life inviting, and start making them happen right now.

P.S. The Last Drop . . .

Shhhh. I have the best secret. When a bottle of Champagne (or any sparkling wine) is empty to the last drop, it's not over. Lay the bottle on its side on the table while you finish your glass, then hold the bottle over your glass again. See? Another one. Sometimes the real last drop—the sweetest—is the one we never even suspected was here.

Acknowledgements

Having been an author exclusively of cookbooks up until now, I understand that it took nerve to give me a chance to get out of my pigeonhole and spread my wings. My publisher Robert McCullough of Appetite by Random House was the brave soul willing to let me fly with this book, and I'll be forever grateful, because it was bliss to write and I learned so much. Thank you, Robert!

My excellent and most amusing editor Tim Rostron was an invaluable filter, preventing me from saying anything idiotic (I hope) and helping me get all the pieces of this puzzle to fit and make sense. My agent Grainne Fox of Fletcher & Company in New York was hands-on from the get-go, encouraging me to keep going when I was still trying to figure out exactly what this book was supposed to be about. Tim and Grainne, heaps of thanks!

Thanks also to whip-smart and eagle-eyed copy editor Lana Okerlund.

The person responsible for this book's gem-like beauty—ahem, other than the illustrator, of course—is its brilliant designer, Jennifer Griffiths. Many thanks to her for all her hard work and her inspired eye.

My husband, Peter Scowen, deserves sainthood. Not only did he act as one of my readers, but he agreed to be written about, to have aspects of our private life exposed, and most of all to let me host dinners on average three times a week for two years straight, for "research." I'm grateful to my agent Grainne, and my friends Isabelle Fish, Jill Horne, Anne Fitzgerald, and Mollie Patterson for taking the time to read the manuscript in the raw stages. I especially thank my mother for going over the final manuscript with her fine-tooth comb (and a bottle of white-out).

Friends who are experts in certain subject areas were very patient in taking my pesky questions whenever I hit a bump. I owe particular thanks to Anne Fitzgerald, Ian Tuck, John Brunner, Stephan Argent, Roxanne Tota-Kosey, and John D. S. Adams.

This book was written after a lifetime thus far as a keen social observer and passionate host. So many people over the years have influenced me in these areas that I couldn't begin to name everyone or I'd need an extra hundred pages. My long-ago employers Anne Willan and her late husband Mark Cherniavsky played a major role in my life, as of course have my parents, John and Doris Calder, who instilled in me so many of the values that have shaped this book. I single these people out, but the truth is that anyone who has ever fed me or welcomed me into their home or given me a tidbit of life advice deserves credit too. If you're one of those people, know that you're remembered by me with gratitude for even the most inadvertent and minor lessons you may have given me in how to make life inviting.

Love,

Laura